SEX WORK AND THE NEW ZEALAND MODEL

Decriminalisation and Social Change

Edited by
Lynzi Armstrong and Gillian Abel

BRISTOL
UNIVERSITY
PRESS

First published in Great Britain in 2021 by

Bristol University Press
University of Bristol
1-9 Old Park Hill
Bristol
BS2 8BB
UK
t: +44 (0)117 954 5940
e: bup-info@bristol.ac.uk

Details of international sales and distribution partners are available at bristoluniversitypress.co.uk

© Bristol University Press 2021

British Library Cataloguing in Publication Data
A catalogue record for this book is available from the British Library

ISBN 978-1 5292-0581-7 paperback
ISBN 978-1-5292-0576-3 hardcover
ISBN 978-1-5292-0578-7 ePub
ISBN 978-1-5292-0577-0 ePdf

The right of Lynzi Armstrong and Gillian Abel to be identified as editors of this work has been asserted by them in accordance with the Copyright, Designs and Patents Act 1988.

All rights reserved: no part of this publication may be reproduced, stored in a retrieval system, or transmitted in any form or by any means, electronic, mechanical, photocopying, recording, or otherwise without the prior permission of Bristol University Press.

Every reasonable effort has been made to obtain permission to reproduce copyrighted material. If, however, anyone knows of an oversight, please contact the publisher.

The statements and opinions contained within this publication are solely those of the editors and contributors and not of the University of Bristol or Bristol University Press. The University of Bristol and Bristol University Press disclaim responsibility for any injury to persons or property resulting from any material published in this publication.

Bristol University Press works to counter discrimination on grounds of gender, race, disability, age and sexuality.

Cover design: Clifford Hayes
Front cover image: Grain detail © Freepik (background),
New Zealand Prostitutes' Collective (NZPC) logo (umbrella)

Contents

Notes on Contributors v
Acknowledgements ix
Glossary of Māori Words xi

Introduction 1
Lynzi Armstrong and Gillian Abel

PART I: Legislative change in New Zealand

1 'On the Clients' Terms': Sex Work Before 17
  Decriminalisation
  Jan Jordan

2 Stepping Forward Into the Light of Decriminalisation 39
  Dame Catherine Healy, Annah Pickering and Chanel Hati

3 The Future of Feminism and Sex Work Activism in 61
  New Zealand
  Carisa R Showden

PART II: The Diversity of Sex Workers in New Zealand

4 The Impacts of Decriminalisation for Trans Sex Workers 89
  Fairleigh Gilmour

5 Fear of Trafficking or Implicit Prejudice? Migrant Sex 113
  Workers and the Impacts of Section 19
  Lynzi Armstrong, Gillian Abel and Michael Roguski

6 "My Dollar Doesn't Mean I've Got Any Power or 135
  Control Over Them": Clients Speak About
  Purchasing Sex
  Shannon Mower

PART III: Perceptions of Sex Workers in New Zealand

7	"Genuinely Keen to Work": Sex Work, Emotional Labour, and the News Media *Gwyn Easterbrook-Smith*	157
8	The Disclosure Dilemma: Stigma and Talking About Sex Work in the Decriminalised Context *Lynzi Armstrong and Cherida Fraser*	177
9	Contested Space: Street-based Sex Workers and Community Engagement *Gillian Abel*	199

Index   223

Notes on Contributors

Gillian Abel is Professor and Head of Department in the Department of Population Health at University of Otago, New Zealand. Over the last 20 years, she has carried out extensive research in the field of sex work, which is decriminalised in New Zealand. Using community-based participatory methods, her exploration of how decriminalisation has impacted on the health, safety and human rights of sex workers has been influential in informing policy in New Zealand and abroad.

Lynzi Armstrong is Senior Lecturer in Criminology at Victoria University of Wellington, New Zealand. She has been involved in sex work research for over a decade and her projects have included exploring street-based sex workers' experiences of violence, and sex worker-led organising in response to anti-trafficking policies. Stigma has long been a key concept underpinning her work; her most recent work focuses on exploring sex work stigma and discrimination in the context of diverse legislative frameworks.

Gwyn Easterbrook-Smith is a researcher based in New Zealand, whose work primarily considers news media representations of sex work under decriminalisation. They completed their PhD at Victoria University of Wellington in 2018, and most recently taught in the School of English and Media Studies at Massey University. Gwyn's research into media productions of transgender sex workers has recently been published in *Feminist Media Studies*. They are interested in considering which sex workers are granted acceptability through media discourses, and how this occurs.

Cherida Fraser is a community liaison, advocate and researcher at New Zealand Prostitutes' Collective (NZPC), established by sex workers in 1987. She has a strong interest in the rights and wellbeing of communities that have historically been marginalised and has worked in the community sector since graduating with a Masters of Cross-cultural Psychology in 2014. Her research contributions include action research with a 'hard to reach' Māori community, and exploring the lived experiences of sex workers in the contexts of the 2011 Canterbury earthquake, the impact of decriminalisation, and in relation to sex workers' experiences of stigma and discrimination.

Fairleigh Gilmour is Lecturer in Criminology and Gender Studies at University of Otago, New Zealand. Their research examines sex work governance and media representations of crime. They completed their PhD at Monash University, Australia, in 2016, and their doctoral research examined the impact of regulations in different Australian jurisdictions on the work conditions experienced by indoor sex workers. Their current research examines the laws and regulations that shape work conditions in multiple jurisdictions (including New Zealand) with a specific focus on the experiences of trans and non-binary sex workers.

Chanel Hati is a community liaison at NZPC and is particularly focused on engaging with street-based sex workers. Chanel is of Nga Puhi decent and is whakawahine (transgender). She has been working with NZPC since the early 2000s. In 2019 she co-curated an exhibition on pioneering transgender women from Carmen Rupe's era at The Portrait Gallery in Wellington.

Dame Catherine Healy is a founding member and current National Coordinator of NZPC. She is a strong advocate for the rights of sex workers and has played a prominent role in the campaign to decriminalise sex work in New Zealand. She built widespread support among the major women's organisations, public health, social justice agencies and politicians for this change in law. She was appointed to the Prostitution Law Review Committee (2003–08) to assess the impact of decriminalisation on sex workers. She has assisted in major research projects and is a co-editor of *Taking the Crime Out of Sex Work: New Zealand sex workers' fight for decriminalisation* (Abel, Fitzgerald, Healy & Taylor, 2010). She was awarded a Public Health Champion Award in 2016 and made a Dame of the New Zealand Order of Merit (DNZM) in the 2018 Queen's Honours List.

Jan Jordan is Professor at the Institute of Criminology at Victoria University of Wellington, New Zealand. Her research involvement with sex work began while researching 19th century women classed as criminal offenders. Subsequently, she brought out the first book of interviews conducted with New Zealand sex workers, *Working Girls* (1991), and was a member of the first Board of Trustees for NZPC. Jan campaigned strongly for decriminalisation and was later a member of the Prostitution Law Reform Review Committee, 2003–08. Although her principal research focus is no longer sex work, she retains a keen interest in the area and also remains connected through supervising postgraduate students in related topics.

Shannon Mower completed a Master of Arts (MA) in Criminology in 2019. She became interested in sex work policy and its impacts after watching a TED talk by sex worker rights activist Juno Mac titled 'The laws sex workers really want'. Her MA research explored the experience of purchasing sex among clients in New Zealand's decriminalised sex industry and involved in-depth interviews with 12 clients in this context. Her thesis was awarded a pass with distinction. Shannon now works in the public sector in Wellington.

Annah Pickering is Regional Co-ordinator of NZPC. Annah has been involved in NZPC since 1999, and was an active campaigner for decriminalisation. She is a passionate advocate for the rights of sex workers globally and has presented on the issue at many local and international events as a representative of NZPC, Global Network of Sex Worker's Projects (NSWP), Asia Pacific Network of Sex Workers (APNSW), and Pacific Sex Workers Leaders Forum in advisory roles on decriminalisation, including the Sex Worker Freedom Festival in Kolkata, India, in 2012. Annah regularly provides commentary for media on sex worker rights issues, participates in field research, and provides guidance to researchers and policy makers.

Michael Roguski is Director of Kaitiaki Research and Evaluation, based in Wellington, New Zealand. Michael's research expertise is in sensitive topic research, and he has carried out research and evaluation on diverse topics including: family and sexual violence, the abuse of disabled people residing in the community, abuse of police discretionary powers and sex worker rights. Michael is a member of the Family Violence Death Review Committee.

Carisa R Showden is Senior Lecturer in Sociology and Gender Studies at the University of Auckland, New Zealand. Her books include *Choices Women Make: Agency in domestic violence, assisted reproduction, and sex work* and (with Samantha Majic) *Youth Who Trade Sex in the U.S.: Intersectionality, agency, and vulnerability*. In addition, she co-edited *Negotiating Sex Work: Unintended consequences of policy and activism* and has published journal articles on questions of trafficking, feminist and queer theories, and third wave feminism, among other topics. She is currently part of a research team looking at what motivates young people's environmental and social justice activism.

Acknowledgements

This book is dedicated to sex workers around the world, who have been tirelessly advocating for their rights for decades. Despite the steadfast advocacy of sex workers, the decriminalisation of sex work is still rare. While the legal framework in New Zealand is far from perfect, the decriminalisation of sex work in 2003 was a critical first step to improving the situation of sex workers and has had many significant impacts. In the context of the ongoing struggle for sex workers' rights globally, we hope that this book will be a helpful resource in shedding more light into how decriminalisation is operating in New Zealand, and that it may help to inform debates elsewhere.

Several chapters forming the basis of this book would not have been possible without the participation of sex workers who shared their perspectives and experiences. Sex workers are frequently called upon to inform research, which necessitates time and emotional labour on their behalf. We wish to sincerely thank all the sex workers who, at different points in time over a period spanning 20 years, have shared insights which have helped to develop this book.

We would particularly like to thank the New Zealand Prostitutes' Collective (NZPC) for their ongoing support of robust and ethical research on sex work in New Zealand, and for their important contribution to this book. We recognise that sex worker led organisations are focused on supporting sex workers first and foremost, and the time and energy required to engage with researchers can be an additional burden. We sincerely thank NZPC for their ongoing guidance and generosity.

Cover image

The image on the front cover of this book was designed for the New Zealand Prostitutes' Collective (NZPC). It combines the silver fern/ponga – a national symbol of New Zealand, with the red umbrella – the global symbol of the struggle for sex workers' rights. The editors were granted permission to use this image as a way of dedicating the book to sex workers in New Zealand and recognising the contributions that sex workers have made and continue to make throughout the world in shifting attitudes and advocating for legislative change.

Glossary of Māori Words

Aotearoa	New Zealand
hoa mahi	colleague
mana wāhine Māori	Māori feminist discourses
mokopuna	grandchild
Pākehā	New Zealand European
pasifika	people from the Pacific region
rangatiratanga	self-determination
takatāpui	lesbian/gay/transgender
tamariki	children/youth
tangata whenua	people of the land
Te Ropu Wahine Māori Toko I Te Ora	The Māori Women's Welfare League
Te Tiriti o Waitangi	Treaty of Waitangi
tikanga	protocol
tima tane	ship man
whakawahine	transgender women
whanau	extended family

Introduction

Lynzi Armstrong and Gillian Abel

Drawing together research and reflections from scholars, activists and sex workers, this edited volume provides cutting-edge insights into New Zealand's decriminalised sex industry. In the context of global politics surrounding sex work laws, the decriminalisation of sex work in Aotearoa/New Zealand[1] remains exceptional. While sex work was first decriminalised in the state of New South Wales, Australia in 1995, New Zealand remains the only country to have decriminalised sex work. Thus, after the Prostitution Reform Act (PRA) was passed in 2003, the situation in New Zealand became a point of interest throughout the world for policy makers concerned with reforming sex work laws, and a beacon of hope for sex workers advocating for decriminalisation.

In the years following the law change in New Zealand, several empirical studies have been conducted that have illustrated the positive benefits of decriminalisation on the occupational health and safety of sex workers (see, for example: Abel et al, 2007; Abel, 2014; Armstrong, 2016). However, despite the weight of this evidence, the New Zealand model remains contentious in the international context. Opponents of decriminalisation argue that it emboldens clients and managers since they are not subject to criminalisation, and that it 'normalises' prostitution, which they believe serves to worsen gender inequality (Bindel, 2018). However, there is no robust evidence to support these speculative claims about the situation in New Zealand. In the face of such conjecture it is particularly important that the findings of research continue to be published so that the situation in New Zealand post decriminalisation – in all its complexity – is well understood within the context of global sex work politics. This collection – featuring contributions from academics across disciplines, including criminology, public health, political science and media studies, as well as sex industry experts with lived experience pre- and post-decriminalisation – provides critical insights and reflections on the story so far, well over a decade since the PRA was passed.

New Zealand and the international policy landscape

Prostitution law is highly contentious globally. While the precise nature of criminalisation differs between jurisdictions, most commonly sex work laws are punitive – with either sex workers and/or their clients and other third parties criminalised. For decades numerous sex worker rights' advocates and organisations around the world have been calling for the full decriminalisation of sex work (Dziuban and Stevenson, 2015). They do so on the basis that criminalisation in its various guises causes harm, and while decriminalisation will not address structural inequalities that impact many sex workers, it is an essential starting point for tackling injustice (Mac and Smith, 2018). In recent years, sex workers have been joined by an increasingly diverse range of allies supporting full decriminalisation, including international bodies such as Amnesty International, the World Health Organization, International Human Rights Watch and UNAIDS (Mac and Smith, 2018). However, despite this steadfast activism and support, the decriminalisation of sex work has not been widely adopted and in the international policy landscape New Zealand remains exceptional.

Debates regarding sex work laws have been characterised by polarised arguments that often obscure the nuances and complexities of sex workers' experiences (Connelly et al, 2015). Choice versus coercion, free versus forced, work versus exploitation – all examples of the binary thinking that has underpinned these debates. Such arguments are particularly pronounced among feminists who, since the beginning of the 'sex wars' in the 1960s, have occupied two opposing positions – one which conceptualises prostitution as exploitation and violence, and another which recognises sex work as a form of labour (Showden, 2016). Feminist voices have greatly influenced legislative debates on sex work, and in the contemporary context internationally the battle lines have been drawn along two opposing policy approaches. One of these approaches is the decriminalisation of sex work – with New Zealand held up as the example – which seeks to reduce harm by defining prostitution as work and affording rights to sex workers. The other is the criminalisation of clients and other third parties, which is commonly referred to as the Swedish or 'Nordic' model, owing to its initial adoption in Sweden in 1999 and subsequent adoption in several other countries in the Nordic region and beyond (Kingston, 2019). Proponents of this perspective construct the sex industry as abusive and seek to abolish it by 'tackling demand' for sex workers' services by criminalising clients and offering 'help' to sex workers, who they see as victims (Scoular and Carline, 2014). In other words, supporters of this approach seek to deter the purchase of sex through the threat of criminalisation, and subsequently ensure that work in the sex industry is not a viable economic option, regardless of the consequences this may have for those who rely on it for their economic survival. Proponents of this perspective have thus in recent years been described as 'carceral feminists', owing to their reliance on the criminal justice system to achieve their desired outcome of ending the sex industry (Mac and Smith, 2018).

Advocates of client criminalisation argue the Nordic model is essential for gender equality, premised on the position that rendering the purchase of sex legally permissible sends a societal message that women are commodities (Bindel, 2018). However, sex work laws are not merely symbolic and have tangible impacts on sex workers. Several studies conducted around the world have highlighted numerous negative impacts of this legislative approach on sex workers – including increased vulnerability to violence (see, for example: Kilvington et al, 2001; Kulick, 2003; Kulick, 2005; Krüsi et al, 2014; Levy and Jakobsson, 2014; Vuolajärvi, 2019; Ellison et al, 2019). However, despite this evidence, a growing number of countries have adopted variants of client criminalisation, including Finland (2006), Norway (2009), Iceland (2009), Canada (2014), France (2016), Northern Ireland (2015), the Republic of Ireland (2017) and Israel (2018).

Debates regarding sex work legislation in the contemporary context are further complicated by the anti-trafficking movement, within which sex work has often been problematically conflated with trafficking (Doezema, 2010). As Yingwana et al (2019) have noted, the inaccurate conflation of sex work and trafficking has maintained support for criminalisation, while undermining calls among sex workers for decriminalisation. Trafficking debates are highly politicised as well as racialised, and anti-trafficking discourse positions sex work as intrinsically harmful; this has, in turn, popularised policies seeking to curb the sex industry rather than policies exploring pathways for safer migration among those who wish to engage in sex work (O'Brien et al, 2013). Thus, fears regarding trafficking have dominated policy debates regarding sex work in recent years. However, while in some corners the risk of trafficking has been cited as a justification for *not* decriminalising sex work, others have argued that decriminalisation is an essential step to prevent trafficking since it is well-documented that punitive policies drive sex workers underground, subsequently ensuring that they are unable to report exploitation and violence (Albright and D'Adamo, 2017).

Thus, discourses which position the sex industry and those in it as dangerous and threatening have proliferated in recent years in the context of concerns regarding the risks of trafficking, and the promotion of approaches to end demand. The international policy landscape has therefore been described by Scoular and Carline (2014) as 'creeping neo-abolitionism'. New Zealand has, however, moved in a very different direction in decriminalising sex work and affording sex workers with rights through the PRA, with the intention of minimising harm. To distinguish the New Zealand model of decriminalisation from other legislative approaches, Östergren (2017) has termed it an 'integrative' approach, to capture how this approach seeks to minimise harm by integrating the sex industry into existing social and legal frameworks instead of setting it apart from wider society. Existing approaches in other countries differ to New Zealand, Östergren argues, in that the sex industry is framed negatively and the legislative approach is either repressive (aiming to eradicate sex work entirely) or restrictive (aiming to clamp down on it) to protect sex workers and/or wider society from harm (Östergren, 2017).

While research is readily available which illustrates the benefits of decriminalisation, as previously noted, opponents of decriminalisation repeatedly malign this approach, arguing that it has been a catastrophic failure for sex workers (see, for example: Coy and Molisa, 2016; Bindel, 2017; Raymond, 2018). Thus, evidence on the New Zealand model and how it is operating is even more important in the context of these ideologically charged international debates, and the continued struggle of sex workers around the world who have been calling for decriminalisation for decades (North, 2019).

The New Zealand model

Central to this book is the New Zealand model of decriminalisation. Thus, it is essential to be clear about what 'the New Zealand model' is, what it looks like, what its intentions are, and its similarities and differences with other legislative approaches. As previously noted, the New Zealand model has been described as an integrative approach since it endeavours to regulate sex work comparably to other commercial businesses; this makes it distinct from frameworks seeking to stop sex work from happening or contain it under certain conditions (Östergren, 2017). However, there are other important differences.

Decriminalisation is often discussed interchangeably with legalisation but, while there are certainly overlaps, these are distinct approaches with different implications. Although decriminalisation is a somewhat murky term, it essentially involves the repeal of laws that make a specific act a crime (Mossman, 2007). Legalisation, which is the framework in place in several jurisdictions (for example Germany, the Netherlands, the State of Victoria in Australia, and the State of Nevada in the US), permits the sex industry to operate only under very narrow government-dictated conditions (Outshoorn, 2012; Herter et al, 2017). While the precise details of legalised regimes differ between jurisdictions, what they share is the requirement that sex workers comply with specific regulations, *not* designed with the express intention of keeping them safe, but to control the sex industry in the interests of wider society. As Mac and Smith (2018) note:

> Under legalisation, *some* sex work in *some* contexts is legal. This legal sex work is heavily regulated by the state – generally not in a way that prioritises the welfare of workers ... By comparison, decriminalisation ... describes a situation where sex work is legal *as the default position* ... The regulations that exist under

decriminalisation tend to prioritise the welfare of people who sell sex. (Mac and Smith, 2018, p 176)

Clarity around what is meant by the term 'decriminalisation' is particularly important in the context of contemporary debates relating to sex work laws, since it is a term used by different people with different ideological positioning. While some commentators discuss decriminalisation and legalisation interchangeably as though they are synonymous, others purport to support a policy of decriminalisation while they are advocating for the Nordic model. For example, journalist Julie Bindel has argued that under the Nordic model the selling of sex is 'totally decriminalised' (Bindel, 2016), a statement echoed by many other abolitionist campaigners and groups. However, using the term decriminalisation to describe such contexts is a misnomer since numerous reports have stated that sex workers remain criminalised and/or penalised in such contexts, either through brothel-keeping laws or eviction from their homes and workspaces (Smith, 2019). This usage of the term decriminalisation indicates that the *idea* of decriminalising sex workers is considered appealing (and perhaps a branding strategy) by proponents of the Nordic model. However, this muddies the waters of how decriminalisation is understood and suggests that sex workers in countries in which the Nordic model is in place are in the same position as those working under New Zealand's model of decriminalisation, which as previously noted does not align with reports from sex workers in these contexts.

The New Zealand model of decriminalisation means that sexual services can be bought and sold freely – sex workers are not criminalised either directly or indirectly, and neither are clients or other third parties. Thus, the sex industry in New Zealand is decriminalised. The law reform, as explored in more detail in Chapter 2, was achieved in 2003 in no small part due to the relentless work of New Zealand's sex worker-led organisation the New Zealand Prostitutes' Collective (NZPC). The New Zealand model of decriminalisation is therefore unique as a model informed by sex workers directly, though as discussed in Chapters 2 and 8, this does not mean that the NZPC had complete control over the final form the law took and the organisation is by no means satisfied with every aspect of it. Regardless, the New Zealand model is distinct in its explicit focus on affording sex workers with rights to challenge exploitation and violence, based on a commitment to minimising harm in the sex industry (Abel et al, 2007).

The Prostitution Reform Act

The PRA – the legislation that underpins the New Zealand model – created a policy framework that safeguards the rights of sex workers and provides protections from exploitation. As such, the legislation is intended to foreground the occupational health and safety of sex workers, while also being conducive to public health in general, and ensuring that young people are protected from exploitation.

Sections 16–18 of the PRA are focused specifically on the protection of sex workers. Section 16 states that it is an offence to induce or compel a person to provide or continue to provide commercial sexual services, which subsequently provides protection from coercion and exploitation. Section 17 outlines the rights to refuse to provide (or continue providing) sexual services at any time for any reason, and explicitly states that payment for sexual services does not equate to payment for consent. Thus, a sex worker may withdraw their consent at any point for any reason. And Section 18 ensures that sex workers who wish to stop working in the sex industry can immediately access the unemployment benefit following the approval of their application,[2] and states that refusal to undertake sex work cannot in any way impact entitlement to unemployment benefits.

A common misconception about the PRA is that it has created an entirely unregulated sex industry. This, as Abel (2014) has noted, is inaccurate since there are numerous sections of the Act that allow for regulation, including restrictions on advertising and the ability for territorial authorities to make bylaws relating to signage and the location of brothels (see Knight, 2010 for a more detailed overview). As discussed in Chapter 9, there have been tensions since the PRA was passed, particularly in relation to street-based sex work, which have meant that attempts have been made to pass bylaws, some successful and some not. However, as Abel demonstrates in Chapter 9, the availability of regulatory options under the PRA does not mean that these must be utilised, and the decriminalised context enables a broad range of options to resolve such tensions.

While the PRA was designed with the rights of sex workers foregrounded, parts of the legislation are problematic from a sex worker rights' perspective. As will be discussed in great depth in subsequent chapters, an aspect of the law that was infrequently discussed in the initial years following its enactment is the inclusion of Section 19, which explicitly prohibits temporary migrants from working in the sex industry. Thus, while overall the PRA is distinct in its explicit focus on improving the situation of sex workers, the presence of this section means that the law is not entirely positive for sex workers, nor does it constitute 'full' decriminalisation since an entire population of sex workers is excluded from its protections.

Impacts of decriminalisation: the story so far

After the PRA was passed and sex work was decriminalised, several studies were conducted to explore the impacts of the law, including a large government-mandated evaluation completed three years following its enactment. This research found that the law change had numerous positive impacts on sex workers. For example, the findings highlighted clear awareness of rights among those who participated, with 90 per cent of the 772 sex workers who responded reporting that they felt they had more rights under the PRA than they did under the previous legal framework. The research also highlighted an evening up of the balance of power between sex workers and clients, with 65 per cent of participants stating that they felt more able to refuse to see clients since the law had changed. There were also positive impacts on the relationship between sex workers and clients, with over half of participants feeling that police had a better attitude towards them since sex work had been decriminalised (Abel et al, 2007). The overall conclusion of the Prostitution Law Review Committee (PLRC) which presided over the review of the PRA was that sex workers were in a better position in terms of their safety and wellbeing than they were previously (PLRC, 2008).

Subsequent studies have continued to highlight positive impacts of decriminalisation. For example, a qualitative study with street-based sex workers in New Zealand found that participants could take their time when deciding whether to see clients, meaning that they could ask detailed questions and assess the client's demeanour before getting into the car (Armstrong, 2014). This finding contrasts with the findings of research conducted in Sweden (where clients of sex workers are criminalised); this has found that sex workers rushed interactions with clients to avoid the detection of the police, which hinders their ability to screen out potentially problematic and/or dangerous clients (Levy, 2014). The ability to take time in these exchanges under the New Zealand model is a consequence of sex workers not having to worry about the possibility of them or their clients coming to the attention of police. The same study also further highlighted improvements in the relationship between street-based sex workers and police (Armstrong, 2016).

Thus, there is robust evidence which indicates that the New Zealand model has, overall, improved the situation of many sex workers in New Zealand. Despite the existence of this evidence, within public debates the nuances and complexities of how the New Zealand model operates and is experienced by sex workers are not often fully captured – decriminalisation is presented as either a catastrophic failure or a utopia. Of course, neither representation is accurate. Decriminalisation is a vital first step to legally recognising sex workers as citizens and ensuring they have access to rights and protections in their work. The weight of evidence clearly shows that decriminalisation has had many benefits for sex workers; however, it is not a panacea and challenges certainly remain.

Well over a decade has passed since sex work was decriminalised in New Zealand. In the years initially following the law change, understanding the fundamental ways that the law was working 'on the ground' was of primary importance – for example the extent to which sex workers were aware of their rights, how comfortable they felt asserting those rights in interactions with clients and other third parties, and how they felt about reporting violence to police. However, at the time of developing this edited volume, more than 15 years had passed since the law changed, and within this period much has changed

– decriminalisation is now well-embedded. In 2014, a sex worker won a sexual harassment case against a brothel operator (Duff, 2014). New Zealand's sex worker-led organisation – NZPC – which spearheaded the campaign for decriminalisation, now has a strong relationship with police and has co-developed a resource to assist sex workers with reporting sexual violence (McKay, 2019). And, in 2018, the founding member of the NZPC – Catherine Healy – was made a Dame in recognition of her services to the rights of sex workers (Manson, 2018). Thus, there is now an opportunity to ask different questions and look towards the future. Does decriminalisation have different impacts for different groups of sex workers? What do media depictions look like in a context in which decriminalisation is firmly embedded? How do sex workers feel about their work and talk about it to others? Are there community tensions and how are these resolved? How is Section 19 of the PRA being experienced by migrant sex workers, and how and why might this change? Has decriminalisation impacted how clients of sex workers perceive and experience the sex industry? And where does New Zealand sit in the context of global feminist debates? With a focus on both looking back and looking forward, this collection seeks to explore these questions to consider the relationship between the decriminalisation of sex work and social change, and the lessons that can be learned by those in other countries seeking to reform prostitution laws.

Impetus for this book

The impetus for this book came following a symposium held in Wellington, New Zealand in February 2018, which brought together scholars, activists and practitioners to focus on the theme of stigma and discrimination in relation to New Zealand's sex work policy framework. The symposium raised many interesting questions and important issues that had not yet been examined in-depth – such as how this context was being experienced by specific populations, including migrant sex workers and transgender and gender diverse sex workers, how sex work was being represented in contemporary New Zealand news media, along with unpacking what stigma and discrimination looks like for sex workers in the decriminalised environment and what more could change to further improve their status.

An earlier book (Abel et al, 2010) provided an account of how decriminalisation was working within the first five years after the enactment of the PRA 2003. Decriminalisation is now well-entrenched in New Zealand society; most sex workers in the current context do not know what it was like to work under any other form of regulation.

The sex industry does not on the face of it appear to be contentious in contemporary New Zealand society. But is everything working well, and are there enduring issues that need to be addressed? This book provides a forum to start thinking through the current situation for sex workers in New Zealand, filling gaps in existing knowledge and providing cutting-edge insights into this unique legislative model.

Overview of the book

This edited collection is divided into three thematic areas: legislative change, diverse sex work populations, and perceptions of sex work. The chapters within each section have been written by New Zealand sex work researchers and activists who have researched a range of topics which have become important to look at in a post decriminalisation context. These chapters all point the way to further thinking and actions which are needed to bring New Zealand closer to full decriminalisation and to progress social change.

Legislative change in New Zealand

The colonisation of New Zealand by Great Britain in the 1820s brought with it the start of sex work in this country and clearly had an impact on Māori, New Zealand's indigenous population. In Chapter 1, Jan Jordan provides a succinct and compelling historical context for sex work in New Zealand. She takes the reader for a walk through colonisation, when trading involved Māori women visiting ships' crew when they docked, to the latter half of the 1800s when the discovery of gold in New Zealand resulted in a gold rush and an influx of single male migrants. It was at this time that legislation which affected sex workers in New Zealand was first introduced. British colonies adopted the Contagious Diseases Act(s) of 1864, 1866 and 1869 enforced in the home country, and they were particularly harsh on sex workers. The Acts provided for any woman identified as a 'common prostitute' to be forced to undergo fortnightly medical examinations (Faugier and Sargeant, 1997; Doezema, 1998). Women found to be infected with a sexually transmitted infection (STI) were incarcerated in locked hospitals until they were 'cured', which lengthened from an original three-month period to nine months (Doezema, 1998). These Acts were repealed in 1886, when the focus shifted to measures designed to end vice (Doezema, 1998). Jordan then moves from the 19th to the 20th century and considers the impact both world wars had on the sex industry, through to the 1970s when the New Zealand government introduced law which criminalised sex workers' activities. Finally, she moves to the 21st century, to 2003 when for the first time a rights-based approach to sex work legislation was adopted and all laws which criminalised sex workers' activities were discarded.

NZPC played a vital role in achieving decriminalisation, and in Chapter 2, members of this organisation – Dame Catherine Healy, Annah Pickering and Chanel Hati – discuss the context in which NZPC was formed and their role in drafting the Prostitution Reform Bill (as the first stage of the PRA). This was a Bill written by sex workers for sex workers. However, the Bill did not stay this way. In its progress through Parliament several amendments were made, and these authors discuss how they viewed those amendments and how they have played out since the PRA was passed. While sex workers are certainly able to assert their rights in New Zealand, and there have been numerous examples to support this, NZPC remains concerned that some of the amendments made to the Bill before enactment have had unintentional and detrimental consequences for some sex workers. They conclude their chapter therefore, with a discussion of their hopes for sex work in New Zealand going into the future and what they believe still needs to change.

Carisa Showden rounds off the section on legislative change in Chapter 3 by discussing feminism in New Zealand and, in particular, the gains that can be made when Pākehā (New Zealand European) feminists and Māori feminists work side by side. New Zealand's bicultural context allowed for a complementary relationship between feminists and sex work activists. The Treaty of Waitangi (Te Tiriti o Waitangi), an agreement signed between Māori and the British in 1840, is the founding document of New Zealand (New Zealand Government, 2018). The Treaty governs relationships between Māori and non-Māori to protect the rights of all. The obligation under the Treaty to consult with Māori has provided a unique context for feminist sex work activism, as this principle of consultation and collaboration to achieve rights is embedded in the New Zealand psyche. Showden argues for the possibilities of a fourth wave feminism where sex workers and feminists work collectively for action for the diversity of sex workers.

The diversity of sex workers in New Zealand

Sex workers are not homogenous; they differ in terms of sex and gender identification, location of work and residential status, to name a few. Some experience more societal stigma then others and therefore face different challenges, even in a decriminalised context. Fairleigh Gilmour starts off the section on diversity by focusing on trans sex workers in Chapter 4. She explores the work experiences of trans street-based sex workers, their perceptions of safety on the street, and their interactions with police. NZPC note in Chapter 2 that, prior to decriminalisation, trans street-based workers were more likely than other sex workers to be harassed and arrested by police. Gilmour finds that while trans sex workers feel they are safer from police harassment post decriminalisation, many still feel stigmatised and have negative interactions with police. So, while police have collaborated with NZPC to make it easier for sex workers to report sexual assaults (as discussed in Chapter 2), and have worked collaboratively to address issues for street-based sex workers in the community (Chapter 9), there still seems to be more work needed to improve police relationships with non-binary sex workers.

In Chapter 5, Lynzi Armstrong, Gillian Abel and Michael Roguski examine how the controversial inclusion of Section 19 in the PRA, which limits the ability to work as a sex worker in New Zealand to residents and citizens of the country, has impacted on migrant sex workers and how it is perceived by other sex workers who are permanent residents or citizens of New Zealand. The chapter highlights the problems caused by this section of the PRA and argues that it creates a context in which exploitation of migrant sex workers can thrive. While Immigration New Zealand acknowledge that they have no evidence of trafficking of migrants into sex work in New Zealand, they remain loathe to challenge Section 19. The chapter argues therefore, that there remains an implicit bias towards sex work post decriminalisation. It is not seen as work as any other but is singled out as an occupation not available to migrants seeking work in New Zealand.

The section on diversity ends with Chapter 6, with Shannon Mower looking at the under-researched client population. While numerous studies have been undertaken with sex workers in the decriminalised context, no dedicated studies have explored the perceptions of clients. This lack of empirical research, Mower argues, has helped to fuel speculation among opponents of decriminalisation about how clients conduct themselves – the assumption being that clients have free rein to behave as they wish in the decriminalised context. However, drawing on the perspectives and experiences of 12 clients, this chapter challenges these assumptions by demonstrating that participants were acutely aware of the rights sex workers have under the PRA, and overall approached their interactions with sex workers with these rights in mind, as well as additional ethical considerations.

Perceptions of sex workers in New Zealand

A common theme among many of the chapters in this volume is that of continuing stigma in a decriminalised environment. This theme runs particularly strongly through this final section on perceptions of sex work. In Chapter 7, Gwyn Easterbrook-Smith reviews the narratives in the New Zealand media around sex work post decriminalisation. They highlight that respectability and acceptability is contingent on where a sex worker chooses to work. Some places of work are destigmatised at the expense of others. Sex workers who work from high-end, low-volume agencies, and present themselves as enjoying their work are represented in media as being more socially acceptable than high-volume workers in low-end brothels or on the street. Easterbrook-Smith therefore argues that acceptance in a decriminalised context is conditional.

Many sex workers respond to stigma through managing information about their sex worker status; for many, this means living a 'double life' that requires considerable emotional labour (Wong et al, 2011). The extent to which sex workers feel they can talk about their sex work to other people in their lives is an important indicator of stigma. In Chapter 8, Lynzi Armstrong and Cherida

Fraser explore sex workers' decisions about who to tell about their sex work, and their experiences when they do decide to disclose. As emphasised in the chapter, the ability to talk openly about sex work can be very liberating, but responses to disclosures can in some cases deepen the emotional burden. The experiences of participants outlined in this chapter indicates that while participants were still, overall, guarded about who they told about their work, none described feeling ashamed of what they did. While decriminalisation cannot eliminate stigma, the increased legitimacy that sex workers have may enable more positive feelings about being a sex worker in this context.

Finally, in Chapter 9 Gillian Abel looks at the different spaces in a city where street-based sex workers are either accepted or not accepted. She talks about how community engagement was successful in reducing tensions between street-based sex workers and other community members in New Zealand. She argues that this is a more effective way than regulation to addressing problems in the community, as it leads all parties to a space where they can respect each other. The cohesion and inclusivity demonstrated through community engagement in the two case studies presented in this chapter provide a positive finale to the book.

Notes

[1] Aotearoa is the Māori name for New Zealand. Aotearoa/New Zealand is used in the first instance in the book. For ease of reading, only New Zealand is referred to thereafter, with the exception of instances where it is contextually more appropriate to refer to Aotearoa.

[2] In other occupations there is a mandatory stand down period of two weeks to access unemployment benefits if a person voluntarily leaves paid employment or is dismissed for misconduct.

References

Abel, G. (2014) 'A decade of decriminalization: Sex work "down under" but not underground', *Criminology & Criminal Justice,* 14, 580–92.

Abel, G., Fitzgerald, L. & Brunton, C. (2007) *The Impact of the Prostitution Reform Act on the Health and Safety Practices of Sex Workers,* Christchurch: University of Otago.

Abel, G., Fitzgerald, L., Healy, C. & Taylor, A. (eds) (2010) *Taking the Crime Out of Sex Work: New Zealand sex workers' fight for decriminalisation,* Bristol: Policy Press.

Albright, E. & D'Adamo, K. (2017) 'Decreasing human trafficking through sex work decriminalization', *AMA Journal of Ethics,* 19, 122–6.

Armstrong, L. (2014) 'Screening clients in a decriminalised street-based sex industry: Insights into the experiences of New Zealand sex workers', *Australian & New Zealand Journal of Criminology,* 47, 207–22.

Armstrong, L. (2016) 'From law enforcement to protection? Interactions between sex workers and police in a decriminalized street-based sex industry', *The British Journal of Criminology,* 57, 570–88.

Bindel, J. (2017) 'This is what really happens when prostitution is decriminalised', *The Independent,* 5 August. Available at: https://www.independent.co.uk/voices/prostitution-decriminalisation-new-zealand-holland-abuse-harm-commercialisation-a7878586.html.

Bindel, J. (2018) *The Pimping of Prostitution: Abolishing the sex work myth,* London: Palgrave Macmillan.

Connolly, L., Jarvis-King, L. & Ahearne, G. (2015) 'Editorial – blurred lines: The contested nature of sex work in a changing social landscape', *Graduate Journal of Social Science,* 11, 4–20.

Coy, M. & Molisa, P. (2016) 'What lies beneath prostitution policy in New Zealand?' Open Democracy. Available at: https://www.opendemocracy.net/en/5050/what-lies-beneath-prostitution-and-policy-in-new-zealand/.

Doezema, J. (1998) 'Forced to choose: Beyond the voluntary v. forced prostitution dichotomy', in K. Kempadoo & J. Doezema (eds) *Global Sex Workers: Rights, resistance, and redefinition,* New York and London: Routledge.

Doezema, J. (2010) *Sex Slaves and Discourse Masters: The construction of trafficking,* London: Zed Books.

Duff, M. (2014) 'Sex worker gets $25,000 over harassment', *The Dominion Post,* 1 March. Available at: http://www.stuff.co.nz/business/industries/9777879/Sex-worker-gets-25-000-over-harassment.

Dziuban, A. & Stevenson, L. (2015) 'Nothing about us without us! Ten years of sex workers' rights activism and advocacy in Europe', International Committee on the Rights of Sex Workers in Europe. Available at: https://ruj.uj.edu.pl/xmlui/bitstream/handle/item/30042/dziuban_stevenson_nothing_about_us_without_us.pdf?sequence=1&isAllowed=y.

Ellison, G., Ni Dhonaill, C. & Early, E. (2019) *A Review of the Criminalisation of Paying for Sexual Services in Northern Ireland,* Belfast: Queen's University.

Faugier, J. & Sargeant, M. (1997) 'Boyfriends, "pimps" and clients', in G. Scambler & A. Scambler (eds) *Rethinking Prostitution: Purchasing sex in the 1990s,* London: Routledge.

Herter, A., Fem, E. & Lehmann, M. (2017) 'Professed protection, pointless provisions: Overview of the German Prostitutes Protection Act', International Committee on the Rights of Sex Workers in Europe. Available at: http://www.sexworkeurope.org/news/general-news/germany-sex-workers-rights-day-icrse-launches-briefing-paper-germanys-new.

Kilvington, J., Day, S. & Ward, H. (2001) 'Prostitution policy in Europe: A time of change?', *Feminist Review,* 67, 78–93.

Kingston, S. & Thomas, T. (2019) 'No model in practice: A "Nordic model" to respond to prostitution?', *Crime, Law and Social Change,* 71, 423–39.

Knight, D. (2010) 'The (continuing) regulation of prostitution by local authorities', in G. Abel, L. Fitzgerald, C. Healy & A. Taylor (eds) *Taking the Crime Out of Sex Work: New Zealand sex workers' fight for decriminalisation,* Bristol: Policy Press.

Krüsi, A., Pacey, K., Bird, L., Taylor, C., Chettiar, J., Allan, S., Bennett, D., Montaner, J., Kerr, T. & Shannon, K. (2014) 'Criminalisation of clients: Reproducing vulnerabilities for violence and poor health among street-based sex workers in Canada - a qualitative study', *BMJ Open,* 4.

Kulick, D. (2003) 'Sex in the new Europe: The criminalization of clients and Swedish fear of penetration', *Anthropological Theory,* 3, 199–218.

Kulick, D. (2005) 'Swedish Model', Beijing Plus Ten Meeting. Available at: http://lastradainternational.org/lsidocs/258%20The%20Swedish%20model%20(Beijing%20Plus%20Ten%20meeting).pdf.

Levy, J. (2014) *Criminalising the Purchase of Sex: Lessons from Sweden*, London: Routledge.

Levy, J. & Jakobsson, P. (2014) 'Sweden's abolitionist discourse and law: Effects on the dynamics of Swedish sex work and on the lives of Sweden's sex workers', *Criminology and Criminal Justice*, 14, 593–607.

Mac, J. & Smith, M. (2018) *Revolting Prostitutes: The fight for sex workers' rights*, London: Verso Books.

Manson, B. (2018) 'Dame Catherine Healy "brought in from the cold" after career advocating for sex workers', 4 June. Available at: https://www.stuff.co.nz/national/104330042/dame-catherine-healy-brought-in-from-the-cold-after-career-advocating-for-sex-workers.

McKay, E. (2019) 'Police and Prostitutes' Collective partnership helps to improve assault reporting', *New Zealand Herald*, 29 October. Available at: https://www.nzherald.co.nz/nz/news/article.cfm?c_id=1&objectid=12280310.

New Zealand Government (2018) 'The Treaty of Waitangi'. Available at: https://www.newzealandnow.govt.nz/living-in-nz/history-government/the-treaty-of-waitangi.

North, A. (2019) 'The movement to decriminalize sex work, explained', *Vox*, 2 August. Available at: https://www.vox.com/2019/8/2/20692327/sex-work-decriminalization-prostitution-new-york-dc.

O'Brien, E., Carpenter, B. & Hayes, S. (2013) 'Sex trafficking and moral harm: Politicised understandings and depictions of the trafficked experience', *Critical Criminology*, 21, 401–15.

Outshoorn, J. (2012) 'Policy change in prostitution in the Netherlands: From legalization to strict control', *Sexuality Research and Social Policy*, 9, 233–43.

Scoular, J. & Carline, A. (2014) 'A critical account of a "creeping neo-abolitionism": Regulating prostitution in England and Wales', *Criminology and Criminal Justice*, 14, 608–26.

Showden, C. (2016) 'Feminist sex wars', in A. Wong, M. Wickramasinghe, R. Hoogland & N. Naples (eds) *The Wiley Blackwell Encyclopedia of Gender and Sexuality Studies*, Malden, MA: Wiley-Blackwell.

Smith, M. (2019) 'Feminists, if you support the "Nordic" approach to sex work, you're co-signing the imprisonment of women', *The Independent*, 11 June. Available at: https://www.independent.co.uk/voices/sex-work-ireland-kildare-brothel-new-york-trades-act-a8954151.html.

Vuolajärvi, N. (2019) 'Governing in the name of caring—the Nordic model of prostitution and its punitive consequences for migrants who sell sex', *Sexuality Research and Social Policy*, 16, 151–65.

Wong, W., Holroyd, E. & Bingham, A. (2011) 'Stigma and sex work from the perspective of female sex workers in Hong Kong', *Sociology of Health & Illness*, 33, 50–65.

Yingwana, N., Walker, R. & Etchart, A. (2019) 'Sex work, migration, and human trafficking in South Africa: From polarised arguments to potential partnerships', *Anti-Trafficking Review*, 12, 74–90.

PART I

Legislative Change in New Zealand

1

'On the Clients' Terms': Sex Work Before Decriminalisation

Jan Jordan

Introduction

Before the passing of the Prostitution Reform Act (PRA) in 2003, the provision of sexual services in New Zealand was effectively illegal and sex workers lived with high levels of risk and fear. The consequences of being charged with soliciting were severe and the implications of having a prostitution-related conviction lasted for life. Their essentially illegal status rendered sex workers vulnerable to abuse, violence and exploitation, and highlighted the double standard of morality that penalised them while protecting the rights and identities of their clients.

This chapter will outline significant features in the history of prostitution in New Zealand, focusing in particular on the social and legal context in the years leading up to the passing of the PRA. It will draw on existing research documenting both the social stigma associated with prostitution as well as the legal sanctions against sex workers. Particular effort will be given to including accounts and quotations from sex workers themselves, some of which will draw on the author's own previously published interviews from the 1990s. This emphasis is important in order to ensure as much as possible that sex workers' own voices inform accounts of the history of their experiences of working in the sex industry.

The primary aim of this chapter is to present a contextual framework for the chapters that follow by providing a window into how sex workers' lives were negatively impacted upon, and their safety compromised, by the legal environment pre-decriminalisation. It begins with a brief overview of the early history of prostitution in New Zealand and developments leading up to the 1970s, before focusing more specifically on the Massage Parlours Act and the experiences of sex workers in the years leading up to the passage of the PRA. Included in the discussion are the voices of sex workers themselves commenting on their experiences of living under a legislative regime that, while not outlawing prostitution itself, nevertheless made it impossible to work within the sex industry without breaking the law. The chapter argues for the necessity of law reform based on the need to eliminate the double standard of morality that prevailed, which privileged men's access to sex workers while leaving the women facing multiple risks and exploitation.

Early history in New Zealand

When New Zealand was first colonised by Europeans in the late 18th century, one of the many social practices introduced to our shores was prostitution. Sailing ships arrived after long voyages with male crews of whalers, sealers and traders eager to obtain sexual services. While no evidence of prostitution exists among Māori before this time, exchanges of muskets and other goods quickly became common between seamen and local women (Belich, 1996; King, 2004). In the 1820s, a naval doctor observed canoes 'crammed' with women arriving when the French ship, *La Coquille*, anchored in the Bay of Islands. He described them as 'a flock of ewes in search of buyers', noting that despite the captain's best efforts, there was no moving the 'lascivious livestock' (Lesson, cited in Kehoe, 1992, p109, quoting Sharp's *Duperry's visit to New Zealand in 1824*). Some chiefs began organising the practice, recognising the potential presented for significantly increasing their tribe's income (Eldred-Grigg, 1984). One commentator observed:

> At this time it was the practice to permit single girls to visit the ship and remain on board over nights, sometimes for several days; the recompense being a nail, gimlet, chisel, hammer, saw, tomahawk, axe, or gun. It is alleged that a chief, named Pomare, maintained in the Bay of Islands one hundred girls, ninety four to be exact, for the purpose of participating in these maritime picnics. (Donne, 1927)

Trade was particularly brisk during the early 19th century in the whaling port of Kororareka (Russell) in the Bay of Islands, and the town gained a reputation as the 'hell-hole of the Pacific' (King, 2004). Whaleboats would frequently stay in port for three weeks, during which time their crews made heavy use of the many taverns and often established short-term 'marriages' with local Māori women (Belich, 1996).

Later, during the 1850s and 1860s, it was the goldfields that were awash with men, money and alcohol, swiftly followed by women seeking their own share of the gold (Eldred-Grigg, 2008). Like the men, many of these women had followed the gold rushes from California and Canada to Australia and now New Zealand. In towns like Dunedin, for example, its proximity to the Otago goldfields resulted in a growing demand for prostitution services. During the mid-1860s its streets 'thronged with more whores than any other city in the colony. Two hundred were still working its streets full-time even three years after the first strike at Gabriel's Gully' (Eldred-Grigg, 2008, p 388).

Meanwhile the rapid growth in immigration during the 1860s and the vastly uneven sex ratio that persisted through the 19th century began to expand men's demands for prostitution services in other towns. While missionaries and ministers lamented the large numbers of 'gin palaces' and 'fallen women', gold-diggers often regretted the amount of money spent on 'finery for the soiled doves' (Eldred-Grigg, 2008, p 390). Complaints were voiced in Christchurch that respectable women risked being jostled on busy streets by whores touting for business, and fears for the new colony's morality were expressed (Macdonald, 1990; Jordan, 2010). 'For many colonists, prostitution and syphilis represented the most degraded Old World ills from which they had fled' (Olssen, 1999, p 47). Women working as prostitutes could be arrested for public drunkenness and rowdy behaviour, and local registers of brothels categorised women according to how 'rowdy' and disruptive they might be (Robinson, 1984). Prostitution, many argued, was a vice that needed to be brought under control.

One strategy involved attempts to attract young single women as immigrants in the hope that they would marry and improve the men's behaviour. The fact that many rejected marriage and domestic servitude on arrival in favour of making money through prostitution produced horrified outrage in some quarters (Eldred-Grigg, 1984; Jordan, 2010). What emerged from discussions at various public meetings was less of a desire to rid the nation of 'the social pest' (Letter to the editor, *Christchurch Press*, 21 February 1868) and more of a concern to find ways to regulate and control the women providing prostitution services (Robinson, 1984; Jordan, 2010). This resulted in New Zealand's introduction of the Contagious Diseases Act 1869, following Britain's lead from 1864, when similar legislation was passed in relation to port and garrison towns in the UK.

The New Zealand legislation was wider-reaching. The Act gave police, initially in Christchurch and later other centres, the power to ascertain who was a 'common prostitute' and subject them to compulsory medical examination, followed by forcible detention if they were found to be suffering from a venereal disease (Eldred-Grigg, 1984; Macdonald, 1986; Knight, 1987). Other legislation was also imported from the UK, including the Vagrancy Act 1824, which remained in place until New Zealand passed its own equivalent legislation in 1866, replaced subsequently in 1884 with the Police Offences Act. Any prostitute acting in a 'riotous or disorderly manner' in a public place ran the risk of being termed 'idle and disorderly' and could be imprisoned for up to three months (Eldred-Grigg, 1984). This legislation reflected the prevailing attitude that saw prostitution tolerated as a necessary evil as long as those plying their trade behaved discreetly and without attracting public attention. It set the tone for how prostitution was policed into the 20th century, while the structure and stratification of the early sex industry also remained evident through later decades, as outlined in the next section.

Twentieth century developments.

By the end of the 19th century sex work was well-established in many towns and cities. Concerns were expressed that demand for prostitution services was so high that many women could live in luxury, and an Auckland clergyman observed that some of the city's most 'magnificent houses' were now owned by whores (Eldred-Grigg, 2008). Prostitutes and barmaids were identified as the two groups of women posing the largest threat to the family unit (Grigg, 1983), and the need to enhance the nation's 'moral purity' became linked to calls to allow women into parliament (Dalziel, 1977; Brookes, 1993). Parallel to the suffrage movement, some women campaigned against prostitution and called for temperance in all matters, but male demand saw the industry continue to flourish.

During the First World War, major concerns were expressed in some quarters about the high numbers of soldiers visiting prostitutes overseas, with Ettie Rout (a safe-sex advocate prominent during the First World War) assuming prominence for her matter-of-fact acceptance of this practice (Tolerton, 1992). She was particularly aware of the risks of venereal and other sexually transmitted diseases that these men faced, and personally travelled to Africa and Europe to assist in the distribution of condoms and other prophylactics.

While sex work seems to have dwindled between the world wars, anxieties about it increased again during the Second World War when American servicemen visited New Zealand for rest and recreation, often finding it in the arms of those known as the 'good time girls' (Jordan, 2005). A veneer of domestic harmony generally dominated official ideology in the 1950s, as ex-soldiers settled into marriage and family life and women vacated the various wartime jobs they had performed. Post-war demand was again said to slump, although the high-class Auckland parlour run by former dressmaker Flora MacKenzie continued to flourish during this period and up until the 1970s (Jordan, 2000). Her Ring Terrace business operated discreetly, providing regular services to many businessmen and politicians while she often employed nurses, teachers and secretaries as part-time workers. As one woman who worked there described it:

> 'Everything was organised for you at Flora's. People didn't come in casually. It was appointments only. And you'd phone up in the morning and be told you had X amount of bookings for the day .... Basically she had very good clients, having come from a very good family herself.' (Hilary, in Jordan, 1991, p 108)

Flora served two short terms in prison but mostly her premises operated with tacit support from the police – she established such good relationships with some that it was said the vice squad held their Christmas parties at Flora's (Jordan, 2000). This attitude of tolerance reflects the dominant police approach of viewing prostitution essentially as a victimless crime requiring only occasional displays of official censure.

Factors of class and ethnicity, often intersected with age, resulted in some sectors of the sex industry receiving no such tolerance during the mid-20th century. One arena of particular scrutiny involved 'ship girls', young mostly Māori women who frequented the wharves seeking to establish liaisons with visiting seamen (Jordan, 1994).

> 'They had bars on the ships, lovely bars. We'd go in there and party, and then back to their rooms. If you got on well with your tima tane [ship man], he'd be with you for the

> whole stay. If you got on extra well, whenever he came back to port, you were for him, you were his girl in this port .... You got paid – or else you went shopping, especially with the Japanese. They'd take you shopping. You'd buy perfumes, clothes, shoes, things like that.' (Poppy, in Wilton, 2018, p 266)

The ships could come from Japan or Korea, England or Denmark, countries sounding faraway and exotic in these years before air travel became commonplace. Some women boarded in one port and sailed round the country with a particular seaman, occasionally even further afield in a practice termed 'ringbolting' (Jordan, 1991). A former ship girl commented "girls were ringbolting then to Holland, the UK, certainly backwards and forwards across the Tasman, like a taxi service. I knew girls who might climb on a ship just to go and visit mother!" (Desna, in Jordan, 1991, p 153).

This was no cruise ship, however, and all those on board were expected to pull their weight working during the voyage, in the kitchen or laundry, even painting the ship (Jordan, 1991). In New Zealand ports it became common practice for the police to wait around the wharves, hoping to arrest the girls and women for being unlawfully on board as they left the boats. During the 1950s and 1960s, many were sent to borstal institutions, such as Arohata Prison, for a mix of both punishment and reform (Templeton, 1981; Jordan, 1994).

The social upheaval was vast when, during the 1970s, the happy families façade was increasingly challenged by the exposure of sexism and racism, and as human rights movements around the world gained traction. Many previously hidden aspects of society became more publicly acknowledged, and in this climate growing attention was given to prostitution and the policing of the sex industry. The street scene attracted particular attention from vice squads into the 1980s, with several of the country's major cities having what everyone recognised as 'red-light districts'. The workers walked or waited on the pavements for 'business' from men soliciting them from their cars, typically accepting lifts to a secluded area where the sexual transactions occurred.

> 'There's a lot more choice out on the streets, for the guys as well as us. If he doesn't like the look of you, he can just drive on by and look somewhere else. And if you don't like the look of him, you can wave him goodbye. You've

got all the freedom in the world to say no.' (Genevieve, in Jordan, 1991, p 121)

The streets were typically the only arena within which transgender sex workers could work (Worth, 2000). The transphobia of this period meant these women had few other employment options available, and they were easy targets for both public and police harassment. A former officer in charge of the Wellington vice squad has recounted how, as well as being highly visible, all that needed to be proved until the passing of the Homosexual Law Reform Act in 1985 was that some form of sexual connection between 'males' (as they were viewed in the eyes of the law) had occurred (Fitzharris, 2010). It was on this basis that he was involved in the arrest of the most prominent transgender woman in the city, Carmen, though in retrospect she believed the publicity surrounding her colourful trial served only to enhance her and her coffee bar's reputation (Fitzharris, 2010).

After the 1985 law changes, any arrests and prosecutions needed to include evidence of payment being offered in exchange for sexual services, with undercover police officers often assisting vice squad operations. An interview with a transgender sex worker included the following description:

> 'There are times I'd go out and I'm a bit overexcited because I'm out for a good night and I feel confident, I've got a nice dress on, looking forward to making a bit of money and going out to a nightclub and having fun – but then hop in a car, don't really care who it is, just being greedy really. You hop in a car, ask for business, and out comes this card – 'Undercover police officer, you're under arrest for soliciting' which is really, really tortuous …. You get driven to the back of a building, to a waiting police wagon, and you know you're going to be in that cell till about eight o'clock in the morning. So you can kiss your good night goodbye.' (Shareda, in Wilton, 2018, p 76)

While the street scene was the public face of prostitution, for decades brothels had operated surreptitiously in many cities. Many were small, backroom affairs servicing local or fishing industry men which mostly flew beneath the radar. *Flora's* was an exception in being so widely known about, in large part due to her larger-than-life personality and the wealthy clientele her business attracted. In Wellington, it was Bill Crowe's house in Mt Victoria that became the famous hub for the city's businessmen and politicians. A former 'hostess', as he called them, described living in a bedsit in his home during the eighteen months she worked there:

> 'I'd like to say you get a much better clientele at Edward's [Bill Crowe's], and to some extent that's true. There used to be a lot of top businessmen, politicians, Olympic athletes – the upper crust. But three-piece suits can get as drunk as anybody else, and they're just as bloody objectionable.'
> (Hilary, in Jordan, 1991, p 111)

Such establishments were mostly allowed by police to operate quietly, with only the occasional visit or raid to keep everyone in line. A vice squad anecdote tells of one famed night when detectives poised to undertake such a raid were quickly ordered to 'stand down' – the prime minister at the time had been spotted waddling up the path. Bill Crowe himself boasted of the dignitaries and celebrities who partied at his establishment, along with the high calibre of international hostesses he recruited for the pleasure of his guests (Bill Crowe, in an interview with author Jan Jordan, 1990).

During the 1970s, concerns had become rife throughout New Zealand regarding perceptions of a growing drug problem. Stereotypes abounded of drug-addicted women forced into prostitution to feed their habits, and the police often believed sex workers were associated with the criminal fraternities involved in the drugs scene (Fitzharris, 2010). It was within the context of this moral panic that the Massage Parlours Act 1978 was passed.

The Massage Parlours Act 1978

'Massage parlour' was a euphemism for a brothel, as was the less frequently used term 'rap parlour'. These terms were used as a means of denying that prostitution services were available in such places. Some sex workers resented the time and effort spent massaging clients, with one noting for example:

> 'The Las Vegas was a rap parlour then, which meant there was no massage. You took a guy to the room, you sat there, you had a chat – rapping was just chatting. Usually within five minutes they got bored and asked about sex, so in that sense it was a lot easier because you didn't have

to go through the rigmarole of giving a massage.' (Sarah, in Jordan, 1991, p 17)

Under the Massage Parlours Act 1978, all parlours were defined as 'public places', despite the transactions being negotiated and conducted in private (Jordan, 2010). This legislation required operators to obtain licences, and enabled existing laws against sex workers, such as soliciting for business on the streets, to be extended to indoor settings. It also required operators to maintain lists of their employees, and police regularly checked these names to ensure no workers had convictions for drugs or prostitution offences (Healy et al, 2010). If any did, they were immediately barred from working in massage parlours, restricting the prostitution arenas within which they could work to the streets or escort services.

Clients walking into a massage parlour were greeted by a receptionist, who told them how much a massage cost and showed them through to a room with one of the women. Some establishments paraded the women in front of the client first so he could choose whom he liked. The woman would typically undress and begin providing a massage, then ask if the man wanted 'extras', with the nature of those extras left deliberately vague in order to avoid any solicitation on her part (Robinson, 1987). If the client requested sexual acts then he paid for these directly to the woman providing them; if he wanted only the massage, or came with limited cash, the woman would receive no recompense for her time while the parlour always kept the money paid upfront for the massage.

> 'All of the girls were giving nude massages. The client would pay a fee at the door, NZ$40, and he got a nude massage, and then it was up to him to negotiate any extras with the girl. So of course a lot of them didn't have the money. They've already seen you in the nude, they've had you massaging them and quite often they've already ejaculated on the towel, then all of a sudden there's no money, they've got what they've needed, and you don't get paid.' (Kelly, in Wilton, 2018, p 114)

A climate of fear surrounded these transactions because of the ever-present risk that undercover police officers might pose as clients in order to arrest the women for selling prostitution services. While a conviction for soliciting carried a relatively low financial penalty, no more than a NZ$200 fine, the consequences for the women were potentially very harmful (Robinson, 1987). These included the stipulation already noted that any woman with a prostitution-related or drugs-related conviction was banned from working in a massage parlour for ten years (Robinson, 1987). This meant that to return to such work, a woman would have to exchange the relative safety and support of the parlour for a potentially riskier working environment. Even longer lasting were the impacts of such a conviction in a range of other contexts, affecting the ability to secure other employment, arrange mortgage finance, travel overseas, or undertake other activities that required criminal history checks (Healy et al, 2010). The heavy stigma attached to sex work also made it virtually impossible for sex workers to be open on their CVs or when job-hunting about where they had worked previously. Ironically, the attitudes and penalties that prevailed made exiting the industry difficult and effectively locked some women into staying longer than they might have wished within this occupational context.

Some parlours and individuals also offered escort services, involving the sex worker going to meet the client in his home or hotel room. Former escort workers have described different kinds of categories of men requesting their services, one large category comprising men away from home on business while others asked to be visited in their homes (Jordan, 1991). One noted that 'a lot of these guys ring up because they don't want to be seen walking into a parlour' (Kate, in Jordan, 1991, p 194), and described how many of the men appeared lonely and in search of companionship.

> 'I tell them I'm quite happy to have a cup of coffee and a chat, but they'll have to pay me for it, otherwise I'm leaving immediately. In fact they always end up fucking me. Nobody wants to shell out NZ$100 just to have a cup of coffee with somebody – despite the wonderful scintillating company!' (Kate, in Jordan, 1991, p 194)

Risks and hazards

For women doing escort work, concerns about the potential risks involved meant some places sent a male driver to wait for the woman, but often they went alone. This prospect was "really scary" for some women, with one reflecting:

> 'You don't know who's going to be there, and if it's his house then he knows where everything is and you don't. Some of

these guys lived on their own, but a lot didn't. I remember one guy in particular was living in a very frilly house with a pink bedroom, dim lighting and women's clothes everywhere – I don't know where his wife was. Another place had kids' toys all over the floor and I wondered, 'My God, did your wife and kids just nip out to see Nana or something and you quickly got on the phone?'" (Jasmine, in Jordan, 1991, p 184)

While the majority of clients posed no risks to sex workers, the legal situation posed a constant risk and created a climate of fear throughout the industry.

'Police entrapment was certainly a thing that happened …. You've got those that would have the sex and then bust you. Nobody is going to take that to court. You're fighting a losing battle because people would not believe you – they would not think the police would possibly do anything like that. Yes they could, and yes they did.' (Kelly, in Wilton, 2018, p 121)

More than ten years before the passing of the PRA, a parlour worker articulated her view:

'If it was decriminalised, we could run the same as we are now but without having to live in constant fear of getting busted. At the moment you've got to be so careful with every client, and so suspicious. And the clients feel paranoid too. Decriminalisation would be the best option for everybody.' (Sarah, in Jordan, 1991, p 29)

When sex workers were arrested in any public place, streets or massage parlours, a strange anomaly existed allowing police officers to seize supplies of condoms as evidence of prostitution. This meant that, while safe sex and anti-HIV/AIDS messages were being strongly disseminated through public health channels, should a sex worker's handbag contain multiple condoms then these could be used against her in court (Healy et al, 2010). This was blatantly unjust in a climate where practising safe sex had always been a priority for those making their living from the sex industry. Pressure from clients for the women not to use condoms was an occupational hazard they learned to negotiate, although some encountered the occasional man insistent on his right to sex without a condom.

> 'I've got a scar up through my eyebrow and under my eye where another client attacked me. He broke two ribs as well as splitting my eye open. We were fighting over a condom. He wanted not to use a condom, and it got really violent, just fighting over a condom. I've always insisted on condoms being used, before AIDS or anything.' (Caroline, in Jordan, 1991, p 236)

Street workers could face additional risks arising from the contexts within which they met clients and provided sexual services. Being picked up by a typically unknown male cruising by in his car necessitated high levels of trust regarding what might follow. While most of the time business was conducted quickly and without trouble, this was not always the case. An Auckland-based sex worker observed:

> 'It can be risky on the street. There are a few guys you have to watch out for. One particular guy up K Road [Karangahape Road in Auckland] seems to do over everybody. He picks them up, beats them up, robs them and rapes them. That's how a mate of mine lost her teeth.' (Liz, in Jordan, 1991, p 173)

Sex workers in parlours were vulnerable also to possible exploitation by the owners and operators of these businesses. The precarious legal position of the workers made them potentially vulnerable to those operating these establishments.

> 'Most of the parlours I worked at were owned by men, and their attitude was pretty terrible. Some of them insisted on sleeping with you first, just to see if you were any good at the job. They tried out every girl before they employed her, and some still felt that they had free access to the girls whenever they wanted. If you refused, you lost your job.' (Caroline, in Jordan, 1991, p 243)

Not only might they not receive any payment for clients whom they massaged without 'extras', but they were often subject to a raft of exploitative employment conditions. These could include paying shift fees every time they worked, as well as incurring costs for laundry and other items essential to the running of the business.

> 'Then there were fines. You're 10 minutes late, NZ$100 fine. Anything to get any money out of people. The woman that managed the place where they introduced shift fees used to hire and fire and fine arbitrarily. Every day people would turn up for work – got a taxi, had to pay for child care – to be told they were no longer on the roster. They wouldn't even get a phone call. No reason – her little whim.'
> (Anna Reed, in Wilton, 2018, p 53)

The women had no protection as workers, and no benefits such as sick pay or annual leave. While such benefits might not be missed during periods of bumper business, changing economic times made a big difference to the women's earnings and employment conditions. Not surprisingly, some women lamented the lack of a union that could champion their rights. This was evident, for example, in one interview: 'I think there's a real need for some kind of organisation to represent the interests of working girls, some kind of union or body that will stand up for the girls' rights' (Sarah, in Jordan, 1991, p 33).

The New Zealand Prostitutes' Collective (NZPC)

During the 1980s there were growing concerns among some sex workers regarding their social and legal vulnerability. Economically, times had been particularly buoyant until events such as the stock market crash and the banning of visits by American warships heralded what some sex workers saw as the end of the golden weather.

The fear of HIV/AIDS was also at its peak, adding to the fears sex workers already had of being arrested or having nowhere to go if a client, real or bogus, robbed or raped them. In describing the social and legal environment, Dame Catherine Healy (national spokesperson for NZPC) has referred to a range of issues that prompted her and other sex workers to establish a collective:

> 'Labour, management, stigma, recognising sex work as work, equal rights, equal protections, public health, HIV and Aids were the major themes – and of course the fact that sex workers were criminalised, and there would be these police raids where they'd come in undercover and

entrap sex workers for soliciting. Then there would be this reality of going to court and being prosecuted, and that was pretty horrific.' (Wilton, 2018, p 135)

NZPC was initially established in 1987 by Wellington women working in massage parlours who soon began reaching out to other sectors of the industry, including transgender and male sex workers. There was a shared anger over laws targeting sex workers and negative public perceptions that stigmatised all those who worked in the industry (Jordan, 2018). Massage parlour workers also held concerns over unfair management practices and the lack of legal protection for workers. Most importantly, 'They wanted sex workers' voices to be heard and for them to inform the discourses that framed their work and lives' (Healy et al, 2010, p 46).

The misinformed but dominant view of sex workers as transmitters of sexual diseases was important in securing initial funding to assist in the establishment of a network. In October 1988, the group received funding from the Minister of Health and opened a drop-in centre for all sex workers in Upper Cuba Street in Wellington (Healy et al, 2010). While NZPC knew of no cases of HIV affecting sex workers or their clients, their awareness of the growing prevalence of the disease in the general population meant they agreed to work with the Department of Health in education and prevention initiatives.

NZPC began publishing its own magazine, *SIREN*, and soon established community bases in other centres, combining these with needle exchange programmes. Different groups of sex workers began developing their own identities beneath this umbrella, including male sex workers (PUMP – Pride and Unity for Male Prostitutes), transgender sex workers (ONTOP – Ongoing Network Transgender Outreach Group) and Māori sex workers (Māori Action Group). While generally well received, the formation of NZPC provoked resistance from some quarters.

> Some controlling and coercive operators forbade their staff to have contact with the NZPC because they did not want their mistreatment of staff to be challenged. Other parlour owners and operators were cautious about being associated with sex work out of fear of being prosecuted for brothel keeping. (Healy et al, 2010, p 50)

Throughout the 1990s, strong arguments were made by NZPC that sex workers could not be effective as safe sex promoters and educators in a criminalised environment. Support from a wide range of sectors was growing for prostitution to be decriminalised, alongside recognition that the constant reality of client demands rendered any thoughts of eradicating the sex industry impossible in a society still etched with the mix of gendered and economic inequalities that are patriarchy's legacy.

Clients

The history of prostitution has been mostly a very one-sided affair, with by far the bulk of attention and opprobrium directed at the women providing sexual services while those demanding to purchase them have remained largely protected and invisible. When we consider who the clients are within the New Zealand context, we can see the demands initially generated by an unequal sex ratio – whalers, traders, gold-diggers. Sailors and soldiers continued this trend through the 20th century, with sex workers themselves referring to particular client groups at different times – American soldiers and sailors during and after the war, later men off the Japanese and Korean fishing boats, and always the teams and supporters during many large male-dominated sporting events (Jordan, 1991; Wilton, 2018).

More recently, however, the majority of men likely to be regular buyers of sexual services have been those who equate to the 'everyman' concept. They may be married or single, young or old, from any employment group, of any ethnic background, and most likely will be seeking very ordinary sexual services (Jordan, 1991). Research has identified some men consider paying money is the only way they will be able to have sex, with many clients in interviews describing how their interactions with sex workers help them to manage the loneliness of their everyday lives (Jordan, 1997; Mower, 2019). Others viewed paying for sex as an easier, less complicated option than hooking up with women at bars or nightclubs (Plumridge et al, 1997; Jordan, 1997).

> 'You can end up picking up somebody you don't really want to pick up and doing some things you don't really want to do, and then you wake up in the morning and sneak out or whatever, and next minute they'll be knocking on your door that they're pregnant or they've got VD or something … or they're crying rape because they've come out of their drunken stupor or whatever and they realize they shouldn't be there or the boyfriend's going to find out, so then you've got all that hassle, just for one thing, for something that

might last for a few minutes to a couple of hours – I just don't see the point, I really don't see it.' (David, in Jordan, 1997, p 60)

Some felt able to request services from sex workers that they would not feel able to request of their wives or partners, or viewed their visits as ways to indulge particular sexual fantasies. One of the more common practices requested involved bondage and discipline sessions. One sex worker, for example, recounted of her business:

'I also did a lot of golden showers and whippings. It was a lot of money for B&D – NZ$150 for a hiding even then. I'd give them a good hiding for that. Some would bring their own horsewhips along. Others liked to have your stiletto shoes stamped and prodded into their bodies. I used to do all that rather than sex.' (Gloria, in Jordan, 1991, p 94)

Married men sometimes justified their visits to sex workers by referring to their wives no longer being interested in sex, or not being sexually adventurous enough for them. Others maintained that sex is such a basic need that if they were out of town without their wife then it was only natural that they would need to buy sex (Jordan, 1997). For example, one married man who bought sexual services during his frequent trips away from home said he felt no sense of betraying his wife: 'Not at all – she just wasn't there. I didn't tell her because I didn't think it would be very diplomatic and it could make her unhappy' (Jansen, in Jordan, 1997, p 59).

The laws that operated against prostitution had little to no impact on clients here, apart from the occasional fear that if caught up in a police raid their wife might hear about it. Clients faced none of the risks that the sex workers did, and New Zealand has never had the kerb-crawling legislation of the United Kingdom (Brooks-Gordon and Gelsthorpe, 2003) or sent clients to 'john schools', as happens in parts of Canada and the United States (Fischer et al, 2002). Men's knowledge of the legal vulnerability of sex workers, however, may have contributed to the violence and robberies experienced by some women. Clients could potentially rely on the women needing to stay discreet and beneath the radar, so that those who did choose to attack them knew there was scant likelihood of the women contacting the police. From this perspective, the legal situation pre-decriminalisation potentially enabled the abuse and exploitation of sex workers as well as denying them any employment rights. It was the inequities of this double standard that encouraged the formation of a diverse support base calling for an end to the discrimination and exploitation inherent within the existing situation.

Campaigning for decriminalisation

Despite the obvious inequities of the double standard, the road to decriminalisation was far from smooth. In a country still coy about talking about 'sex', the capacity to have frank and open conversations about 'sex work' was initially limited. Gradually support for changing the law grew, in large part due to the steadfast way in which NZPC, and Catherine Healy in particular, built relationships of trust through large cross-sections of the community.

Healy has spoken of her efforts garnering support from diverse sectors, and identifying key individuals whom it would be useful to have on board. As she described the passing of the PRA: 'There wasn't actually a campaign for decriminalisation – there was just a series of rolling events' (Catherine Healy, in Wilton, 2018, p 142).

The seemingly ad hoc way in which networks emerged and energies were harnessed nonplussed some observers. Healy recalled:

> '... after it happened I remember people saying, well, can you share your ideas on your strategy? And that wasn't what happened at all. It was just a constant chip, chip, chip, chip, you know, almost obsessive. And using every situation that presented an opportunity to nudge it forward.' (Catherine Healy, in Wilton, 2018, p 143)

The opportunities that arose involved accepting speaking invitations from a wide cross-section of community, business and professional groups, as well as participating in as many media interviews and television documentaries as possible. Engagement with the wider public to challenge the stigma surrounding sex work had grown since 1991. when there was nationwide publicity and speaking tours following the publication of the first book of interviews documenting sex workers' lives (Jordan, 1991). This helped in building the momentum for change that grew through the 1990s and was undertaken by academics and community groups willing to work collaboratively alongside NZPC. One of the most important strands of support came from women's organisations, once their members could see that the abuses and double standards enabled by the existing legislative framework violated basic human rights and, for some, contradicted the principles of feminism (Laurie, 2010). A second critical strand involved doctors, venereologists and other medical professionals who could see how the existing laws worked against public and sex worker health interests (Healy et al, 2010).

Politicians likely to be supportive of law change were also identified and approached, initially Maurice Williamson and Katherine O'Regan and later Labour MP Tim Barnett, who agreed to sponsor the Bill. The goal was decriminalisation, but the exact wording of the clauses necessitated considerable consultation and legal drafting. The specific aims sought to recognise the human rights of sex workers and reflected a harm minimisation approach (Abel et al, 2010). One particular clause prohibited the use in prostitution of any person under 18 years of age, a significant outcome given that the age of consent generally was 16. Consistent with the safeguarding of sex workers' rights were the provisions stipulating there was to be no coercion of any person to accept any client or perform any service they did not wish to.

Despite widespread support across diverse sectors, the debates enacted in the early 2000s leading up to the Bill's passing were often intense, at times vitriolic (Laurie, 2010). Church communities were typically polarised in their views, some Christian groups were supportive on humanitarian grounds while others condemned laws that they believed sanctioned sin. One commonly voiced argument expressed the fear that removing the legal sanctions against sex workers would result in swarms of women leaving homes and marriages to make their fortune selling sex (*New Zealand Herald*, 2003).

Debates on the proposed legislation before a Select Committee underscored the polarised perspectives in place, even from *within* some quarters. For example, of the total number of 222 submissions received, approximately one quarter came from feminist groups or individuals or were based on feminist arguments. Of these 56 feminist submissions, however, 40 supported decriminalisation while 16 vigorously opposed it (Laurie, 2010). While some of the latter claimed prostitution itself was a violation of women's human rights, many of the former saw the existing legal framework as the greater abuser. Significantly, many large, mainstream women's organisations supported the bill, among them the National Council of Women, the Young Women's Christian Association (YWCA), and the New Zealand Federation of Business and Professional Women (Laurie, 2010). Explaining the YWCA's stance, its Executive Director asserted:

> The law is structured so that it acknowledges that the act of prostitution occurs, but ensures that it occurs only on

the clients' terms. It labels sex workers as the criminals and their customers as victims ... Allowing women to work without fear of prosecution would at least help provide a safer working environment. (Keenan, 1996)

Sex workers were among those making submissions, often providing graphic accounts of how the existing legal situation left them vulnerable to violence and abuse. Said one:

'... it is often nearly impossible to refuse a client. There's no discussion of this in parlours, but women who have tried to refuse a client, say if they have seen them before and they are rough or extremely unhygienic, they have been told "you're in no position to be refusing clients, young lady", or, one which seems to be a favourite around Wellington, "your cunt's not golden, get upstairs"'. (PRB 107A, 2001, p 4)

Not surprisingly, the lead-up to the passing of the legislation in June 2003 was a tense affair with the factions in Parliament appearing equally divided. No one felt confident enough to predict the outcome, with several MPs saying they remained undecided right to the bitter end. The speeches in Parliament that night reflected this division, although a moving account provided by transgender MP, Georgina Beyer, appeared to influence both sides of the House. She described how, when she was working the streets years earlier, she was raped by a client yet knew she would receive no support if she went to the police. It was her aspiration, she said, to create a safer climate for today's sex workers so they would not have to endure what she did (O'Connor, 2003; Venter, 2003). Her delivery of this speech was so heartfelt and impassioned that, when she finished, even MPs from the opposing National Party crossed the floor to embrace and congratulate her. When the vote was finally taken on 25 June 2003, for many of those there it was a 'pinch me' moment when the count came in at 60 to 59 – prostitution in New Zealand was now decriminalised.

Conclusion

The sex industry has been an ever-present strand of New Zealand society since its early colonisation and shows little sign of abating. Throughout its history it has been characterised by different levels of stratification providing services to clientele across a wide range of income and occupational groups. While some sectors have been blatantly visible and attracted high levels of stigma and attention, others have operated with a quiet discretion protecting both workers and clients. The legal environment dominating most of this history reflected a double standard of morality that justified men's seeking of sex while simultaneously penalising those providing them with sexual services. By the 1990s, there was growing awareness in many sectors of the injustices perpetrated by the prevailing legal system, and NZPC was able to harness widespread support for adopting a rights-based approach to law reform. The passing of the PRA in 2003 reflected a harm minimisation stance oriented towards maintaining an environment conducive to public health while empowering sex workers in their occupation. The rest of this book explores what this legislative sea change has subsequently meant for New Zealand, and particularly for those connected in any way with the sex industry.

References

Abel, G., Healy, C., Bennachie, C. & Reed, A. (2010) 'The Prostitution Reform Act', in G. Abel, L. Fitzgerald, C. Healy & A. Taylor (eds) *Taking the Crime Out of Sex Work: New Zealand sex workers' fight for decriminalisation*, Bristol: Policy Press, pp 75–84.

Belich, J. (1996) *Making Peoples: A History of the New Zealanders. From Polynesian settlement to the end of the nineteenth century*, Auckland: Allen Lane/Penguin Press.

Brookes, B. (1993) 'A weakness for strong subjects: The women's movement and sexuality', *New Zealand Journal of History*, 27(2): 140–56.

Brooks-Gordon, B. & Gelsthorpe, L. (2003) 'What men say when apprehended for kerb crawling: A model of prostitutes' clients' talk', *Psychology, Crime & Law*, 9(2), 145–71.

Dalziel, R. (1977) 'The colonial helpmeet: Women's role and the vote in nineteenth-century New Zealand', *New Zealand Journal of History*, 11(2): 112–23.

Donne, T. E. (1927) *The Maori, Past and Present*, London: Sealey Service.

Eldred-Grigg, S. (1984) *Pleasures of the Flesh: Sex and drugs in colonial New Zealand 1840–1915*, Wellington: A. H. and A. W. Reed.

Eldred-Grigg, S. (2008) *Diggers, Hatters and Whores: The story of the New Zealand gold rushes*, Auckland: Random House New Zealand.

Fischer, B., Wortley, S., Webster, C. & Kirst, M. (2002) 'The socio-legal dynamics and implications of "diversion": The case study of the Toronto "John School" diversion programme for prostitution offenders', *Criminal Justice*, 2(4): 385–410.

Fitzharris, P. (2010) 'Review of the Prostitution Reform Act', in G. Abel, L. Fitzgerald, C. Healy & A. Taylor (eds) *Taking the Crime Out of Sex Work: New Zealand sex workers' fight for decriminalisation*, Bristol: Policy Press, pp 105–18.

Grigg, A. R. (1983) 'Prohibition and women: The preservation of an ideal and a myth', *New Zealand Journal of History*, 17(2): 144–65.

Healy, C., Bennachie, C. & Reed, A. (2010) 'History of the New Zealand Prostitutes' Collective', in G. Abel, L. Fitzgerald, C. Healy & A. Taylor (eds) *Taking the Crime Out of Sex Work: New Zealand sex workers' fight for decriminalisation*, Bristol: Policy Press, pp 45–56.

Jordan, J. (1991) *Working Girls: Women in the New Zealand sex industry*, Auckland: Penguin Books.

Jordan, J. (1994) *Ship Girls: The invisible women of the sea*, Wellington: Institute of Criminology Occasional Paper Series.

Jordan, J. (1997) 'User pays: Why men buy sex', *Australian and New Zealand Journal of Criminology*, 30(1): 55–71.

Jordan, J. (2000) 'Flora McKenzie', in C. Orange (ed) *The Dictionary of New Zealand Biography, Volume Five, 1941–1960*, Auckland: Auckland University Press, pp 386–7.

Jordan, J. (2005) *The Sex Industry in New Zealand: A literature review*, Wellington: The Ministry of Justice.

Jordan, J. (2010) 'Of whalers, diggers and "soiled doves": A history of the sex industry in New Zealand', in G. Abel, L. Fitzgerald, C. Healy & A. Taylor (eds) *Taking the Crime Out of Sex Work: New Zealand sex workers' fight for decriminalisation*, Bristol: Policy Press, pp 25–44.

Jordan, J. (2018) 'New Zealand Prostitutes' Collective', in *Women Together – Ngā Rōpū Wāhine o te Motu*. Available at: https://nzhistory.govt.nz/women-together (Ministry for Culture and Heritage), updated 1 May 2019.

Keenan, D. (1996) 'YWCA backs prostitutes' collective', *The Press*, 31 Oct 1996, edn 2, p 4.

Kehoe, J. M. (1992) 'Medicine, sexuality and imperialism: British medical discourses surrounding venereal disease in New Zealand and Japan: A socio-historical and comparative study', PhD thesis, Wellington: Victoria University of Wellington.

King, M. (2004) *The Penguin History of New Zealand*, Auckland: Viking.

Knight, A. (1987) 'Prostitution and the law', *Race, Gender, Class*, 5: 57–70.

Laurie, A. (2010) 'Several sides to this story: Feminist views of prostitution reform', in G. Abel, L. Fitzgerald, C. Healy & A. Taylor (eds) *Taking the Crime Out of Sex Work: New Zealand sex workers' fight for decriminalisation*, Bristol: Policy Press, pp 85–101.

'Letter to the Editor', *Christchurch Press*, 21 February 1868.

Macdonald, C. (1986) 'The "Social Evil": Prostitution and the passage of the Contagious Diseases Act (1869)', in C. Macdonald, M. Tennant & B. Brookes (eds) *Women in History: Essays on European women in New Zealand*, Wellington: Allen and Unwin/Port Nicholson Press, pp 13–34.

Macdonald, C. (1990) *A Woman of Good Character: Single women as immigrant settlers in nineteenth-century New Zealand,* Wellington: Allen and Unwin/Historical Branch.

Mower, S. (2019) 'Clients coming out – Men speak out about purchasing sex in New Zealand's decriminalised environment', MA thesis, Wellington: Victoria University of Wellington.

New Zealand Herald (2003) 'If we encourage prostitution, we will get more of it', *New Zealand Herald*, 18 February, p 7.

O'Connor, T. (2003) 'Lightening up on red light zone', *The Nelson Mail*, 1 July 2003, edn 2, p 7.

Olssen, E. (1999) 'Families and the gendering of European New Zealand in the colonial period, 1840–80', in C. Daley & D. Montgomery (eds), *The Gendered Kiwi,* Auckland: Auckland University Press, pp 37–62.

Plumridge, E., Chetwynd, J., Reed, A. & Gifford, S. (1997) 'Discourses of Emotionality in Commercial Sex: The Missing Client Voice', *Feminism & Psychology,* 7(2): 165–81.

PRB 107A, Private submission to the Select Committee on Prostitution Reform, 2001.

Robinson, J. (1984) 'Canterbury's rowdy women: Whores, madonnas and female criminality', *Women's Studies Journal*, 1(1): 6–25.

Robinson, J. (1987) 'The Oldest Profession', in S. Cox (ed) *Public and Private Worlds: Women in contemporary New Zealand*, Wellington: Allen and Unwin, Port Nicholson Press, pp 177–91.

Templeton, C. (1981) *Pillpopper: Live and die,* Martinborough: Alister Taylor.

Tolerton, J. (1992) *Ettie: A life of Ettie Rout*, Auckland: Penguin Books.

Venter, N. (2003) 'MPs have late changes of heart', *The Dominion Post*, 26 June 2003, edn 2, p 1.

Wilton, C. (2018) *My Body, My Business: New Zealand sex workers in an era of change,* Dunedin: Otago University Press.

Worth, H. (2000) 'Up on K Road on Saturday night: Sex, gender and sex work in Auckland', *Venereology*, 13(1): 15–24.

2

Stepping Forward Into the Light of Decriminalisation

Dame Catherine Healy, Annah Pickering and Chanel Hati
(New Zealand Prostitutes' Collective)

Introduction

Sex workers' rights activists began organising themselves into collectives to advocate for their rights from the early 1970s. COYOTE (Call Off Your Old Tired Ethics) was the first sex workers' rights organisation to emerge in 1973 (Jenness, 1993). Based in San Francisco, COYOTE has aimed to decriminalise sex work, challenge negative attitudes towards sex work and argue for health and safety. Other sex workers' rights organisations have since been established worldwide. They have had a variable influence on law reform but most, if not all, advocate for full decriminalisation of sex work. This chapter is written by members of one sex workers' rights group, New Zealand Prostitutes' Collective (NZPC), which did have success in changing law. Much of this chapter comes from information held in the NZPC archives and its institutional memory.

In this chapter, we first discuss the formation of NZPC. The establishment of NZPC gave sex workers a collective voice as advocates for law reform on behalf of sex workers and provided them with a legitimacy that had been absent until that time (Lichtenstein, 1999; West, 2000). We have played an active role in educating the public and the media about issues affecting sex workers and we were strong lobbyists for decriminalisation. In the sections that follow, we outline the main issues facing sex workers prior to law reform, before talking about the rationale behind the Prostitution Reform Bill to decriminalise sex work, which was drafted by and for sex workers. This Bill was debated in Parliament and several amendments were made, some of which we were able to live with, but others of which are highly controversial – and have kept us lobbying with the aim of more closely achieving full decriminalisation. This will be discussed prior to exploring some implementation issues with the Prostitution Reform Act 2003 (PRA), the most troublesome being the implementation of bylaws by territorial authorities. There has been a noticeable change in sex workers' access to justice since decriminalisation and we examine some examples of this before looking at NZPC's hopes for the future of sex work in New Zealand.

In 1987, NZPC was formed by sex workers from all sectors of the sex industry – including women who worked in massage parlours and escort agencies, and transgender Māori street-based sex workers (Healy et al, 2010). We started to meet in pubs and, in a typically New Zealand way, at the beach. In 1988, NZPC was contracted by the then Department (now Ministry) of Health (Chetwynd, 1996) and continues to be funded to date. The initial contract was to provide health promotion and education to sex workers in an effort to minimise the spread of HIV/AIDS, which was particularly concerning to the government at that time. The current rationale for the contract, however, supports the aims and purposes in Section 3 of the PRA 2003, which are to create a framework that:

a) safeguards the human rights of sex workers and protects them from exploitation;
b) promotes the welfare and occupational health and safety of sex workers;
c) is conducive to public health;
d) prohibits the use in prostitution of persons under 18 years of age.

Some of the activities in this contract include building healthy public policy by advocating for, and supporting the adoption of, best practice to support the health and wellbeing of sex workers. It also includes the empowerment of sex workers to advocate for change in policies and practices and support participation in policy-making decisions. In addition, the contract allows us to develop and maintain strategic alliances and interagency networks to support action to address the unique challenges and health inequities that sex workers face. The contract with the Ministry assists in building collaborative governance systems where an external organisation drafting a policy that may affect sex workers (such as a territorial authority, government body, or non-governmental organisation) consults with us to ensure that the health and safety of sex workers are upheld (Wagenaar et al, 2017; Rottier, 2018;). We, as NZPC, are frequently a party to effective decision making. Of course, we cannot control government, but we can use our place around the table to significantly influence outcomes for sex workers.

NZPC is peer-led, governed by a board of current and former sex workers, with representation from brothel-based, street-based, and independent sex workers (sex workers who manage their own sex work) as well as the full range of sex, gender and sexual diversity that make up the population. Māori, the indigenous population of New Zealand, have always formed a large part of NZPC, and the governing board of trustees of NZPC has consistently included 30 to 50 per cent Māori in order to reflect this representation. As Chanel states:

> 'Māori have always been a big part of NZPC right from its inception. Māori have regarded NZPC as a place of safety, and we always felt we could raise our concerns and discuss issues affecting us within NZPC. The peer support and information provided by NZPC has been an important part in dealing with and solving issues that impact upon Māori sex workers.' (Chanel Hati, NZPC Community Liaison, Wellington)

The board develops the broad aims and policies of NZPC and these are implemented throughout the organisation with guidance from NZPC's national office and significant input from each region. NZPC staff are sex workers, current and past; however, some specialist positions, such as legal expertise, are filled by allies. Management roles are always held by peers to reflect the organisation's peer-led ethos. Staff are representative of the New Zealand sex worker demographics, with Pākehā (New Zealand European), Māori, Pasifika, and Asian staff, paid and unpaid. Clinical services are provided by complementary organisations, such as Family Planning and Sexual Health Services.

Migrant population groups are also represented on the staff of NZPC. Migrant workers, particularly those from Asia, have always had an influence on, and a role to play within, NZPC right from its inception. This has varied with the types of immigration occurring at a given point in time. During the 1990s for instance, NZPC had a Thai outreach project in collaboration with sexual health services as Thai people were the predominant migrants entering New Zealand to work in the sex industry at that time. Since 2008, NZPC has had the Migrant Education and Information (MEI) project led by Chinese people for Chinese migrant sex workers, who are now the dominant migrant population group: on occasion NZPC has promoted this project in Chinese language newspapers as part of community outreach. NZPC resources have been translated into other languages for migrant sex worker communities.

Prior to reform

Māori, the indigenous people of New Zealand, are paramount as the tangata whenua (people of the land). Prior to decriminalisation, they were often the worst affected by police actions against the sex worker population, particularly Māori street-based sex workers. It was therefore important that their voices were heard loudly when NZPC was formed and throughout the process of law reform. Jordan (2005) reported that in 2000, 70 per cent of those convicted for soliciting were Māori (compared to 10 per cent Pasifika and 10 per cent European). This is significant when the ethnic make-up of the New Zealand population is taken into account: Māori comprise only 15 per cent of the general population. Although police reports show that, in 2000, 70 per cent of those convicted for soliciting were men, Jordan noted:

> These figures are useful, however, in indicating a pattern of law enforcement that tended to focus on street prostitution and resulted in *the arrest, prosecution and conviction of significant numbers of transgendered workers in particular* .... (Jordan, 2005, p 33: emphasis added).

Māori whakawahine (transgender women) were recorded as 'male' when apprehended by police and their treatment was often humiliating and dehumanising. For example, police often referred to them using the wrong pronoun or by the name they were given at birth, or improperly searched them. Māori sex workers who faced violence at work felt powerless to approach police and report it due to this treatment as well as the illegal nature of sex work itself at that time (NZPC, 2013).

Street-based sex workers and those working in massage parlours experienced undercover police officers pretending to be clients, trying to get sex workers to offer sex for money (Healy et al, 2010) so that they could be charged with soliciting, an offence that carried a NZ$200 fine (Summary Offences Act 1981, s26). Section 18 of the Massage Parlours Act 1978 stated that people who had been convicted of a prostitution or drug offence within the previous ten years could not work in a massage parlour. This often meant these sex workers' choice of places to work were reduced. Consequently, some chose to meet their clients through street-based sex work, while others chose to work independently, often by themselves from home. Others created new identities or shifted to new cities to circumvent detection. The impact of this was destabilising for the sex workers and their peer groups by placing them in an unfamiliar environment in which they were uncomfortable.

Labour rights for sex workers were fanciful at the time. The overwhelming majority of sex workers were dependent on managers of massage parlours for work, and therefore vulnerable to their whims. Also, massage parlour proprietors were required to maintain a list of people employed or engaged under the Massage Parlours Act 1978. They had to provide that list to the police for inspection on a regular basis and police could copy any entry. Police went beyond this legal requirement and enthusiastically extended it to all sex workers, capturing the names and other personal information of people who were sex workers, including their sex work history, and, in some places, a photograph on a 'known prostitute' database. Once someone was on this database, it was unknown as to whether or not their details could ever be removed. In 1995, the police wrote to Wellington Newspapers Limited, the publishers of the local Wellington newspapers *The Dominion* and *The Evening Post*, where sex workers advertised in the classified columns, stating:

> The Police are concerned with the activities of persons placing advertisements in the classified entertainment sections of both The Evening Post and The Dominion. … *Those persons, with few exceptions, are in breach of certain sections of the Crimes Act 1961 relating to crimes against public welfare.* (Correspondence obtained through the Official Information Act)

In a letter to 'The Advertiser' in the classified columns, police stated the register '… is not designed to screen sex workers, but rather to give Police an ability to monitor the sex industry' (Correspondence obtained through the Official Information Act). Nevertheless, the police commander of the Nelson Bays District at the time scrapped the register in his area, stating: 'It is not the role of the Police to vet people to advertise in newspapers. What makes one prostitute better than another?' He also noted that sex work was a health issue rather than a criminal one (Plenio, 1995).

Sex workers found the register intrusive and demeaning. This register implied the police were monitoring sex workers as criminals. NZPC discovered that the register was kept on the police national database and was therefore available to all police officers. Sex workers feared details from the register could be used in court cases not related to sex work, such as custody cases over children, or included in police vetting for employment outside the sex industry. This no doubt resulted in former sex workers being refused positions they were otherwise qualified for.

Police also used the presence of condoms as part of the evidence to convict someone on soliciting charges or for other prostitution-related crimes (Jordan, 2005). One escort agency even hid condoms in the freezer, and massage parlour proprietors would not mention the word 'condom' when ordering supplies from NZPC on the phone. One agency manager would always phone and say: "Can you bring some of those little things round please?" As late as 2002, condoms and other sex paraphernalia were considered evidence of prostitution-related activities. No sex worker would say, "I'm going to call the police" if confronted with the threat of violence. The feeling among sex workers was that the police could never be trustworthy. There was always the sense that they could turn against sex workers and arrest them. This was the context in which the Prostitution Reform Bill was drafted.

Prostitution Reform Bill: Parliamentary process

The rationale for the Prostitution Reform Bill[1] as it entered the Parliamentary process was to address the harms caused by the existing laws. The Bill, as written by NZPC and its allies, was simple and to the point, focused on repealing as crimes soliciting, brothel keeping, living on the earnings of sex work, and procuring. The bicultural[2] grounding and the lived experience of sex workers that NZPC had, gave us the impetus needed to work through issues that could affect sex workers at that time, or which would affect sex workers in the future. It would clearly benefit those sex workers most affected by the enforcement of the law.

The Bill was debated for the first time in Parliament in October 2000 and passed its first reading on 8 November 2000, with 87 Members of Parliament (MPs) voting for it to be sent to a Select Committee, and 21 voting against it (Prostitution Reform Bill, First Reading, 2000). The Select Committee, comprising of 11 MPs from varying political parties, called for public submissions on the Bill. There were a number of submitters who were against the Bill, and the New Zealand Police Association sought strong regulation of what they saw as a criminal activity, yet admitted that heavy regulation elsewhere had '… led to a black market type prostitution for those not able to work legally in the industry' (Submission: New Zealand Police Association, 2001). Nevertheless, a number of organisations, including faith-based organisations, supported the Bill, with the Salvation Army saying:

> Although we might be philosophically and theologically opposed to prostitution, it is important that sex workers are respected as individuals, and their safety, health, and human rights are upheld. It is in this context that The Salvation Army accepts the necessity of the law reforms proposed in this Bill. (Submission: Salvation Army, 2001)

Te Ropu Wahine Māori Toko I Te Ora/The Māori Women's Welfare League submitted in favour of the Bill, supporting Māori women and young people (tamariki/mokopuna[3]) and said:

> The introduction of the legislation to decriminalise prostitution will allow sex workers to have the same rights as workers involved in other industries. This will improve their working conditions and encourage them to attain quality health care. (Submission: Māori Women's Welfare League, 2001)

The Select Committee also called for oral submissions to be made in support of the 222 written submissions so that they could ask submitters specific questions. NZPC was the first organisation called to publicly address the Select Committee and present the case for decriminalisation. A total of 65 oral submissions were heard after our submission, including a number of individual sex workers who were able to have closed hearings. The committee spent a total of 23 hours and 10 minutes hearing oral evidence, and a total of 42 hours and 25 minutes considering the Bill.

In 2002, there was a Parliamentary election, and the Bill was carried over to the new Parliament, which had a change in composition. United Future, a minority party with a number of fundamentalist Christians, sought a second set of Select Committee oral hearings as they now had a seat on the Committee. Additional sections were added to the Bill during the Select Committee process, incorporating the suggestions of submitters, advisors from government departments, and politicians.

We were able to accept some of these additions, such as the application of the Health and Safety in Employment Act 1992, and limits on signage for brothels. Worthy of note as an addition to the Bill was a clause which stated that, if a sex worker decided to stop work as a sex worker, they would not have additional penalties when applying for an unemployment benefit, and would only be subject to the standard two-week wait for receipt of benefits, rather than an additional 13-week stand-down for leaving a job voluntarily. We were also relieved that an amendment was added that police would no longer have automatic right of entry into brothels, but would have to apply for, and be granted, a search warrant, as is normal in other workplaces.

However, some suggestions were against our advice and were very concerning. One such addition was the requirement that sex workers and clients use condoms for vaginal, anal and oral sex, and can be prosecuted if they do not. Although we accepted the requirement that operators and clients be held responsible for promoting safer sex, as proposed in the original Bill, we were opposed to the addition of sex workers also being held responsible. It allows for the entrapment and recriminalising of sex workers who do not use condoms with clients, and is stigmatising in specifically targeting sex workers, while not being applicable to the general population. Our position is that it would have been more appropriate to rely on existing public health norms, as these cover concerns related to the prevention of sexually transmissible infections (STIs). Interestingly, however, in the period since the PRA was passed, some individual sex workers have been enthusiastic about the requirement to take all reasonable steps to use a condom and quote this part of the law to their clients to reduce tensions and debate with clients in relation to condom use for all penetrative acts (Abel et al, 2007). Occasionally clients or the police phone NZPC about accusations of sex workers practising unsafe sex. We are only aware of one formal investigation by the police in respect to a sex worker. It is our impression from these contacts that the police respect our advice in using peer-based health promotion as a mechanism to support sex workers in creating a safe-sex culture, and thus this aspect of the law is rarely used against sex workers.

However, there are situations where sex workers have used this section of the PRA to support the prosecution of clients who have deliberately removed condoms. There have also been situations where police have spoken to clients and warned them, or laid charges, under this section and have achieved convictions. However, we are aware of situations where the sex worker affected has negotiated with the police to use this section where the client admits to removing a condom, as it was more likely to achieve a conviction than a charge of sexual violation.[4] We are concerned that an unintended consequence of this section is that it may be used to replace a charge of rape or other forms of sexual assault/violation against a client who has deliberately removed a condom.

After these amendments were made, the Bill passed its second of three readings on 19 February 2003 by 62 to 56 (Prostitution Reform Bill, Second Reading, 2003). It was apparent that support for the Bill was reducing. Close to its final stages, we met with a number of MPs, including those who were undecided or opposed to the Bill – such as Dame Luamanuvao Winnie Laban, a Pasifika MP. This MP was swayed by the arguments of the Pasifika sex workers and some of our members she spoke with; she realised that, if passed, the Bill would aid Pasifika sex workers, and changed her mind from opposing decriminalisation to supporting it:

> Over the last few weeks I have talked with, and listened to, many prostitutes and others working in the sex industry. I have been particularly touched by the stories of several Polynesian transsexuals and fa'afafines [Samoan males who behave in feminine-gendered ways]. Their stories tell me that the current laws serve to make their working life unsafe, and to increase the risk in a risky occupation. They are struggling to live a life of dignity. The current laws do not protect them. Whilst this bill has its imperfections, it does provide greater protection for prostitutes and affords them the same rights as other workers. (Prostitution Reform Bill, Second Reading, 2003)

Some of the more contentious additions to the Bill occurred during the Committee of the Whole House stage, where several further amendments were proposed and voted on by MPs. Some of these amendments were publicised in advance and we could work behind the scenes to support or oppose them. However, we were under pressure to make decisions and to compromise where required. There were some proposed amendments that were presented as a fait accompli. We had no control over these aspects of the Parliamentary process. The whole process was very quick and pressure was building as the final vote approached. There were a total of 18 amendments proposed, of which five passed. We felt that two of these amendments would have little effect on the autonomy, anonymity and choices available to sex workers and found it easy to accept amendments restricting advertising to classified sections of newspapers and magazines (Section 11), and to the ability of medical officers working as health and labour inspectors to enter brothels in accordance with other workforce norms (Sections 24–29). We tried to keep home-based workers out of the definition of 'brothel' workers (Section 4), as we wanted to avoid them being included in potential controversy related to the location of brothels, as had happened in New South Wales, Australia. The requirement for operators to hold an operator's certificate was certainly contentious for NZPC (Sections 34–41). There were concerns that such certification of brothel operators belonged in a model of legalisation rather than decriminalisation and would undermine inclusiveness, creating a two-tiered regime where some sex workers could work legally and others would be in breach of the law. This certification regime was requested by operators themselves. Certificates are issued by the Auckland District Court, not by the police, and police, councils, or other persons cannot have access to the list of brothel operators. There are no regular inspections, and the certificates are the same size as a credit card and not on public display. They must only be produced when requested by a police officer who 'believes on reasonable grounds [a person] is an operator' (Section 40(1), PRA). To date, it is our impression that the certification regime does not add value and should therefore be removed. Sex workers know who the operators of brothels are, and it is easy for officials to obtain this information should they seek to have formal engagement with operators. For example, the Auckland City Council withdrew an additional tier of licensing requiring brothel operators to register their premises with the Council.

The section requiring an evaluation of the PRA five years after it came into force (Sections 42–46) was contentious, but, although it generated a lot of work for NZPC, it also produced good evidence-based research that supported the success of the Act. The most confrontational section added to the Bill, however, was one that stated migrant sex workers would not be allowed to enter New Zealand, or, if discovered working in New Zealand, may be deported (Section 19). This section was added as an anti-trafficking measure. One MP (Dianne Yates, National Party) who was opposed to the Bill stated the proposed amendment 'borders somewhat on racism and protectionism' (Prostitution Reform Bill, Third Reading, 2003). We were opposed to this clause because it meant that migrant sex workers would be excluded from the protections offered by the Bill. The majority of migrant sex workers at the time were on visitor visas or student visas and would have been working in breach of these, which would have been covered under general immigration law. There was therefore no need for this section to be added. Unlike street-based sex workers, migrants were not being targeted by the police (who raided the Auckland streets the night before the Bill passed its final reading). With the actions against Māori street-based sex workers occurring at the time, and the pressures of waning support from MPs, it did not occur to us to ask to have the Bill removed from Parliament at this late stage. There was a sense that we were losing ground rapidly, and that we had to fight to hold onto what we could achieve at that time.

With these amendments added, the Bill passed the third reading on 25 June 2003, with the narrowest of margins, 60 for and 59 against, with one abstention. It was signed into law by the Governor General two days later. There was jubilation among the sex worker community, especially from those street-based sex workers who were Māori:

> 'I remember on the night the Bill was passed, I stepped forward out of the shadows into the light and said "Ladies, we're free". Its passage meant that we had the right to be free, to be seen, that's why I stepped into the light. Another stepped forward into the light as well and started clapping, then we all came out and started hugging each other and said it was time for a celebration.' (Tiana, NZPC outreach worker, sex worker, and board member)

Dame Catherine Healy recalled the successful fight for decriminalisation, stating:

> 'We were walking a tightrope. We had pushed hard for years for decriminalisation, and it was unimaginable that so much effort would amount to a loss. We knew we weren't getting everything we wanted, but had to focus on what we could get for those sex workers who were being knocked around so frequently by the enforcement of the then law. We were incredibly proud to fully decriminalise street-based sex work. This affected Māori and transgender workers the most.' (Dame Catherine Healy, National Co-ordinator, NZPC)

Implementing the Prostitution Reform Act

The transition from a repressive criminalised and illegal system to an integrative decriminalised system was, on the whole, smooth. In the first few months following the passage of the PRA, we worked with the Department of Labour to develop 'A Guide to Occupational Health and Safety in the New Zealand Sex Industry' based on those developed by Scarlet Alliance[5] (Department of Labour, 2004). The Medical Officers of Health throughout the country also had a role to play after the passage of the PRA and organised a training day where we helped by providing resources and case studies.

Many police stations around the country held records of sex workers' names that had been legally obtained under the newly repealed Massage Parlours Act 1978. The Select Committee, in its Report, stated 'the practice should be discontinued (and where these records are kept separate they should be destroyed)' (Prostitute Reform Bill, 2002). Nevertheless, there were attempts by some police at the frontline level to continue documenting the identities of sex workers, and we had to push back.

While the crimes of soliciting, brothel keeping, living on earnings from prostitution and procuring were repealed on the day the PRA came into force – 27 June 2003 – some parts did not come into effect until six months later. On 27 December 2003, Part 3 of the PRA, dealing with operators' certificates, came into force and the Massage Parlours Act 1978 and related regulations were repealed. There had been a move to encourage brothel operators to apply for certification prior to the date, but the associated forms and other administrative elements were not in place until the following year.

Following the passage of the PRA some territorial authorities expressed resentment at having the control over the location of brothels placed upon them by Parliament. Several councils were lobbied to prohibit brothels by those who were opposed to the PRA. As a result, there were some extreme responses, which played out in the passing of motions and enactment of bylaws. The Local Government Association were of the opinion banning brothels would be illegal (TVNZ, 2003). They wrote a set of guidelines for territorial authorities in New Zealand to follow and held a training day for people who were involved in town planning. Only a small number of local authorities (eight of 74) brought in bylaws specific to the location of brothels. Some councils sought to restrict sex workers from working from home. However, in a few cities such as Wellington, under the district plan independent sex workers were allowed to work from home, either by themselves or with up to two more people, putting sex work on the same basis as any other home-based occupation (Wellington City Council, 2000). Some councils, like Hastings District Council, reviewed the situation and concluded, 'There is no evidence of a pressing need for a bylaw at this time' (Hastings City Council, 2004). This reflects the experience of those city councils which have chosen not to have bylaws or have introduced bylaws which minimally intrude on sex worker rights.

Hamilton City Council, on the other hand, passed bylaws that are repugnant to the laws of New Zealand, with fines of up to NZ$20,000. This Council not only prohibits street-based sex work, but limits the area in which brothels (large managed brothels and independent workers who are operating from their own home) may run to a small area of the central city and of the industrial zone. Both areas are not conducive to the safety and health of sex workers, and the Council has been made aware of this. The bylaw was first put in place in 2004 and reviewed in 2009 (Hamilton City Council, 2009). More recently, Hamilton City Council completed another review of their bylaw. They have chosen to retain the NZ$20,000 fine and criminal convictions for breaches of the bylaw. The area in which brothels may be established has shrunk considerably due to changes in the district plan meaning that there may be no 'retail' in industrial zones (Hamilton City Council, 2019). We continue to state that the bylaw does not support the rights, health, or welfare of sex workers in this city.

Another authority with whom we have fought the same battles repeatedly is Manukau City Council. In 2004, the Council passed a bylaw that had the effect of banning most home-based sex work, and unreasonably restricting where brothels could establish in the centre city (Manukau City Council, 2004b). This bylaw barely had time to have effect when the Manukau City Council decided they would seek to have a Local Bill presented to Parliament to enable them to have the ability to control street-based sex work (Manukau City Council, 2004a). The Select Committee considering this Bill discussed it extensively, and eventually recommended that it not proceed because it was contrary to the PRA and was in breach of the Bill of Rights Act 1990:

> While local legislation typically addresses issues unique to a particular locality and does not involve itself with the criminal law, this local bill creates offences that criminalise behaviour that exists throughout New Zealand. If the bill were passed, citizens would be subject to conflicting criminal laws, depending on their current geographical location. Unlike federal states, New Zealand does not have an established framework for enforcing different criminal offences on a region by region basis. (Local Government and Environment Select Committee, 2006)

The Bill was defeated 46 to 73 at its second reading, nevertheless, community tensions between street-based sex workers and local residents continued to run high in Manukau City (TVNZ, 2009). A local MP introduced a second Bill to Parliament in 2009 seeking to control street-based sex work in Manukau. Manukau City Council amalgamated with eight other councils in Auckland to form the Auckland Council in October 2010, and Auckland Council took the Bill over from the former Manukau City Council. There were several meetings of the Select Committee from 2010 to 2014 as they sought a consensus between the Local Community Boards, the Auckland Council, the police and NZPC. We suggested a collaborative approach as an option to address the main issues raised by the Manukau City Council (noise, litter, kerb-crawling and disorderly behaviour) instead of legislation (discussed further by Abel in Chapter 9). The Committee then recommended that the Bill not be passed. The vast majority of MPs therefore voted against the Bill, 109 to 11.

In Christchurch, we were confronted with another attempt to change the PRA or put blocks in the way of it operating effectively. The initial Christchurch bylaw, which located all brothels (including home-based brothels) to the city centre, had been overturned by the court ('Willowford Family Trust v Christchurch City Council', 2005). Then the earthquakes of 2010 to 2011 had a major impact on where street-based sex work took place, with sex workers moving into residential areas (Law, 2017). Residents in the areas affected by this displacement sought redress through a council bylaw. However, following our submissions, Christchurch City Council followed a collaborative approach with NZPC and local residents taking initiatives that would reduce tensions. Abel provides a detailed account of this in Chapter 9 of this book.

Access to justice

Prior to the passage of the PRA, sex workers would rarely have adequate access to justice. It was difficult for sex workers to report crimes against them due to the criminalisation of their work (Abel and Fitzgerald, 2010; Jordan, 2010). Following the passage of the PRA, in preparing a report for the Prostitution Review Committee[6] (PLRC), Mossman and Mayhew (2007, p 11) noted that despite existing barriers, 'Police were now seen more as a "protector" than as a "prosecutor"' and as a result there was an 'increase [in] the reporting of violence to the Police, particularly by street workers. There were also indications that incidents of violence against sex workers were being taken more seriously, and that in some cases the Police response assisted in resolving situations' (Mossman and Mayhew, 2007).

Street-based sex workers were among the first to notice the difference, with police in South Auckland often providing assistance, including ensuring sex workers were paid if a client tried to underpay them or not pay them (Wynn, 2014). In 2006, street-based sex workers in Wellington stated that they rang the police because a man came onto the street with a piece of timber, threatening them. They said the police arrived and arrested the person, taking them away and thanking the street-based sex workers for making the complaint.

In order to facilitate and make it easier for sex workers to complain to the police about violence, particularly sexual violence, we worked with police to produce a resource in the form of a booklet, which was launched on 17 December 2018 to commemorate International End Violence Against Sex Workers Day (NZPC and New Zealand Police, 2018; McKay, 2019). This resource is not only for sex workers but provides the police with information on how to address issues affecting sex workers who may be reluctant to come forward, while also making it easier for sex workers to report sexual violence against them.

There have been numerous other instances where sex workers have successfully achieved justice for wrongs committed against them. A case was taken to the Human Rights Commission by a sex worker who was being sexually harassed by a brothel operator, asking her sexually explicit questions (Dudding, 2014). The sex worker won the case and was awarded a cash settlement of NZ$25,000 and the operator ordered to attend sexual harassment training ('DML v Montgomery', 2014). The operator also had to pay costs to the Human Rights Commission amounting to NZ$11,250. This was the first time the Human Rights Review Tribunal had given a ruling on a case involving a sex worker.

In another case, a sex worker had her work used against her by the ex-partner of a man she was in a relationship with (Nightingale, 2018). His ex-partner posted untrue allegations online about the sex workers' sexual health as well as personal details and images. Following a complaint from the sex worker, the ex-partner was found guilty in 2018 under the Harmful Digital Communication Act 2015, which was passed to target online bullying, and the sentence passed recognised that emotional harm had been caused.

Another example of increased access to justice for sex workers in a decriminalised environment was a case of a sex worker who was being harassed by a former client. The sex worker exercised her right to say no and refused to see the client. When he told her that she had to go through with the agreement, she offered him his money back and he refused to take it. He kept on contacting her to demand that she complete their arrangement. She initially laid a restraining order against him, but he continued to harass her, including appealing against the order. As a result, she laid charges under the Harassment Act 1997, and when he was convicted, he appealed to the High Court, and later to the Court of Appeal. The Court of Appeal dismissed all his appeals, including those against restraining orders ('NR v MR', 2016). The courts also noted that his continued use of the court to appeal cases involving her amounted to a form of harassment. This example demonstrates that the right of a sex worker in New Zealand to say no trumps the contract to provide services.

When it comes to sentencing, the judiciary takes violence towards sex workers very seriously, proactively denouncing crimes committed against sex workers, deeming their vulnerability an aggravating factor (Clarkson, 2014). When sentencing a defendant to imprisonment, Justice Dunningham noted ('R v Daly', 2014) that:

> I ... accept that the complainant was in a position of vulnerability. A prostitute does place herself in a position where she must trust her client not to take advantage of the circumstances by harming or taking advantage of her. Your actions that morning were a significant abuse of that trust. ('R v Daly', 2014)

These cases are only the tip of the iceberg. There have been numerous other cases before the courts, from the Disputes Tribunal to the High Court, which show that the PRA has been working, and sex workers have the ability to access justice if they so wish. Nevertheless, societal stigma, encouraged by those opposed to the PRA, remains evident. This is well illustrated by a violent attack in 2019 on a sex worker where, after arrest, the perpetrator stated that he was 'a bit rough' with her 'but she was just a prostitute' (Angeloni, 2019). Stigma continues to affect a number of sex workers and prevents them from reporting violence against them.

Hopes for the future

As discussed in this chapter, there have been a number of positive outcomes for New Zealand sex workers following decriminalisation.

One positive outcome not previously mentioned has been the emergence of social media where sex workers can form peer support groups and share information. Also, we are consulted on a range of issues which pertain to sex workers, including being consulted by the New Zealand Reserve Bank about a future cashless society and what its impact is likely to be on sex workers, clients and brothel operators. Anti-trafficking groups take the lead from us in think tanks relating to trafficking. They support our knowledge and experience that migrant sex workers are not being trafficked.

However, there is still work for us to do to pave the way for a more inclusive and less discriminatory approach to sex workers. In particular, we would like to address issues raised by Section 9 of the PRA, which criminalises sex workers who, for whatever reason, are unable to use a condom. As noted, this section is being used in cases where charges of sexual assault should be used, either because it is generally easier to prove or the person who did sexually assault a sex worker is more willing to plead guilty to a charge under Section 9, with a maximum fine of NZ$2000, than to a charge of sexual violation, which carries a maximum term of imprisonment of 20 years. It is only sex workers and their clients who are subject to criminal responsibility for failure to use a condom. This treats them differently to other members of society who do not face a corresponding criminal liability, and is therefore unfair.

Another area we would like to see discussed is Section 19, which states that migrants may be refused entry to New Zealand if it is suspected they may be coming with the intention of being sex workers, or may be deported if they are found to be working as sex workers. As discussed in this chapter and in Chapter 5 this leaves these migrant sex workers vulnerable to exploitation and violence. This is an issue that needs to be revised. In May 2019, we were a party to a group of non-government organisations that addressed the United Nations Convention on the Elimination of All Forms of Discrimination Against Women (CEDAW) Committee. During oral submissions, the issue of migrant sex workers was raised with the CEDAW Committee, which recommended to the New Zealand Government that Section 19 of the PRA be amended to reduce its negative impact on migrant women, and revise migration laws by adopting 'measures aimed at preventing discrimination against women in prostitution in the State party, with a view to preventing and addressing the factors and structures that render migrant women vulnerable' (CEDAW, 2018, p 8).

We would also like to address societal stigma. One way to do this is to amend the Human Rights Act 1993 to include the wording 'being, or having been, a sex worker' in the list of prohibited grounds of discrimination, subsection 21(1). This would prohibit discrimination against sex workers and act as a powerful educational tool. It would improve the situation on the ground for sex workers who experience such things as evictions by body corporations who lease apartments and allow home-based occupations, but not sex work. Sex workers should be supported to be fully fledged participants in society. We will continue to fight for this right and the achievement of full decriminalisation in New Zealand.

Notes

1. The New Zealand Parliament is unicameral, having only one House, and operates under a modified Westminster system. A Bill – which is what an Act is called until it passes all three stages – has several stages as it progresses through Parliament. The 'first reading' is when a Bill is introduced to the House, and it can be thrown out at this reading; the Select Committee stage is where public submissions are sought; then comes the 'second reading', which confirms or rejects changes made by the Select Committee and is a point where a Bill can be defeated. The next stage is the Committee of the Whole House, where individual MPs can propose changes they want to see in a Bill. All MPs can vote on these proposals and can confirm or reject them. There is no vote on the whole Bill at this time. The final stage is the 'third reading', and if a Bill passes this, it becomes an Act of Parliament, and awaits the Royal Assent.
2. In New Zealand, society is described as bicultural as it consists of Māori (tangata whenua – people of the land), who have a specific attachment to the lands in Aotearoa and non-Māori (manuhiri – NZ European and all other ethnic identities) and is based on the relationship between Māori and the Crown through the Treaty of Waitangi (Te Tiriti o Waitangi). See https://teara.govt.nz/en/biculturalism.
3. Children/grandchildren
4. 'Sexual violation' under the Crimes Act 1961 comprises rape and unlawful sexual connection. The conviction rate for sexual violation is low in New Zealand, which is an ongoing concern. See https://www.justice.govt.nz/about/news-and-media/news/how-sexual-violence-cases-progress-through-the-justice-system/
5. Scarlet Alliance is the 'peak body' (group or association) sex worker organisation in Australia.
6. There was a section in the Prostitution Reform Act which required the Act be evaluated and reviewed within five years of its enactment. The Prostitution Law Review Committee was formed under the Ministry of Justice and oversaw the review of the Act.

References

Abel, G. & Fitzgerald, L. (2010) 'Introduction', in G. Abel, L. Fitzgerald, C. Healy & A. Taylor (eds), *Taking the Crime Out of Sex Work: New Zealand sex workers' fight for decriminalisation,* Bristol: Policy Press, pp 1–21.

Abel, G., Fitzgerald, L. & Brunton, C. (2007) 'The impact of the Prostitution Reform Act on the health and safety practices of sex workers: Report to the Prostitution Law Review Committee', Christchurch: University of Otago. Available at: https://www.otago.ac.nz/christchurch/otago018607.pdf.

Angeloni, A. (2019). 'Man abducted and raped sex worker in Blenheim motel room', Stuff, 9 October. Available at: https://www.stuff.co.nz/national/crime.

CEDAW (2018) 'Concluding observations on the eighth periodic report of New Zealand'. Available at: https://women.govt.nz/sites/public_files/CEDAW_C_NZL_CO_8_31061_E%20%283%29.pdf.

Chetwynd, J. (1996) 'The Prostitutes' Collective: a uniquely New Zealand institution', in P. Davis (ed), *Intimate Details and Vital Statistics: AIDS, sexuality and the social order in New Zealand,* Auckland: Auckland University Press, pp 136–48.

Clarkson, D. (2014) 'Man jailed for slapping, choking sex worker', Stuff. Available at: http://www.stuff.co.nz/national/crime/10382961/Man-jailed-for-slapping-choking-sex-worker.

Department of Labour (2004) *A Guide to Occupational Health and Safety in the New Zealand Sex Industry.* Available at: http://espu-usa.com/espu-ca/wp-content/uploads/2008/02/nz-health-and-safety-handbook.pdf.

Dudding, A. (2014) 'Sex worker stands up to "overbearing" boss', Stuff. Available at: http://www.stuff.co.nz/national/64332562/sex-worker-stands-up-to-overbearing-boss.

Hamilton City Council (2009) *Prostitution Bylaw 2009.* Available at: https://www.hamilton.govt.nz/our-council/policies-bylaws-legislation/bylaws/Documents/Prostitution%20Bylaw%202009.pdf.

Hamilton City Council (2019) *Elected Member Briefing.* Available at: https://www.hamilton.govt.nz/AgendasAndMinutes/Elected%20Member%20Briefing%20Topic%20List%20and%20Presentations%20-%2028%20February%202019.pdf.

Hastings City Council (2004) *Agenda Item 3, Friday 11 June 2004.* (TRIM File No: CG-02-01-19-04-113).

Healy, C., Bennachie, C. & Reed, A. (2010) 'History of New Zealand Prostitutes' Collective', in G. Abel, L. Fitzgerald, C. Healy & A. Taylor (eds), *Taking the Crime Out of Sex Work: New Zealand sex workers' fight for decriminalisation*, Bristol: Policy Press, pp 45–55.

Jenness, V. (1993) *Making It Work: The prostitutes' rights movement in perspective*, New York: Aldine de Gruyter.

Jordan, J. (1991) *Working Girls: Women in the New Zealand sex industry talk to Jan Jordan*, Auckland: Penguin.

Jordan, J. (2005) *The Sex Industry in New Zealand: A literature review*. Available at: http://www.justice.govt.nz/pubs/reports/2005/sex-industry-in-nz-literature-review/index.html.

Jordan, J. (2010) 'Of whalers, diggers and "soiled doves": A history of the sex industry in New Zealand', in G. Abel, L. Fitzgerald, C. Healy & A. Taylor (eds), *Taking the Crime Out of Sex Work: New Zealand sex workers' fight for decriminalisation*, Bristol: Policy Press, pp 25–44.

Law, T. (2017) 'Pressure builds for Christchurch City Council to ban sex workers from residential areas', *Christchurch Press*. Available at: https://www.stuff.co.nz/the-press/news/91494073/pressure-builds-for-christchurch-city-council-to-ban-sex-workers-from-residential-areas.

Lichtenstein, B. (1999) 'Reframing "Eve" in the AIDS era: The pursuit of legitimacy by New Zealand sex workers', in B. Dank & R. Refinetti (eds), *Sex Work and Sex Workers*, Oxon: Routledge, pp 37–59.

Local Government and Environment Select Committee (2006) *Report on Manukau City Council (Control of Street Prostitution) Bill*. Available at: https://www.parliament.nz/resource/en-NZ/48DBSCH_SCR3539_1/22df7c96077d21f06b04235250e83df8d5b26eb9.

Manukau City Council (2004a) *Agenda for the Community Safety Committee*.

Manukau City Council (2004b) *Letter to submitters on the proposed bylaw affecting the location of brothels notifying them of the passage of the bylaw*.

Māori Women's Welfare League (2001) Submission to Justice and Electoral Select Committee on 2001 Prostitution Reform Bill, JL/PRB/65.

McKay, E. (2019) 'Police and Prostitutes' Collective partnership helps to improve assault reporting', *New Zealand Herald*, 29 October. Available at: https://www.nzherald.co.nz/nz/news/article.cfm?c_id=1&objectid=12280310.

Mossman, E. & Mayhew, P. (2007) *Key Informant Interviews: Review of the Prostitution Reform Act 2003*. Available at: http://www.justice.govt. nz/prostitution-law-review-committee/publications/key-informant-interviews/report.pdf.

New Zealand Police Association (2001) Submission to Justice and Electoral Select Committee on 2001 Prostitution Reform Bill, JL/PRB/86W.

Nightingale, M. (2018) 'Jilted wife sentenced for exposing sex worker online', *New Zealand Herald*, 15 November. Available at: https://www.nzherald.co.nz/nz/news/article.cfm?c_id=1&objectid=12160462.

NZPC (2013) *Decriminalisation of Sex Work in New Zealand: Impact on Māori*. Available at: https://www.nzpc.org.nz/pdfs/Impact-on-Maori-Decriminalisation-of-Sex-Work-in-New-Zealand.pdf.

NZPC & New Zealand Police (2018) *What To Do: A guide for sex workers who have experienced sexual assault*. Available at: http://www.nzpc.org.nz/pdfs/WHAT-TO-DO-A-guide-for-sex-workers-who-have-experienced-sexual-assault.pdf.

Plenio (1995) *Police Chief Stops Unauthorised Vetting*.

Prostitution Law Review Committee (2008) *Report of the Prostitution Law Review Committee on the Operation of the Prostitution Reform Act 2003*. Available at: http://www.justice.govt.nz/policy/commercial-property-and-regulatory/prostitution/prostitution-law-review-committee/publications/plrc-report/report-of-the-prostitution-law-review-committee-on-the-operation-of-the-prostitution-reform-act-2003.

Prostitution Reform Bill 66-2, 29 November 2002, Available at: https://www.parliament.nz/en/pb/sc/reports/document/47DBSCH_SCR2281_1/prostitution-reform-bill-66-2

Prostitution Reform Bill, First Reading, 11 October 2000.

Prostitution Reform Bill, Second Reading, 19 February 2003. Available at: https://www.parliament.nz/en/pb/hansard-debates/rhr/document/47HansD_20030219_00001132/prostitution-reform-bill-second-reading.

Prostitution Reform Bill, Third Reading, 25 June 2003. Available at: https://www.parliament.nz/en/pb/hansard-debates/rhr/document/47HansD_20030625_00001319/prostitution-reform-bill-procedure-third-reading.

Rottier, J. (2018) *Decriminalization of sex work: The New Zealand Model*, The Hague: Eleven International Publishing.

Salvation Army (2001) Submission to Justice and Electoral Select Committee on 2001 Prostitution Reform Bill, JL/PRB/59W.

TVNZ (2003) 'Council seeks to ban brothels', TVNZ, 11 July. Available at: http://tvnz.co.nz/content/204834/2556418/article.html.
TVNZ (2009) 'Group defend actions against prostitutes', TVNZ, 20 April. Available at: http://tvnz.co.nz/national-news/group-defend-actions-against-prostitutes-2659695.
Wagenaar, H., Amesberger, H. & Altink, S. (2017) *Designing Prostitution Policy: Intention and reality in regulating the sex trade,* Bristol: Policy Press.
Wellington City Council (2000) 'Chapter 3', *District Plan General Provisions.* Available at: https://wellington.govt.nz/~/media/your-council/plans-policies-and-bylaws/district-plan/volume01/files/v1chap03.pdf?la=en.
West, J. (2000) 'Prostitution: collectives and the politics of regulation', *Gender, Work and Organization,* 7(2), 106–18.
Wynn, K. (2014) 'Police help short-changed sex worker', *New Zealand Herald,* 13 July. Available at: https://www.nzherald.co.nz/nz/news/article.cfm?c_id=1&objectid=11292537.

Court cases
DML v Montgomery [2014] NZHRRT 6 (12 February 2014). Available at: http://www.nzlii.org/nz/cases/NZHRRT/2014/6.html.
DML v Montgomery (Costs) [2014] NZHRRT 18 (6 May 2014). Available at: http://www.nzlii.org/nz/cases/NZHRRT/2014/18.html.
NR v MR [2016] NZCA 430 (12 September 2016). Available at: http://www.nzlii.org/cgi-bin/sinodisp/nz/cases/NZCA/2016/430.html.
R v Daly [2014] NZHC 1922. Available at: http://www.nzlii.org/nz/cases/NZHC/2014/1922.html.
Willowford Family Trust v Christchurch City Council HC Christchurch CIV 2004-409-002299 [2005] NZHC 493; [2006] 1 NZLR 791; (2005) 17 PRNZ 867 (21 September 2005). Available at: https://www.nzpc.org.nz/pdfs/Willowford-Family-Trust-and-Brown-v-CCC.pdf.

3

The Future of Feminism and Sex Work Activism in New Zealand

Carisa R Showden

'If you're a surfer, you know that waves come in sets of three, but if there is a fourth wave in the set, that is the really powerful one, and I think that's what we're living in now.'
Michèle A'Court, 'Contemporary Feminism 1: Feminism – the Morning After' (Radio New Zealand, 8 March 2017a)

The starting assumption of this chapter is that a fundamental goal of feminism is to challenge the political, social, and economic structures that support gender oppression, with a focus on the exploitation of women through sexual relationships and practices. Feminism in the Global West has had an uneasy relationship with sex work activism over the past 40 years. Some feminists have viewed 'prostitution' as a signature form of violence against women and exploitation of women's embodied labour, while others have argued that sex work is part of a larger project to dismantle the strictures of gender and sexuality norms. On this second account, sex work is a key battleground for challenging the economic exploitation women face in paid employment and their unremunerated, socially reproductive labour or embodied care work. Despite the persistent skirmishes following the feminist sex wars of the 1980s and 1990s that pitted feminists, and sex workers, against each other over matters of commercial and public sexual labour, many sex workers are feminists, and many feminists are committed to working collaboratively with sex workers to understand their needs (O'Neill, 2010; Harrington, 2017).

This chapter considers how feminism in New Zealand has arrived at its current state and what future possibilities for feminist sex work activism spring from its history. As the historical survey in the first section reveals, feminist and sex work activism in New Zealand have been more complementary here than almost anywhere else in the Global West, setting up a tantalising promise of continued mutually reinforcing visions and praxis. Pointing to certain limits – some necessary, some unfortunate – in both movements to date, it considers how the current political moment offers the opportunity for feminist sex work activism to tackle ongoing forms of oppression rooted in material and cultural structures and practices that feminist and sex worker movements still need to address.

To do this, the chapter first provides a brief overview of second and third wave feminist activism in New Zealand, focusing specifically on connections between feminist and sex work decriminalisation activism in the late 1990s and early 2000s. It then explores the emerging fourth wave of intersectional feminist activism. Just as in the second and third wave, the fourth wave is a period of contentious and diverse modes of feminist theories and practices. While acknowledging this diversity, the discussion in this chapter examines the more intersectional and radical fourth wave activism – 'radical' in the sense of targeting the structural roots of gender oppression *but not* in a trans-exclusionary or gender essentialist mode. Intersectional radical feminism assumes that gender is a fundamental basis of social stratification that has consequences for the development of individual gender identities, the cultural expectations for how men and women will interact, and the distribution of institutional resources and material goods (Risman and Davis, 2013). It is a political, collective, social movement feminism, one whichchallenges heteronormativity and has the explicit goal of substantive gender equity (Arruzza et al, 2019). This is in contradistinction to an individualist, liberal feminism focused on formal equality. After setting out the foundations of this fourth wave, sex-worker inclusive feminism, this chapter concludes by considering key challenges such a feminism faces and the lessons a New Zealand fourth wave might offer activists elsewhere.

From the second to the fourth wave of feminism and sex work activism

Feminism in New Zealand has moved through a few different configurations. While these are frequently described as distinct 'waves' of feminist activism, the wave language is somewhat misleading, if useful as a heuristic, in that periods and types of feminist activity overlap. Still, we can think roughly of three periods of activity from the 1970s until about 2010, which is when what we might call a fourth wave started to emerge. As social movement scholar Sandra Grey (2009, p 35) describes it, New Zealand's second wave was 'the contentious politics era of the women's liberation movement' in the 1970s, which led to a more 'institutional approach' in the 1980s and 1990s. This shift from radical to institutional, or state, feminism occurred as a result of the rapid neoliberalisation of New Zealand government and society in the mid-1980s as well as activist fatigue (Grey, 2008, 2009). State feminism, which includes the development of the Ministry for Women, privileges certain women's interests, and is most successful (as a state actor) when aligned with dominant state policies (Kantola and Squires, 2012). Through state feminism, liberal feminist ideals of using existing political structures and processes to achieve gender equality obscured 'socialist and radical feminist voices (at least in public forums)' (Grey, 2009, p 55). As a result of this neoliberal tsunami, feminists left out of this institutionalisation dispersed into other left movements for social justice and women's professional organisations (Taylor, 2002; Grey, 2008; Hyman, 2009; Schuster, 2014, 2016), actions described by Grey (2009, p 35) as 'unobtrusive mobilisations in which political activism by women [was] subsumed within other major projects for social and political change'.

There was also a late-arriving and relatively quiet individualist post- and third- wave feminism in New Zealand at the turn of the 21st century,[1] which engaged with online feminist communities in a modified form of 'consciousness-raising' and virtual community building (Schuster, 2013; Ashton, 2014), but lacked the *social movement* focus that makes feminism a political force. The individualism of third wave feminism alienated Pasifika and Māori social justice activists who wanted to advance communities rather than individuals (Hyman, 2009), further splitting feminist activists. Its significant presence online and focus on identity claims rather than redistributive politics also led to its lack of visibility and to concerns that feminism was dead (Grey, 2008; Schuster, 2013, 2014). More precisely, social movement feminism was in a period of 'abeyance' rather than rigor mortis because waves ebb and flow (Grey, 2009; Schuster, 2013). And feminists themselves had already taken gender concerns into other left social movements, which is itself a form of continuation, as 1970s feminism was far from unified. This fragmentation and dispersal was healthy, according to Prue Hyman (2009) because it reflected changes in society and an expansion of coalition and rights-based activism with groups organising around poverty, indigenous rights and anti-racism, and queer activism.

Again, while these are clear shifts in tactics and foci, there were then, as now, overlaps in these approaches. In the 1980s and early 1990s, when feminism moved from the streets to the state, there were still individuals and small civil society organisations engaging in occasional political protests, but overall this period is marked by the dispersal of radical, social movement feminism. A weakened state feminism persists today, and its mainstreaming coincided with both the third wave and the strengthening of mana wāhine Māori (Māori feminist discourses). The remainder of this section highlights those features of the mid-1980s–2010 period that are most significant for understanding the possibilities for feminist sex work activism in the near future, rather than providing a comprehensive historical overview of the second and third waves.

Linking institutional feminism and sex work decriminalisation

Grassroots feminism of the 1990s was deradicalised through incorporation into liberal and neoliberal state bureaus and the social development approach they championed in the 1980s and 1990s. Here the government's quest to 'build capacity' in women's civil society organisations by 'professionalizing' volunteers and pushing groups to 'manage issues' rather than challenge patriarchy (Aimers, 2011, p 305) was especially notable. Issue management was necessary as the state turned to civil society organisations to undertake the social welfare work it was no longer doing, and feminist organisations were tied to government values and priorities if they wanted to secure funding (Grey, 2009). As a result, much feminist activism shifted from an internal process to an outcome or 'deliverable' (Aimers, 2011), from radical politics to professional, single-issue service provision (Aimers, 2011).

Institutional feminism, alongside the social development, capacity-building approach the state took in its engagement with feminism, was a central feature of the success of sex work decriminalisation. The Prostitution Reform Bill was first read into Parliament in September 2000, passing its third reading in June 2003, well into the liberal, institutional state feminism period, and 16 years after the formation of the sex workers' advocacy organisation, the New Zealand Prostitutes' Collective (NZPC) in 1987. In 1988, NZPC contracted with the Department of Health to provide STI (sexually transmitted infection) services for sex workers (Harrington, 2017), a move that fitted well with the privatisation and public-private partnership model for service delivery instituted through neoliberal government reforms. This work, and the firmly established state feminism, shaped both the feminist response to sex work and how decriminalisation policy was framed. The legitimacy and connections facilitated by NZPC's sexual health services work provided support for its mission to help get decriminalisation on the government agenda. Not surprisingly, given the pragmatic and consultative culture of New Zealand, the winning arguments for decriminalisation offered in Parliament stressed harm reduction and public health, with concerns about the sexual double standard of punishing women but not men for sexual activity also raised, but to a lesser degree (Laurie, 2010). Many parliamentarians made clear they would not want their daughters working in the sex industry, and the preamble to the Prostitution Reform Act (PRA) states that 'the purpose of this act is to decriminalise prostitution (while not endorsing or morally sanctioning prostitution or its use) and to create a framework that (a) safeguards the human rights of sex workers and protects them from exploitation …'. Thus, the debates and resulting law still made clear that sex work was not morally endorsed, but sex workers should be treated with respect (Bruckert and Hannem, 2013).

Feminist submissions to Parliament on the Bill favoured decriminalisation 40 to 16 (Laurie, 2010). Submissions supporting decriminalisation came from an array of groups and individuals, ranging from the liberal feminist group the National Council of Women of New Zealand to the more conservative YWCA and New Zealand Federation of Business and Professional Women and the more left-leaning UniQ Victoria (Laurie, 2010). Supportive submissions mirrored public feminist discussion of sex work before and around the PRA's passage, focusing on harm minimisation and free choice, while discussion of gender as a social structure and how commercial sex does (or does not) support heteronormativity appeared much less frequently (Laurie, 2010; Abel, 2017). One notable exception was Professor Ngahuia Te Awekōtuku's submission, stating:

> 'Prostitution has been here in the Māori world since the earliest social encounters with people from the northern hemisphere. During the first encounters … those providing sexual services were in control. The exchange was uncomplicated; the provider set the terms. I would suggest that the proposed Bill puts forward an opportunity for similar arrangements. It has occurred on these islands before; it could happen again.' (quoted in Laurie, 2010, p 96)

Other feminist submissions noted that decriminalisation would make it easier for women to leave sex work and harder for violent partners to use a history of sex work against women in child custody disputes or as a form of harassment (Laurie, 2010).

Feminists opposed to decriminalisation included a mix of individuals and groups from overseas and in New Zealand. They argued that gender equality is inconceivable while prostitution exists because it relies on women's degradation and the violation of their human rights (Laurie, 2010); in short, prostitution is a foundation of patriarchal exploitation of women. Notably, few submissions either in favour of, or opposed to, the PRB considered male or transgender sex workers, promoting a highly gendered view of the industry and whose interests needed protection in it (Laurie, 2010). This attention to women sex workers remains today, particularly among those opposed to decriminalisation.

Indigenous feminisms in the second and third waves

Another consequence of state feminism is the reduction of feminist and women's issues to a single-axis, women/men plane. But while middle-class Pākehā (a New Zealander of non-Māori, predominantly European descent) women's interests were favoured by state feminism, other voices were also part of the discourse for women's liberation in the 1980s and 1990s. Notably mana wāhine Māori was addressing intersectional gender and colonial oppressions.

Te Awekōtuku (1991, p 10) defines mana wāhine Māori as:

> ... reclaiming and celebrating what we have been, and what we will become. It is not a re-action to males, and their violence against us; it is a pro-action, a determining of ourselves as Māori women, with authenticity and grace. And its ultimate aim is a rediscovery and renaming of that essential strength and harmony, that complementary relationship between genders that may have occurred on these islands two centuries past.

Mana wāhine Māori understands that Māori women 'are the makers of [their] own authenticity' (Te Awekōtuku, 1991, p 12). Critical education scholar Te Kawehau Clea Hoskins (2000, p 44) adds that while 'the primary site of struggle for Māori women is within a struggle for Māori independence ... this necessarily includes the struggle for gender equality both within [Māori] culture and in the wider society'.

Most feminist theory from the second wave to today comes to New Zealand from the US, UK, Europe and Australia (Taylor, 2002; Fairburn, 2008). Thus, mana wāhine is an essential thread of New Zealand's politics and social justice activism not only because of the central role colonialism has played in shaping every feature of contemporary society and politics, but also because mana wāhine is the only truly 'local' feminist theory in New Zealand. Indeed, Gay Simpkin, a founder of both Women for Aotearoa and Auckland Feminist Teachers, argues that the Māori sovereignty movement has been so critical to left thought in New Zealand because it is the rare 'shattering' that comes innately from within our local context (Taylor, 2002).

A feminism specific to New Zealand should interweave mana wāhine Māori and Pākehā feminisms so that class, ethnicity and gender are fully integrated into any postcolonial analysis and feminist praxis. That said, while New Zealand is de jure bicultural, it is de facto multicultural. In terms of sex work activism, tensions arise because the PRA limits legal sex work to citizens and permanent residents. Some tourists and migrants – especially young Asian women – are targeted by immigration authorities as likelier 'sex trafficking victims' or persons who want to work in the sex trades illegally. The near-silence in the New Zealand feminist literature on migrant women, Asian women, and queer male sex workers (but see Armstrong, 2017b and Ting, 2018) demonstrates how feminism in New Zealand must be more expansive in its approach to working with sex workers, as well as the narrow gender and risk frame that still permeates research in this area.

A unique context for feminist sex work activism

Feminist sex work research and activism are closely related in New Zealand. Due in part to commitments arising from Te Tiriti o Waitangi and Māori rangatiratanga (self-determination) activism, both research norms and academic institutional requirements in New Zealand include an ethical obligation for consultation with indigenous and vulnerable groups (Harrington, 2017). Such norms can and should, and generally do, extend beyond academic studies to feminist activism more broadly. When it comes to research with sex workers, sociologist Carol Harrington (2017) notes that feminist commitments to collaborative and participatory methods buttress consultation obligations and require research *with*, rather than on or about, sex workers. Sex workers may or may not be indigenous, but even post decriminalisation they remain vulnerable due to stigma. Consultation norms combined with the small size of the country mean that, in practice, the polarising divisions of the sex wars have not been sustained here to the degree that we see in the US and Europe. As Mary Holmes (2000) observes, New Zealand's small population means that community relationships are prioritised, and activists and politicians need to operate in ways that respect close social networks across the regions.

Further, Harrington (2017) explains that consultation and collaboration have precluded broad feminist support for criminalisation. This is important for a few reasons. First, it matters that New Zealand decriminalised rather than legalised sex work. Decriminalisation positions sex work as an industry regulated like most others, while legalisation would have continued to mark out sex work as uniquely dangerous and sex workers in need of protective legislation (Bruckert and Hannem, 2013). Research collaborations and decriminalisation have made sex worker feminisms not just more likely but more visible here than in most other places in the Global West. Frequently generated by current and former sex workers, sex worker feminisms aim to unsettle heteronormativity, deconstruct the 'whore stigma', and produce 'richer analyses of gender oppression' (Nagle, 1997, p 1) that 'reveal how many arguments against female prostitution reify the very cultural notions of femaleness they often purport to challenge' (Nagle, 1997, p 11). Their goal is to generate and affirm a 'positive and autonomous view of female sexuality' while accounting for 'the minefield of sexual oppression within which the struggle to define our sexuality takes place' (Nagle, 1997, p 7).

Developing a sex worker feminism in a decriminalised context is a first step in shifting to a materialist and anti-racist feminist politics of sex work, and by extension, a feminist politics of sex. Where sex work is defined as legitimate labour, it is easier to highlight what's exploitative about the *work* as opposed to emphasising the moral quandary of commercial sex. And, conversely, it is easier to consider how what's exploitative about the sex in sex work is precisely what is also exploitative about sex (full stop) under patriarchy and capitalism.

A second reason feminist support for decriminalisation is important is that the future of feminist sex work activism builds from the possibility for closer collaboration with the most vulnerable groups of sex workers based on the self-articulated needs and the intersectional interests of migrant, transgender, and impoverished sex workers, among others. So as public-private partnerships form the basis of state feminism, researcher-activist collaborations set a framework for fourth wave feminist praxis. Participatory methods rely on a model of feminist reflexivity – a model of listening and re-evaluating priorities to build a feminist praxis of accountability for working in solidarity with those most vulnerable in a community (Russo, 2019; Majic and Showden, 2019). Since consultation obligations rest in part on the status of vulnerability, then feminist praxis with, for example, street workers or migrants, should include them to the fullest degree possible. Such collaborations are made significantly easier in a decriminalised environment where sex workers are less likely than in criminalised systems to be a hidden population who are difficult to reach or to face significant legal risks when visible.[2]

The period of feminist dispersal into other social movements that occurred alongside a strengthening mana wāhine Māori has reshaped feminist possibilities in New Zealand. The next section discusses the increasing political opportunities for a more robust intersectional, social movement feminism to emerge in New Zealand. This intersectional feminism is not based primarily on identities but rather in structures of racialisation, gendering and class (Moran, 2018). Recent local and global events have cascaded in such a way that gender is very much back in the public consciousness, indicating that radical social movement feminism is ready to have another moment.

The near-future of feminist sex work activism

Grassroots feminist activism has been reanimated in New Zealand as part of local and global discussions of rape culture, sex trafficking, domestic violence, and gender norms. For example, prominent sexual assault and sexual harassment cases in New Zealand involving perpetrators ranging from high school boys to major law firm partners, alongside national debate over family violence law reforms and recent high-profile murders of women by men they were dating, have all raised public discussions of sexual and gender relations, with a renewed interest in rethinking toxic and hegemonic masculinities as well as norms of femininity (see, for example, Clifton, 2011; Trotter, 2013; Bennett, 2018). Evidence of grassroots feminism re-emerging in New Zealand includes actions such as SlutWalk, HollaBack Wellington, local 'women's marches' tied to events in the US and Europe, and the formation or revival of feminist groups such as Ace Lady Network, Thursdays in Black, and high school feminist clubs. These build on successes of earlier 'waves' and share political space with more established feminist-friendly organisations such as ActionStation, Children's Poverty Action Group, and the Auckland Women's Centre.

Discourses of gender and sexuality are changing in New Zealand in ways that are important for undoing some of the stereotypes and expectations of cisgender women's sexuality. In 2017, a panel of prominent 'second wave feminists' noted that the 1960s and 1970s helped to open the door for the wonderful number of people no longer defining themselves as male or female. 'That population is increasing ... and our responsibility is to never let those doors close' (Radio New Zealand, 2017a). Actively supporting a panoply of lived gender embodiments helps to undermine the norms and expectations that lead to 'slut-shaming' in general and stigma for sex workers specifically. One panellist, Ngahuia Te Awekōtuku, argued that the art and music scene has helped move feminism in New Zealand beyond the sex wars, and this means that the rifts between trans and gender-queer people, ciswomen, and lesbians can be bridged.

This queer and sex work positive feminism was hard-fought for in the second wave. And while there are still other feminist voices and activists active in contemporary public feminism in New Zealand, adopting individualised, third wave approaches or opposing sex work decriminalisation and the inclusion of transgender women under the feminist umbrella (Gerlich, nd), these views remain marginalised.[3] So, while the history of feminist support for sex workers' rights to work, to be free from stigma, and to challenge their working conditions from within a feminist frame has been fraught, the fourth wave of feminism is starting from a position of supporting sex workers' agency and right to dignity.

Partly this is because the PRA has been hugely successful in its harm reduction goals. Both a government-mandated five-year follow up study and more recent academic investigations find that, post decriminalisation, sex workers experience greater workplace safety alongside greater freedom to refuse clients and better relations with police (Abel et al, 2007; Abel, 2014; Armstrong, 2017a). The report to the Prostitution Law Review Committee found the number of sex workers had remained stable since the PRA's passage, with some movement of workers 'from the managed sector to the private sector' (Abel et al, 2007, p 6). One consequence of the PRA's successes is that whether some feminists ultimately want to abolish sex work or argue for its merits, most favour decriminalisation as the best strategy here and now. Thus, support for decriminalisation and the treatment of sex work as work is not just the state feminist position, but the view of a majority of public feminists. For example, when pressed on whether their comments on the harms of pornography were anti-sex work, one panellist on a second forum on contemporary feminism

(Radio New Zealand, 2017b) stated simply, 'I don't think any of us on this panel would say that sex work is a bad thing … and I think we all agree that women have their rights to their bodies'. Similarly, when *Vice* provided its candidate scorecards for the 2017 national elections, 'feminism' was one measure of assessment, with support for 'sex worker rights' being one of the five policy positions key to supporting feminism (McClure, 2017).

With alliances built through years of working in and with a range of left social justice groups, and the near-universal adoption of online and social media tools (especially Facebook) (Radio New Zealand, 2017b) blurring the lines between online and offline lives and activism, the generational digital divide is ebbing and intersectional analytics have matured. Alliances that build on older models of cooperation rather than individualism are finding themselves poised to exploit a political opportunity structure (Meyer and Minkoff, 2004) ripe for feminist action. SlutWalk, #MeToo, and renewed attention to the damaging nature of restrictive gender norms such as toxic masculinity have created spaces for feminist mobilisations aimed at decreasing stigma for sex work while raising more sympathetic awareness to how poverty and globalisation serve as push factors into both domestic sex work and migration for sex work. Taken together SlutWalk, #MeToo, and sex worker rights underscore how women are sexualised whether or not they are sex workers, and that sex is always potentially dangerous for women, which makes sex work not that different *as a matter of potential sexual violence*, for many women in and out of the industry. The current heightened attention to the pervasiveness of gendered sexual violence offers a real possibility to more successfully shift the conversation to sexual violence as a problem of masculinity, money and power, not of sex work per se.

The point here is not to say that sex work is just another form of violence against women. Rather, the current mainstream global discussions about rape culture rooted in norms of gender and power have brought longstanding feminist analyses of sex and gender into a mainstream spotlight, highlighting that systemic, pervasive sexual violence against women exceeds sex work – indeed is an all-too-common feature of women's lives regardless of their occupation. But sex workers are on the front line of challenging ideals about 'proper womanhood'. Feminism provides a structure of analysis for unpacking gender and stigma in sex work.

Shifting feminist questions and tactics

In a country where sex work is legally understood as legitimate labour, longstanding feminist questions can be addressed anew: why does the feminisation of poverty persist? What kinds of political and economic alliances would shift gender and economic norms to address the gender wage gap – a gap that starts with workers as young as 14 (Besen-Cassino, 2018) and sits at an overall rate of 9.2 per cent as of 2018 (Ministry for Women, 2018)? New Zealand has the highest rates of domestic violence and fifth highest rates of child abuse in the Global West (Gammon, 2016; Adams, 2017) while 24 per cent of women and 6 per cent of men in New Zealand report experiencing sexual violence at least once in their lifetime (New Zealand Family Violence Clearinghouse, 2017). Are these normalised experiences of violence and exploitation fuelled, at least in part, by particular understandings of masculinity and gender relations in New Zealand? If so, what macro and meso structures and discourses feed into those gender relations? These conversations, and any political, material and rhetorical shifts that result, will directly affect how sex work is situated in both economic markets and gender relations. Sorting out how women and vulnerable members of society are treated across multiple public and private domains is the next big task for a feminism that wants to reconfigure gender and tackle the problem of violence.

Clearly the problem of sexual violence is not unique to sex work. It is also not the only point where sex work activism and feminism are fruitful allies. Feminists and gender migration scholars increasingly agree that sex work is a form of care work, or socially reproductive and emotional or embodied labour, which also includes nursing, child and elder care, and domestic work (Outshoorn, 2005; Agustín, 2007; Vershuur, 2013; Henry and Farvid, 2017). Socially reproductive labour comprises the material and symbolic activities and relationships that are necessary to support wage labour and to reproduce human beings over time (Kofman, 2012). The global crisis in care work, and 'the globalization of care' are significant interdependent factors in both legal and illegal migration (Lan, 2008; Federici, 2012).

As such, sex work deftly illustrates how gender ideology affects the material conditions of women and gender nonconforming people globally. Advocating for sex workers from a feminist perspective demands an analysis of the material conditions producing normative gender categories and the continued 'naturalising' of skilled tasks when women do them. Here is where labour activism around other feminised socially reproductive labour, such as nursing and midwifery, could profitably operate in coalition with sex workers and feminists to critique the ongoing devaluing of care labour, primarily because it is viewed as 'feminised' labour. In short, while earlier feminist discussions of sex work in New Zealand were primarily liberal, harm reduction, and choice orientated (Laurie, 2010; Abel, 2017), a more radical and intersectional feminism would emphasise gender structures and heteronormativity within and beyond sex work.

Fourth wave feminists must be committed to reshaping, if not dismantling, multiple forms of mutually supportive exploitation (Kwateng-Clark, 2019). This will require a critical unpacking of macro and meso structures in addition to rethinking the individual relationships and identities that were the focus of third wave feminism. This is not simply a matter of multiplying categories of people who are included in sex work studies, but also of rethinking the kinds of political, economic and social formations that shape our research questions and that get included in analyses of 'sex work'. The PRA addressed issues of individual harm in the job, but did not specifically address child poverty, racism and transphobia as push factors into the more vulnerable sectors of the sex industry, even as these concerns were raised occasionally in the parliamentary debates leading up to the Act's passage (Showden, 2017). The housing crisis and diminishing state support for lone mothers are also directly related to who opts to undertake sex work yet are still to be investigated as related issues of gender inequality (Abel, 2018). All of these beg for feminist analysis and action, as questions of sex work politics.

What is particularly exciting for a local sex work feminism is its potential to draw on feminism as it has developed in this specific context. Pākehā and Māori feminists have historically had difficulty effectively engaging in intersectional politics together (Te Awekōtuku, 1991; Schuster, 2016), partly due to Pākehā feminists wanting Māori women to join Pākehā groups rather than working in partnership or following Māori women's lead. Yet Pākehā feminism has failed in many ways to grasp the ontology, epistemology, and political needs of Māori (Irwin, 1992). The period of feminist dispersal seems potentially to have opened the necessary space for Pākehā women to listen more effectively and be led by and alongside other activist groups, including sex worker, Māori, and/or queer activists.[4] If, and how, this potential evolves remains to be seen.

Especially useful would be further building of an intersectional politics through coalition and accountability within and among activist groups. This differs from a politics of inclusivity that seeks to 'diversify' memberships of existing (often white/Pākehā) groups (Schuster,

2016; Moran, 2018; Russo, 2019). Coalition and accountability politics among people from different socio-structural standpoints can expand activists' understandings of different lived experiences of gender inequality. Such a politics of solidarity turns feminists into 'co-strugglers' whose solidarity is based on active participation in collective struggles, 'working side by side with those most impacted, not as privileged outsiders' (Russo, 2019, p 27). It can orient activist attention to productive differences (Simmonds, 2011; Murphy, 2017) and 'relationships of mutuality and responsibility' rather than emphasising group integration and 'helping' (Russo, 2019, p 28). This is one approach for thinking about what feminism is (as a political argument) rather than who feminists are, moving feminist activism further away from identity-based politics. Such an intersectional and materially orientated analysis will be particularly promising for addressing two of the biggest issues facing sex workers and sex work politics now: trafficking and stigma.

The next frontiers

During the legislative debates about the PRA, many conservative and liberal feminist groups supported decriminalisation because they hoped it would prevent sex trafficking (Laurie, 2010). More recent feminist rhetoric has been split about whether decriminalisation helps reduce or promote sex trafficking, due in part to the increasingly vocal global discourse stipulating that sex work and sex trafficking are indistinguishable (Showden and Majic, 2018). While there is no clear definition of what constitutes 'trafficking', exploitation of illegal and irregular migrants is a significant and growing global concern. New Zealand has been under pressure, particularly from the US in the form of its annual Trafficking in Persons (TiP) Reports[5], to get tougher on sex trafficking, with the TiP Reports asserting in part that decriminalised sex work is conducive to trafficking. In 2016, the New Zealand government enhanced its anti-trafficking provisions and removed cross-border movement from the definition of trafficking, defining it instead through a specific condition of labour: 'exploitation' (Showden, 2017). There are some concerns that the current methods for addressing trafficking will hamper efforts to protect migrant workers in the industry or open the door to rollbacks of some sections of the PRA (Ting, 2018). These concerns are not baseless, as anti-trafficking efforts have a history of making life more difficult for all sex workers, but especially those more vulnerable due to poverty or immigration status. For example, the recent US-led crackdown on using the internet for advertising sexual services because this is considered a front for trafficking has worked in New Zealand to undermine some of the safety gains accrued post-PRA (*New Zealand Herald*, 2018).

More effective than raids and internet advertising bans in combating trafficking would be a sex worker feminism laser-focused on the structural causes of poverty, because poverty limits people's work and education opportunities. Poverty keeps sex work as the only, or most viable, option for some members of the community. Poverty, transphobia, racism and the global care crisis are root causes of trafficking (Agustín 2007; Showden and Majic, 2018). Addressing these concerns goes a significant way to making sex work more fully a labour of choice rather than one of structural coercion. An intersectional and materialist feminism will emphasise the ways globalised labour, poverty, and gender discrimination lead to migration; the ways that discourses conflating sex work and trafficking rely on a rhetoric of unavoidable victimisation; and the ways a dual system making some adult sex workers legal and others illegal not only pushes risks of exploitation and violence onto the most marginalised people in the industry but in fact increases these risks (Outshoorn, 2014).

While it is true that the PRA was largely focused on harm reduction, it did address structural stigma by instituting decriminalisation rather than legalisation, that is by instituting minimal regulations akin to other business sectors rather than holding sex work out as a 'special category' (Bruckert and Hannem, 2013, p 61). Still, the PRA perpetuates the moral and social stigmas through its preamble (noted earlier) and, arguably, provisions that reflect stereotypes about sex work as uniquely violent or inseparable from coercion (Warnock and Wheen, 2012). In this way, the law reveals the heteronormative notion that sex work is inherently (more) violent than other sexual interactions, that sex workers are trafficking victims and that sex work is, indelibly, a form of exploitation (Bruckert and Hannem, 2013). Thus, the PRA has not had as much effect on the social and symbolic stigma faced by sex workers as it has had on promoting labour rights (Bruckert and Hannem, 2013).

Bruckert and Hannem (2013) are optimistic that addressing structural stigma is a first step that precedes and facilitates breaking down symbolic and social stigma, offering the history of gay rights legislation as an example. But, this chapter is arguing, a progressive narrative of structural destigmatisation does not inevitably lead to social acceptance. Such progress is in fact contingent upon how feminists reframe rhetorics of risk, morality, and gender in relation to sex work. These frameworks are rooted in heteronormativity, and it is heteronormativity that feminist sex work activism needs to challenge.

As Joanna Schmidt (2017, p 37) explains, 'the discourse of heteronormativity results in understandings of heterosexuality that are gendered in ways which have a direct impact on how prostitution is practised, regulated, and understood'. Heteronormativity posits heterosexual sex as best and 'natural', and reproductive sex rather than recreational or commercial sex as preferred within it. On this view, men and women have different motivations for sex: women as 'natural' caregivers want a limited number of children, while men want many partners to maximise their offspring. Both the concept of male sex drive and the sexual double standard spring from this tenacious view of sexuality. With heteronormative framings of risk, morality and gender in prostitution, the PRA has been beneficial to sex workers on a practical level, but has failed to challenge heteronormativity and gender hierarchy (Harrington, 2012). While centring harm reduction, the PRA continues to foreground both inequality and exploitation – not to mention dominant gender norms – as inevitable in sex work. That there are still efforts to make street work more difficult or illegal in certain jurisdictions (see Chapter 9) is one example that highlights the precarity of the challenge offered by the PRA to sex worker stigma rooted in heteronormativity. Efforts to ban street work or corral it into small and undesirable areas target poorer, younger, and transgender workers in particular, those already the most vulnerable and in violation of middle-class gender norms (Abel and Fitzgerald, 2012). Here we see an earlier law change from the state feminist era that was an essential first step in reshaping gender norms, but that needs to move beyond a single-axis understanding of vulnerability if it is to address social stigma.

Thus, a key task of fourth wave, sex worker feminism is to confront the heteronormative power relations that shape the gendered dynamics of the sex industry (Schmidt, 2017). And this is why the current moment – with the visibility of rape culture, sexual harassment, and the violence of gender norms – is a promising one for targeting the structural dilemmas of sex work. This challenge can build on the PRA's success in addressing individual concerns in sex work (Healy et al, 2017), but it is not inevitable that it will do so. The conditions are in place for an intersectional, materialist, anti-racist feminism to coalesce. And this is needed to tackle the heteronormativity that makes violence and exploitation look inevitable in sex work, through articulating how such violence and exploitation are in fact rooted in capitalist, racist and gender structures producing sex work as we currently know it, but not sex work as it has to be. Such argumentation will include fighting for rights to live and work in public spaces regardless of the 'normativity' of one's body, tackling push factors in the industry like poverty and racism, and addressing the wide-ranging needs of young, takatāpui (lesbian/gay) and other workers often left out of feminist discussions of sex work's exploitative or liberating potential vis-à-vis women and sexual expectations.

Yet counter-hegemonic politics is difficult. Our lives are directed by legal and material rules and barriers that smooth the flow of human interactions in a steady and singular direction (Murphy, 2017). 'Heterosexuality, marriage, the nuclear family, religion, morality, education, advertising, politics, health care, policing, prisons, psychology, and many other structural, discursive institutions are imbued with explicit and implicit' rules for how bodies interact socially and politically (Murphy, 2017, p 13). Feminism aims to disrupt this seamless flow. Such protest works against the imperatives of neoliberalism that privatise and individualise sources of poverty, discrimination and crime. To be successful activists, then, feminists must collectively occupy spaces and challenge norms they are meant to avoid (Murphy, 2017). Mana wāhine Māori, state feminism and fourth wave feminism working together are well-positioned to infiltrate these spaces and address the intersections of sex work and the broader sexual and gender politics that authorise ongoing stigma against sex workers.

Conclusion

Māori feminist Ngahuia Te Awekōtuku has argued that 'feminism is what we make it' (cited in Murphy, 2017, p 6); thus feminism in New Zealand 'must include Māori mythology, song, dance, art, storytelling to develop our contextually specific and appropriate voicings of and responses to violence' (Murphy, 2017, p 6). Feminist sex work activism in New Zealand has developed into an affirmation of decriminalisation and listening to sex workers as allies in feminist struggle because of Māori tikanga (protocol) for consultation and reciprocity. Successful feminist and socialist politics rely on understanding the history and current contexts *where you are* (Taylor, 2002), which is why Māori sovereignty and mana wāhine Māori are central to any future feminist movement in New Zealand.

By working with Māori, Pākehā feminists and sex workers can take part in the ongoing reimagining of 'postcolonial' gender formations that Māori are undertaking as they excavate and deliberate about what pre-colonial gender structures looked like. Māori feminists have argued that pre-colonial gender roles were understood through land

and genealogical relationships, through reciprocity, collectivity and responsibility, but not on sexed hierarchies as in Western cosmologies (Mikaere, 1994). While these pre-colonial gender epistemologies are promising starting points, the postcolonial reconstruction of gender is a fully political and contentious undertaking. The kinds of gender stories that are told depend on who is telling them and for what ends (Hoskins, 2000). Cultures are dynamic; a simple 'reclamation' of pre-colonial gender structure is neither possible nor desirable (Hoskins, 2000, p 35). Thus:

> ... any reconstruction will inevitably be shaped at least in part by contemporary and historical discourses ... this should not be considered a totally bad thing; an acknowledgement of it may relax or free-up the parameters of those discourses, creating gaps/spaces where our reconstructive work can draw from the obvious integrity of our value base while creating new and imaginative possibilities for the construction of tikanga/practice and structures consistent with our needs and aspirations today. (Hoskins, 2000, p 36)

The point here is not that Pākehā feminism can simply appropriate Māori women's work; rather, Pākehā feminists can listen to and learn from the hard fought battles of Māori women. Using reflexivity, accountability, and consultation, Pākehā feminism can work as hoa mahi (a friend who works alongside) with Māori feminists in reconceiving gender relations in ways that neither simply capitulate to an existing capitalist, neoliberal system nor seek to usurp Māori women's leadership roles in defining the meaning of their own cultural gendered practices (Mikaere, 1994; Simmonds, 2011). With this as a framework for future activism, feminists can rethink the way sex work functions in New Zealand culture and economy, as well as who is pulled – and who is pushed – into it and why. A postcolonial, intersectional, materialist feminist approach would promote collaborative alliances and advocacy with (rather than for) sex workers and challenge the gender norms that continue to make sex work the only viable employment option for some, exploitative for many, and stigmatised for most.

This work can happen here and now because, in addition to the spaces opened up by SlutWalk, #MeToo, transgender rights and queer activism, New Zealand has over 15 years' experience of sex work decriminalisation. During that period, plenty of evidence has amassed to demonstrate that harm reduction has improved working conditions. Sex workers (and) feminists can build on this success at the individual level to make claims for more structural changes, and they can do so alongside contemporary social movements looking at sexual violence as a phenomenon rooted in colonial, patriarchal gender structures and norms of cisgender masculinity, along with critiques of neoliberal globalisation that drives gendered migration patterns for and into gender-segregated labour markets.

Some of the possibilities outlined in this chapter are unique to the New Zealand political context: its particular colonial formations and resulting formal biculturalism amid lived multiculturalism; its remoteness and small population; and the embeddedness of consultation as a fundamental value. But other aspects of this analysis could travel and inform feminist analyses beyond New Zealand's shores. The political opportunities of the current moment that arise out of activism surrounding queer gender categories, #MeToo, and revived debates about the gendering, racialising and valuing of social reproductive labour are global phenomena (Arruzza et al, 2019). While the specifics of mana wāhine Māori and Pākehā feminisms in this relatively more secular Western nation are unique, the model of consultation, reflexivity, and materially focused arguments can be adapted to local contexts elsewhere.

Further, much feminist activism around sex work in other parts of the Global West concentrates on legal and policy questions, notably debates about whether the Nordic model of criminalising clients or other models of regulation and criminalisation are most appropriate. But in New Zealand, the broad policy question has largely been settled, though the scope of whose sex work should be decriminalised is still a very live political issue. As concerns about trafficking continue to influence sex work politics, it is important to remember that only permanent residents and citizens can legally engage in sex work. Still, with decriminalisation having become normative, sex work discussions in New Zealand can target cultural, social, and economic questions regarding stigma, harm reduction, and protecting labour rights more than is possible in regimes where criminalisation and carceral rhetorics still hold sway.

Here and abroad, future feminist research with and about sex workers must bring male and transgender sex workers of all ethnicities and immigration/citizenship statuses into 'regular' sex work studies rather than dividing research by sub-groups. Different groups of workers have specific needs, and so some targeted studies are important. But broadening what counts as both sex work and a sex worker also means not persisting in conducting studies of 'sex workers' that look at cisgender women while leaving them unmarked or as the normalised group while studies of 'other sex workers' ('gay sex workers'; 'takatāpui sex workers' and so on) continue to be made a niche. Language matters. Heteronormative gender is reproduced through the social and legal labels and distinctions that continue to pervade how the employment sector and research studies organise our knowledge of and interactions with sex workers.

In this way, the feminism outlined in this chapter is not just intersectional, materialist and postcolonial, it is a queer feminism. A queer feminism is one that tackles the gendered meanings of sexuality, power and embodiment (Showden, 2012). And it interrogates masculinity and gender performativity, so that current forms of economic and gender power are critiqued but so are the possibilities for a productive politics of embodiment and new modes of sexual economics.

Rejecting the individualism of third wave feminism, the possibilities for fourth wave feminism in New Zealand come from collective action among and between feminists and sex workers, two groups with significantly overlapping membership. As Leola Murphy (2017, p.13) writes, '… activism involves collectively getting in the way of mechanized systems, occupying spaces which were not intended for certain bodies'. Sex workers and feminists have a long history of demanding access to spaces they have been deemed inappropriate for and to. They are poised to have a long future of doing the same. Together.

Notes

[1] Though to a lesser degree, and with none of the generational 'mother/daughter' angst of North American third-wave feminism (Grey, 2009, p 50).
[2] Although, even in New Zealand's decriminalised regime, not all sex workers have legal protections, for example, temporary visa holders. This is one reason they are largely missing from the New Zealand sex work scholarship.
[3] In addition to Gerlich, the group Speak Up for Women has recently formed to protest transgender protective policy proposals. While they do not currently campaign on sex work issues, one of their eight principles states 'Women and girls have the right to live free from commercial sexual exploitation'. See: https://speakupforwomen.nz/about-us/our-principles/
[4] I base this claim largely on preliminary data collected as part of ongoing research into young people's political activism in New Zealand undertaken by myself and three other researchers. Murphy (2017) makes a similar argument about the potential for active listening to Māori feminists to instigate an intersectional feminism in New Zealand that begins to address the legacy of colonial violence.
[5] The US publishes an annual Trafficking in Persons (TiP) Report. See https://www.state.gov/trafficking-in-persons-report/ for more information.

References

Abel, G. (2014) 'A decade of decriminalization: Sex work "down under" but not underground', *Criminology and Criminal Justice*, 14(5): 580–92.

Abel, G. (2017) 'In search of a free and fair society: The regulation of sex work in New Zealand', in E. Ward & G. Wylie (eds) *Feminism, Prostitution and the State: The politics of neo-abolitionism*, Abingdon: Routledge, pp 140–55.

Abel, G. (2018) 'Decriminalisation and social justice: A public health perspective on sex work', in S. Fitzgerald & K. McGarry (eds) *Realising Justice for Sex Workers: An agenda for change*, London: Rowman & Littlefield, pp 123–40.

Abel, G.M. & Fitzgerald, L.J. (2012) ' "The street's got its advantages": Movement between sectors of the sex industry in a decriminalised environment', *Health, Risk & Society*, 14(1): 7–23.

Abel, G., Fitzgerald, L. & Brunton, C. (2007) 'Decriminalisation and the rights of migrant sex workers in Aotearoa/New Zealand: Making a case for change: Report to the Prostitution Law Review Committee', Christchurch: University of Otago.

Adams, A. (2017) 'NZ's highest rate of family violence in the developed world - Amy Adams has "had enough"', *Stuff*, 21 March. Available at: https://www.stuff.co.nz/national/politics/90657034/nzs-highest-rate-of-family-violence-in-the-developed-world--amy-adams-has-had-enough.

Agustín, L.M. (2007) *Sex at the Margins: Migration, labour markets and the rescue industry*, New York: Palgrave Macmillan.

Aimers, J. (2011) 'The impact of New Zealand "Third Way" style government on women in community development', *Community Development Journal*, 46(3): 302–14.

Armstrong, L. (2017a) 'From law enforcement to protection? Interactions between sex workers and police in a decriminalized street-based sex industry', *British Journal of Criminology*, 57: 570–88.

Armstrong, L. (2017b) 'Commentary: Decriminalisation and the rights of migrant sex workers in Aotearoa/New Zealand: Making a case for change', *Women's Studies Journal*, 31(2): 69–76.

Arruzza, C., Bhattacharya, T. & Fraser, N. (2019) *Feminism for the 99%: A manifesto*, New York: Verso.

Ashton, L. (2014) 'Dis/identifications and dis/articulations: Young women and feminism in Aotearoa/New Zealand', Master of Social Practice thesis, Unitech.

Bennett, C. (2018) 'One year on: what impact #MeToo has had on New Zealanders', *Next Magazine Online*, 12 November. Available at: https://www.nowtolove.co.nz/lifestyle/career/metoo-in-new-zealand-impact-one-year-on-39634.

Besen-Cassino, Y. (2018) *The Cost of Being a Girl: Working teens and the origins of the gender wage gap*, Philadelphia, PA: Temple University Press.

Bruckert, C. & Hannem, S. (2013) 'Rethinking the prostitution debates: Transcending structural stigma in systemic responses to sex work', *Canadian Journal of Law and Society /Revue Canadienne Droit et Société*, 28(1): 43–63.

Clifton, J. (2011) 'Slutwalk arrives in New Zealand', Noted, 27 June. Available at: https://www.noted.co.nz/archive/archive-listener-nz-2011/slutwalk-arrives-in-new-zealand.

Fairburn, M. (2008) 'Is there a good case for New Zealand exceptionalism?', *Theses Eleven*, 92: 29–49.

Federici, S. (2012) *Revolution at Point Zero: Housework, reproduction, and feminist struggle*, Brooklyn, NY: Common Notions.

Gammon, R. (2016) 'Family violence: New Zealand's dirty little secret'. Available at: http://www.massey.ac.nz/massey/about-massey/news/article.cfm?mnarticle_uuid=C61AEFE4-B1D7-0794-48A1-CFA90FEDDEFF.

Gerlich, R. (nd) 'Writing by Renee'. Available at: https://reneejg.net/.

Grey, S. (2008) 'Out of sight, out of mind: The New Zealand women's movement', in S. Grey & M. Sawer (eds) *Women's Movements: Flourishing or in abeyance?*, Abingdon: Routledge, pp 65–78.

Grey S. J. (2009) 'Women, politics, and protest: Rethinking women's liberation activism in New Zealand', in J. Leslie, K. McMillan & E. McLeay (eds) *Rethinking women and politics: New Zealand and comparative perspectives*, Wellington: Victoria University Press, pp 34–61.

Harrington, C. (2012) 'Prostitution policy models and feminist knowledge politics in New Zealand and Sweden', *Sex Research and Social Policy*, 9: 337–49.

Harrington, C. (2017) 'Collaborative research with sex workers', in M. Spanger & M. Skilbrei (eds) *Prostitution Research in Context: Methodology, representation, and power*, London: Routledge, pp 85–100.

Healy, C., Wi-Hongi, A. & Hati, C. (2017) 'Reflection from the field: It's work, it's working: The integration of sex workers and sex work in Aotearoa/New Zealand', *Women's Studies Journal*, 31(2): 50–60.

Henry, M. V. & Farvid, P. (2017) '"Always hot, always live": Computer-mediated sex work in the era of "camming"', *Women's Studies Journal*, 31(2): 113–28.

Holmes, M. (2000) 'Second-wave feminism and the politics of relationships', *Women's Studies International Forum*, 23(2): 235–46.

Hoskins, T. K. C. (2000) 'In the interests of Māori women? Discourses of reclamation', in A. Jones, P. Herda & T. M. Suaalii (eds) *Bitter Sweet: Indigenous women in the Pacific*, Dunedin: University of Otago Press, pp 33–48.

Hyman, P. (2009) 'Feminist agendas and action in 21st century New Zealand: Violence against women', in J. Leslie, K. McMillan & E. McLeay (eds) *Rethinking Women and Politics: New Zealand and comparative perspectives*, Wellington: Victoria University Press, pp 62–86.

Irwin, K. (1992) 'Towards theories of Māori feminism', in R. Du Plessis (ed) *Feminist Voices: Women's studies texts from Aotearoa/New Zealand*, Melbourne: Oxford University Press, pp 1–21.

Kantola, J. & Squires, J. (2012) 'From state feminism to market feminism?', *International Political Science Review*, 33(4): 382–400.

Kofman, E. (2012) 'Rethinking care through social reproduction: Articulating circuits of migration', *Social Politics: International Studies in Gender, State, and Society*, 19(1): 142–62.

Kwateng-Clark, D. (2019) 'Angela Davis addresses the whitewashing of feminism and Islamophobia', Broadly, 20 March. Available at: https://broadly.vice.com/en_us/article/wjmab9/angela-davis-intersectional-feminsm-apollo.

Lan, P. (2008) 'New global politics of reproductive labor: Gendered labor and marriage migration', *Sociology Compass*, 2(6): 1801–15.

Laurie, A. (2010) 'Several sides to the story: Feminist views of prostitution reform', in G. Abel, L. Fitzgerald, C. Healy & A. Taylor (eds) *Taking the Crime Out of Sex Work: New Zealand sex workers' fight for decriminalization*, Bristol: Policy Press, pp 85–101.

Majic, S. & Showden, C. R. (2019) 'Redesigning the study of sex work: A case for intersectionality and reflexivity', in S. Dewey, C. Izugbara & I. Crowhurst (eds) *Handbook of Sex Industry Research*, London: Routledge, pp 42–54.

McClure, T. (2017) 'We've selected just a few hot points regarded as central to the feminist movement: paid parental leave, sex-worker rights, the gender pay gap, abortion, and support for single mothers', Vice, 6 September. Available at: https://www.vice.com/en_nz/article/gyy7k9/for-the-record-how-feminist-are-new-zealands-mps-really.

Meyer, D. S. & Minkoff, D. C. (2004) 'Conceptualizing political opportunity', *Social Forces,* 82(4): 1457–92.

Mikaere, A. (1994) 'Māori women: Caught in the contradictions of a colonised reality', *Waikato Law Review,* 2: 125–49.

Ministry for Women (2018) 'Gender pay gap'. Available at: https://women.govt.nz/work-skills/income/gender-pay-gap.

Moran, M. (2018) '(Un)troubling identity politics: A cultural materialist intervention', *European Journal of Social Theory* (online first), DOI: 10.1177/1368431018819722.

Murphy, L. (2017) 'Intersectional feminisms: Reflections on theory and activism in Sara Ahmed's *Living a Feminist Life* (2017)', *Women's Studies Journal,* 31(2): 4–17.

Nagle, J. (1997) 'Introduction', in J. Nagle (ed) *Whores and Other Feminists*, New York: Routledge, pp 1–15.

New Zealand Family Violence Clearinghouse (2017) 'Data summaries 2017: Snapshot'. Available at: https://nzfvc.org.nz/sites/nzfvc.org.nz/files/Data-summaries-snapshot-2017.pdf.

New Zealand Herald (2018) 'How the FBI has disrupted NZ's sex work industry', *New Zealand Herald,* 23 April. Available at: https://www.nzherald.co.nz/lifestyle/news/article.cfm?c_id=6&objectid=12037972.

O'Neill, M. (2010) 'Cultural criminology and sex work: Resisting regulation through radical democracy and participatory action research (PAR)', *Journal of Law and Society,* 37(1): 210–32.

Outshoorn, J. (2005) 'The political debates on prostitution and trafficking in women', *Social Politics: International Studies in Gender, State and Society,* 12(1): 141–55.

Outshoorn, J. (2014) 'The contested citizenship of sex workers: The case of the Netherlands', in C. R. Showden & S. Majic (eds) *Negotiating Sex Work: Unintended consequences of policy and activism*, Minneapolis: University of Minnesota Press, pp 171–93.

Radio New Zealand (2017a) 'Contemporary feminism 1: Feminism - the morning after', Radio New Zealand, 8 March. Available at: https://www.radionz.co.nz/programmes/contemporary-feminism/story/201833265/contemporary-feminism-1-feminism-the-morning-after.

Radio New Zealand (2017b) 'Contemporary feminism 2: digital feminism', Radio New Zealand, 26 March. Available at: https://www.radionz.co.nz/programmes/contemporary-feminism/story/201834051/contemporary-feminism-2-digital-feminism.

Risman, B. J. & Davis, G. (2013) 'From sex roles to gender structure', *Current Sociology Review,* 61(5–6): 733–55.

Russo, A. (2019) *Feminist Accountability: Disrupting violence and transforming power*, New York: New York University Press.

Schmidt, J. (2017) 'The regulation of sex work in Aotearoa/New Zealand: An overview', *Women's Studies Journal*, 31(2): 35–49.

Schuster, J. (2013) 'Invisible feminists? Social media and young women's political participation', *Political Science,* 65(1): 8–24.

Schuster, J. (2014) 'Where have all the feminists gone? Searching for New Zealand's women's movement in the early 21st century', PhD thesis: University of Auckland.

Schuster, J. (2016) 'Intersectional expectations: Young feminists' perceived failure at dealing with differences and their retreat to individualism', *Women's Studies International Forum*, 58: 1–8.

Showden, C.R. (2012) 'Theorizing maybe: A feminist/queer theory convergence', *Feminist Theory*, 13(1): 3–25.

Showden, C.R. (2017) 'From human rights to law and order: The changing relationship between trafficking and prostitution in Aotearoa/New Zealand policy discourse', *Women's Studies Journal*, 31(1): 5–21.

Showden, C.R. & Majic, S. (2018) *Youth Who Trade Sex in the U.S.: Intersectionality, agency, and vulnerability*, Philadelphia, PA: Temple University Press.

Simmonds, N. (2011) 'Mana wāhine: Decolonising politics', *Women's Studies Journal*, 25(2): 11–25.

Taylor, K. (2002) 'Feminism and the left: An interview with Gay Simpkin', in P. Moloney & K. Taylor (eds) *On the Left: Essays on socialism in New Zealand*, Dunedin: Otago University Press, pp 133–49.

Te Awekōtuku, N. (1991) *Mana Wāhine Māori: Selected writings on Māori women's art, culture, and politics*, Auckland: New Women's Press.

Ting, D. A. J-R. (2018) 'Understanding the experiences of migrant Asian sex work in New Zealand: An exploratory study', MA thesis: University of Auckland.

Trotter, C. (2013) 'Our distorted perceptions of gender: Reflections on the roastbusters scandal', The Daily Blog, 7 November. Available at: https://thedailyblog.co.nz/2013/11/07/our-distorted-perceptions-of-gender-reflections-on-the-roastbusters-scandal/.

Vershuur, C. (2013) 'Theoretical debates on social reproduction and care: The articulation between the domestic and the global economy', in L. Oso & N. R. Mateos (eds) *The International Handbook on Gender, Migration and Transnationalism: Global and development perspectives*, Cheltenham: Edward Elgar, pp 145–62.

Warnock, C. & Wheen, N. (2012) 'Sex work in New Zealand: The re-importation of moral majoritarianism in regulating a decriminalized industry', *Canadian Journal of Women and the Law*, 24(2): 414–38.

PART II

The Diversity of Sex Workers in New Zealand

4

The Impacts of Decriminalisation for Trans Sex Workers

Fairleigh Gilmour

Introduction

The decriminalisation of sex work in New Zealand, through the passing of the Prostitution Reform Act (PRA) 2003 resulted in significant improvement to police/sex worker interactions and relationships (Armstrong, 2016a), as well as improving work conditions for sex workers on a range of fronts: greater powers of negotiation of safer sex and ability to refuse clients, protection from violent attacks, and enabling workers to feel supported and safe (Abel et al, 2007). The international data indicates that decriminalisation is best practice in terms of public health (Shannon et al, 2015) and there have been positive research findings related to the health and safety of workers in the New Zealand context (Abel et al, 2007; Prostitution Law Review Committee, 2008; Armstrong, 2014). Decriminalisation in New South Wales, Australia, the only other jurisdiction to have decriminalised sex work, has also been found to benefit workers, including street workers and migrant workers (Harcourt et al, 2005, p 126); these two groups are most often excluded in legalised frameworks, which often create a two-tiered system by continuing to criminalise some forms of sex work. However, while some studies, particularly Abel et al's (2007) study into the impacts of the PRA, do include trans participants in their sample, there is an absence of research that specifically addresses the safety needs of, and law enforcement responses towards, trans sex workers. They may face additional challenges in terms of work safety and police protection, and suffer disproportionately from violence and intolerance in the community (Harcourt et al, 2001).

This chapter looks first at some of the factors that may specifically impact trans sex workers. It draws from international literature on gender-identity-based discrimination and on LGBT+ interactions with the police, before discussing the empirical literature on trans sex workers' work conditions. This chapter then explores the experiences of trans sex workers in Christchurch, New Zealand, and draws from qualitative interviews with eight participants that the author conducted in 2018. It looks at participants' perceptions of street work and barriers to safety when working on the street. It then examines participants' experiences with law enforcement and their perspectives on decriminalisation. While emphasising the benefits of decriminalisation, this chapter also highlights the ongoing barriers for some workers in accessing safe working conditions, including police attitudes, exclusion from public space and ongoing stigma.

Trans experiences of work, discrimination, and law enforcement

Both the LGBT+ population and the sex work population have a history of fraught relationships with law enforcement. While this chapter will focus on the work conditions and contemporary interactions between trans sex workers and law enforcement in Christchurch, it is important to contextualise experiences of work and relationships with law enforcement within the broader patterns of discrimination that trans people experience. These broader patterns of discrimination delimit employment options, shape attitudes and make some populations more vulnerable to police abuses.

In a society that sanctions people for failing to conform to stereotypical gender norms, trans people face a pervasive pattern of discrimination – experiencing both economic disadvantage and increased rates of violence. Economic marginalisation is a key issue, with many trans people experiencing unemployment, job discrimination and difficulty in accessing social services (Jacobs et al, 2008). While research indicates that sex workers primarily enter the sex industry for economic reasons (Groves et al, 2008; Pickering et al, 2009; Weldon, 2010; Maher et al, 2013), international research suggests that trans women may face additional difficulties in finding alternative forms of employment due to gender-based labour market discrimination; this may contribute to poverty, and to trans women migrating to non-traditional economies, including the sex industry (Clements-Nolle et al, 2001; Sausa et al, 2007; Hill et al, 2017). This finding has also been noted in large studies that have included trans workers in the sample and which indicated that trans workers have difficulty in leaving the industry and finding other forms of employment because of discrimination (Abel et al, 2007).

While many gay communities celebrate the Stonewall rebellion of 1969[1] as symbolising the birth of the 'gay rights' movement, what is often omitted is the fact that this event was a collective struggle against the police, and was just part of an ongoing struggle between LGBT+ people and law enforcement (Russell, 2017). Dwyer's (2011) summary of the extant global literature indicates that LGBT+ communities continue to be both under-policed, in that law enforcement fails to respond adequately to reports of victimisation against LGBT+ people, and over-policed, in that they remain overly subject to harassment by the police, particularly when navigating public space (see Dwyer, 2015). Numerous studies have documented discriminatory actions by police against members of the LGBT+ community (Amnesty International, 2005; McCandless, 2018). While much of the literature tends to collapse varied identities under the LGBT+ umbrella, trans people in particular are much more likely to experience violence and discrimination by law enforcement personnel than those who fit binary conceptions of gender (Amnesty International, 2005; Stotzer, 2014). Due to these experiences of harassment and violence, trans people are cautious of police contact and often do not trust the police or do not see the police as a legitimate organisation (Miles-Johnson, 2015). A perception of both homophobia and heterosexism in the police force contributes to the reluctance within LGBT+ communities to report victimisation to the police. While there are ongoing efforts in the contemporary era to improve police-community relations with diverse community members, these top-down efforts are often stymied by negative police attitudes towards reform. This resistance to reform may be based on negative perceptions of trans people for defying social conventions that uphold gender boundaries, as well as a police culture that fosters strong in-group identification (and the resulting othering of those perceived as out-group) and which involves the dominance of masculine and heteronormative behavioural norms (Praat and Tuffin, 1996; Miles-Johnson, 2016). Even where shifts have been made towards less aggressive policing practices, law enforcement engagement with trans sex workers has remained underpinned by stigmatising stereotypes around both sex work and gender identity which hamper the possibility of positive police-worker interactions

(Krüsi et al, 2016). The uncomfortable relationship between the trans community and law enforcement is related to, among other issues, the harassment of trans women by police – who often assume they are engaging in sex work, regardless of the activities they are actually observed engaging in (Carpenter and Barrett Marshall, 2017). This results in the exclusion and marginalisation of trans people, with particularly pernicious effects on trans people of colour, immigrants and those who are poor (Daum, 2015).

Social discrimination and stigma are therefore especially heightened for trans women who are also members of communities of colour or also engage in sex work (Sausa et al, 2007) and these women also have particularly negative experiences with law enforcement (Nichols, 2010). While research on police-sex worker interactions in New Zealand has not had a specific focus on trans experiences, individual narratives have detailed significant police harassment. Wilton's (2018) collection of oral history life narrative interviews with New Zealand sex workers included four trans participants. While one did not discuss the police at all, the three narratives that explored work conditions prior to decriminalisation all described police harassment and experiencing gender-based verbal abuse from police officers. While sex workers experience stigma due to societal expectations around appropriate expressions of feminine sexuality (Pheterson, 1993), trans women experience the intersection of stigma related to their actual or perceived sex work status as well as stigma related to their gender identity and expression.

Trans sex workers and street sex work

Research into safety in the sex industry has repeatedly shown that there is significant variation in terms of safe working conditions among sex workers (Weitzer, 2007). Some studies have highlighted the difficulties facing street-based sex workers (Plumridge and Abel, 2000) and trans workers (Nemoto et al, 2011) in accessing safe working conditions. Sex work varies enormously in its forms and social contexts (Zatz, 1997; Harcourt and Donovan, 2005; Bernstein, 2007), and studies have shown significant differences between sex workers working in different sectors in terms of violence and other occupational risks, particularly between indoor and outdoor sex workers (Whittaker and Hart, 1996; Church et al, 2001; Sanders and Campbell, 2007; Seib, 2007). While New Zealand has historically been fairly tolerant of discreet forms of sex work, there has been less acceptance of street sex work. Street-based sex workers in New Zealand are significantly more likely than managed or private workers to identify as transgender (Abel et al, 2007, p 7). As Jordan (2005, p 47) observes, for 'many years the visible sex industry in New Zealand was characterised by transgendered workers operating in the "red-light" streets of our major cities'.

While trans workers have been included in several large studies of the sex industry in New Zealand, there are few qualitative studies that specifically examine the lived experiences of trans people in the industry. One of the few qualitative studies to examine the experiences of trans sex workers in New Zealand is that of Worth (2000) who spoke with six gender liminal Māori and Pasifika workers in Auckland. Her participants began sex work at a young age, usually precipitated by violence or abuse at home. Worth's study, as did Wilton's (2018) life narrative interviews, indicated that trans sex workers experienced significant violence and disadvantage, but that they also demonstrated resilience and courage, and developed strong networks. This chapter contributes to the literature on trans sex worker experiences in New Zealand, which includes the work of Worth (2000) and Wilton (2018), with a specific focus on expanding our understanding of the impacts of decriminalisation on the experiences of trans workers.

Methods

This chapter explores a subset of findings from a larger ongoing study. The purpose of the broader study is to explore safety at work for trans and non-binary people, in multiple jurisdictions with different laws around sex work, in order to analyse the impact of regulatory schemas on worker safety. In recruiting for this study, the author sought participants who self-identified as trans, non-binary, gender diverse or takatāpui.[2] While the sample in other jurisdictions included transmasculine and non-binary people as well as crossdressers, this chapter draws only from a subsection of interviews: those undertaken in Christchurch, New Zealand, during 2018[3] where all eight participants identified as trans women. While the broader study explores safety at work in a holistic way, this chapter has a specific focus on two aspects of the interviews – the impacts of decriminalisation and interactions with law enforcement. Participants from the Christchurch sample ranged in age from 24 to 62 at the time of interview. Four were of Māori descent and four were Pākehā (the Māori term for people of European descent). While other studies have indicated that trans sex workers may be more likely to start sex work at a young age (Worth, 2000; Abel et al, 2007), only two participants in the Christchurch sample, Faye and Bonnie, started sex work as teenagers. The rest started in their early twenties, except for Esme, who started at 40. All participants have been assigned pseudonyms to protect their identities. Ethical approval for this project was obtained from the University of Otago Human Ethics Committee (Ref: 16/127).

Work in the sex industry: participant experiences

A survey undertaken by Abel et al (2007) indicated that, for New Zealand sex workers, financial incentives were not as important for trans workers as they were for cisgender women or men, with social factors and the perceived excitement and glamour of the industry playing a significant role in decisions to enter the industry. Reasons for entering the industry were multiple for participants in this study: money, discrimination in other jobs, validation of their gender identity, fun, excitement and camaraderie were all mentioned. Anahera's description of her reasons for working highlights the varied reasons why participants chose to enter or remain in the sex industry:

> 'It pretty much started because I wanted some sort of validation for myself. To feel like somebody wanted me. Or needed me. So I guess now I do it for drugs. And there was a point in time when I was doing it to try to fund my gender reassignment surgery.' (Anahera)

While motivations for sex industry work were thus complex, participants often discussed employment discrimination as a key reason for entering the industry. Esme had worked in the building industry and felt that she was unable to transition while remaining in her current employment, as if she turned up to work dressed as a woman "they would have found a way to quietly stop that ... It wouldn't go down very well". Chloe also described starting street sex work after experiencing a lack of other options due to employment discrimination:

> 'When I first left my hometown and I knew that I was transgender ... I moved up here because I thought that it'd be easier with people who were doing transgender as well, going through the change and all that. And I just met other people. I ended up working the street and it was sort of quick money at the time. Because being a transgender

[person], it's really hard to, I mean the stigma, it was really hard to get jobs, like a 9 to 5 job.' (Chloe)

Gabriella, who is now in her sixties, observes that, while she feels things are improving for trans people, sex work was one of the only options available when she was growing up. She also suggested that trans people these days may still have fewer options, employment discrimination being an ongoing issue faced by the trans community:

'Back then, it was like if you're going to be transgender, you kind of have to go through that. [Now if] a transgender person came to me and said they [wanted to start working], I would really want to know why. Why? Why do you want to be a prostitute? Like, do you feel that's all? I just think that that's sometimes all we have.' (Gabriella)

Seven of the eight interviewees had done at least some street work, with most working predominantly or exclusively on the street during all or part of their sex work careers. Research by Plumridge and Abel (2000) with cisgender women in New Zealand has indicated that street workers were more likely to use money from sex work for drugs and to have reported more, and more extreme, violence. Participants in the current study generally described the streets as less safe than their other available options. When asked if she liked working for an escort agency, Chloe replied:

'Yeah, it was the safety part around it. Because I'd just started out. It was safer that way. You're in an environment where they look after the money, they look after you as well and they sort of screen clients as they come through.' (Chloe)

Anahera, one of the few participants who had worked in a parlour, also suggested that "safety" was the key benefit of parlour work, even if her circumstances meant that she still often worked the street: "I've done a bit of work in some brothels ... I felt safe there. Lately, it's just mainly been the street. Just because I'm pretty much homeless and haven't got a place to safely do it. So the streets is where I go".

Four participants self-identified as "addicted" to drugs: two participants were in active addiction and two were in recovery. Participants frequently linked street work and drugtaking in their narratives. Some participants worked to fund their habits, yet they had all started street work before they developed drug addictions and many were introduced to hard drugs on the street. Just as Armstrong's (2011) research with cis street workers in New Zealand indicated, some participants reported minimising drug use when working as this was seen to add to potential risks – "I won't work under the influence" (Anahera), while some participants found that drug use made street work easier and gave them more confidence: "You feel like there's nothing can stop you" (Gabriella). However, drug use and street work formed a complex web for some participants, in which they felt quite trapped:

> 'From the day that I started transitioning, I started street working, drug dealing, and basically living a very transient lifestyle ... I went to a rehabilitation programme and managed to get clean ... and then it kind of just sucked me back in again. Like I just found myself back working on the street again. Yeah, and taking drugs, and it was a vicious cycle ... with sex work came the drugs, and with the drugs came all the illegal activities ... you know, it was just really chaotic.' (Gabriella)

Esme, who is the only participant to have never undertaken street work, considered herself "lucky" not to have had to work in what she perceived as the unsafe street environment:

> 'I'm lucky. I never had to go down to the street or anything ... I'm not addicted to drugs. So nobody can push me into doing anything. [I'm] not down on the street getting into strangers' cars.' (Esme)

Participants discussed violence from both clients and the public. Most participants described the majority of their clients as nice and respectful but with notable and unpleasant exceptions. Gabriella describes how clients would sometimes "start getting a bit rough and start doing things that you don't want them to do". She went on to add: "I was nearly raped once. And I thought I could fight this guy off but I couldn't". Gabriella no longer worked on the street at the time of the interview specifically because, "all it takes is one psycho. It only takes one person and you can be killed". Other participants also described violence from clients:

> 'I had a gun pulled on me in Auckland once ... you know anything could have happened, it could have gone either way.' (Faye)

However, while some participants had been repeatedly victimised and most participants had experienced one or two violent encounters with clients, these were sometimes interpreted as very rare or manageable occurrences:

> 'In all the years of doing it, I've only ever had one incident ... I've just been really, really lucky.' (Hana)

> '[If] they get a bit rough with you, you just ... you're the boss at the end of the day. If you don't like it you say: "Sorry, stop dear, get out". But no, it's usually pretty good. Pretty safe.' (Dalia)

Participants reported multiple strategies for managing potential violence, including mentorship from other workers, trusting their gut instinct, learning to diffuse violent situations and, as already mentioned, not working when high. For Chloe, it was the camaraderie among street workers that saved her from a potentially bad experience:

> 'There was one [bad experience] in Auckland, after I'd got into the car, he started taking off, and some of the queens yelled out to me to get out of there, get out. So I actually opened the door and he was speeding up, but I opened the door and I rolled out the car and landed in the gutter. And they said that he's a really freaky client so luckily I escaped from that.' (Chloe)

While research tends to indicate street sex work may be more risky than indoor work, research with cis workers has also indicated that there are benefits to working on the street, particularly in terms of the social environment of street work (Armstrong, 2011). Several participants preferred street work to other forms of work because of the social engagement and friendship with other workers. Participants in this study extended this point though: the street was also understood as a key place to meet other trans women and be part of a trans community, particularly for those participants who moved from rural areas to the city to find a sense of community.

'So here in New Zealand, for transgenders, [the street] was the meeting place.' (Gabriella)

'I made my way up to Christchurch; I just wanted to go see some queens on the street … I just wanted to go see some sisters. Get that sisterhood feeling. … And I just walked out on the street and I was like "Hello mas, sisters!" and I just wrapped my arms around them and cuddled them.' (Dalia)

This camaraderie on the street was felt to not only add to the enjoyment of work, but, as was apparent in Chloe's description of narrowly avoiding a violent client, was also understood to help keep workers safe. Anahera was unusual in this sample in that she did not spend her social time with other workers. For most participants, friendship with their trans sisters was a fundamental part of their narrative and an aspect of their stories that clearly brought them much happiness, a positive aspect of sex work that Wilton's (2018) trans interviewees also described. While Anahera stated "I like to keep my social circle small", she nonetheless went on to add:

'I will keep an eye out for the other girls and make note of who is on the streets, and you know, say hi to them and whatnot … Just so you know that they are safe as well. And that you can look after them, and they can look after you.' (Anahera)

There was thus a sense of community on the street, a feeling of belonging that was often articulated in whanau[4] terms. As several participants had experienced neglect in childhood or had felt that they did not belong in school or in the workplace, the community of trans sisterhood on the street was a fundamental resource. As with Worth's (2000) study with street-based gender liminal workers, participants experienced little social isolation and displayed resilience, courage and often joy, despite their often difficult circumstances, largely due to the close friendships among workers. Women supported each other by providing assistance – in the form of shelter, money and so on – while also giving each other information, emotional support and a sense of family on the street:

'The girls have each other's back. … If they see a guy trying anything … they'll all come over and attack him.' (Faye)

While the presence of, or intervention by, other workers was perceived by participants to prevent or limit client violence on the street, street work also exposes workers to abuse from the wider public. International studies have suggested that workplace harassment is so commonplace among transgender people that it is the norm (Lombardi et al, 2002) and this is particularly the case for transgender sex workers. Even in the context of a decriminalised sex industry, street harassment in the workplace is an ongoing issue for cisgender street workers in New Zealand due to societal views on women and sexuality (Armstrong, 2016b). Street-based sex work is often constructed as a social nuisance, or a form of sexual and social disorder, and is subject to gendered social control (Sanders, 2009) and influenced by media representations of sex workers as an abject and often criminalised other (O'Neill et al, 2008). Trans street-based sex workers are at a heightened risk of harassment due to their visibility and participants in this study reported harassment from the general public:

> 'People who are either going for a cruise with their mates, or just wandering home or wherever drunk and that sort of thing, who can get a bit mouthy or a bit aggressive or whatever ... Street work [is] definitely the more dicey feeling when working. But that was not so much actual clientele but other people who happened to be in the area at the time.' (Bonnie)

For Bonnie, not having to deal with abuse from the public was one of the key reasons she preferred escort work to working on the street: " ... you don't have to deal with abusive drunken people and that sort of thing if you're not working on the street".

While participants mostly described experiencing verbal harassment, or having things thrown at them, others described incidents of serious physical violence. Members of the public had assaulted Faye while she was working on the street: "so I got beaten up once with a baseball bat ... . I was unconscious, stripped of all my clothes".

Thus, while the street had numerous positive aspects for many participants, safety from both clients and from the broader public remained key areas of concern for many street-based sex workers. In this context, where safety at work can be precarious, it is important to explore the impacts of decriminalisation and the extent to which law enforcement can be interpreted as a safety resource for trans workers.

Decriminalisation, stigma, and law enforcement

Decriminalisation had largely impacted positively on participants with all reporting either a neutral or positive impact on their working lives. Two participants felt that it had made little difference. Hana said that "it made absolutely no difference"; Faye had not worked prior to decriminalisation so it was difficult for her to reflect on its impacts: "I don't know because I don't know what it was like before. So I can't compare. I guess it's been ok. I don't know". The remaining participants all saw decriminalisation as largely positive. Esme argued that "It's ridiculous that it was ever criminalised anywhere" while Anahera observed:

> 'I think that because it's not a jailable or finable offence, that the girls do feel a lot more comfortable to be able to do their stuff and do their thing. Without having the fear of: "Am I going to be charged for [this]?" ... So yeah, I think it is a good idea that it is decriminalised.' (Anahera)

The positive impacts of decriminalisation were articulated in two key ways: decriminalisation was understood to have both decreased stigma around sex work to some extent, as well as improved relationships with law enforcement. The former reflects the broader research findings in New Zealand, which indicate that decriminalisation reduces stigma, although ongoing work is needed to counter stigmatising narratives (Armstrong, 2019). 'Stigma' refers to an adverse reaction to individuals who are defined as being different in some way, due to a 'discrediting' attribute that reduces a person from the social position of a whole and usual person to a 'tainted, discounted one' (Goffman, 1963, p 3). Stigma against sex workers has significant negative effects on their working conditions, personal lives and health; it constitutes a fundamental cause of social inequality (Benoit et al, 2018) and is one of the factors underpinning difficult relationships with law enforcement. Participants in this study indicated that decriminalisation was one factor that had helped to shift attitudes around sex work:

> 'With the decriminalisation, I think it just makes it a wee bit easier for new queens ... or new workers, trans or heterosexual, to be able to not have to hide ... It's just a wee bit more ... it's not frowned upon now. It's kind of like me being transgender. Nowadays, it's everybody seems to

know somebody who's trans or a drag queen or something like that, so it's just a wee bit ... it's not as frowned upon as much now as it used to be.' (Chloe)

While reducing stigma is in and of itself an important shift, particularly in the context of the often-stressful work environment of the sex industry, this reduction in stigma was also seen to impact sex workers' ability to access available resources and support. Bonnie emphasised that NZPC (New Zealand Prostitutes' Collective) was an excellent source of information for new workers, and added:

> 'That ties to the decriminalisation aspect as well. ... Having that openness with information and resources can be really useful for people ... I do think that it is really beneficial. Yeah, I think that it's probably helped a lot of people who have been in situations where they need assistance from the likes of police etc, to reach out for that [support] where they otherwise may not have. I think there's also been a change in social attitude as well. Yeah, I think that's shifted a bit too. So yeah, I definitely see it as a hugely beneficial move.' (Bonnie)

Participants' descriptions of their relationships with the police did largely suggest that these had improved post decriminalisation, reflecting existing research (Abel et al, 2007; Armstrong, 2016a), but participants' narratives were nonetheless complex. Some felt that decriminalisation had had a significantly positive impact on relationships between trans sex workers and law enforcement. When asked whether things had improved over time, Dalia said:

> 'Yeah, absolutely, absolutely. The police are a lot better with us. And they're actually to be called upon; they are there to help you now. Back in the day, when you used to call the police, they'd just blame you for everything, and give you no time. Like, nah. But they're really, really good. I really like them.' (Dalia)

Armstrong's (2016a) study on the impacts of decriminalisation on law enforcement-sex worker relationships for cis workers found that while some still had significant distrust of the police, decriminalisation was nonetheless empowering in that it reduced the scope for police harassment of sex workers. Similarly, several participants in this study felt that the primarily positive impact of decriminalisation was that they simply saw less of the police:

> 'You probably don't see the police as much now, because they're probably out on different more important calls and stuff, and they don't hassle the queens.' (Chloe)

Overall, however, participants described significant distrust towards the police, based primarily on the perception that they were being over-policed, particularly in the sense of being harassed when working the streets, including harassment specifically aimed at their gender representation. Several participants reported unease with police-worker interactions in public space and felt that the police deliberately harassed workers: Gabriella observed that there were some nights that she was "bugged constantly by the police. Because there were some nights where you would be bugged two or three times". She goes on, "They want you to fight with them so that they could arrest you". Bonnie was also uncomfortable with the continued police interaction she experienced on the street:

> 'It can feel a little interfering in a way. Yeah. And slightly unnerving. ... I've had occasions where I'd had one drive past and sort of do a U-turn and come and stop and then ask "So what are you doing out here?" And those sorts of questions. Where it's ... I would have thought it's fairly obvious. But it just hasn't felt ... comfortable ... it just feels slightly disconcerting at times.' (Bonnie)

Hubbard et al (2008, p 137) argue that, since the identification of prostitution as a distinctive social problem from the 18th century onwards, 'different techniques of state-sponsored governmentality and surveillance have been used to contain, exclude or control prostitutes on the assumption they threaten social cohesion'. That participants who worked the street reported continued interactions with the police which largely made them uneasy seems to indicate that even in this decriminalised era, urban space is still being regulated in such a way as to exclude street-based sex workers, even if these interactions are considerably less hostile than in the past. As Sabsay (2011) notes, the regulation of sex work can be tied up with the very questions of citizenry and the right to use public space. Public fears around street sex work, and the frequent focus on transgender sex work in these contexts, can be understood not just in that sex work can be read as a nuisance, but that visible transgender sex workers challenge the 'profoundly heterocentric' nature of the socio-sexual imaginary (Sabsay, 2011, p 219). There is an intersection between the exclusion of sex workers from public space and the over-policing of transgender people in public space.

Sometimes police harassment went beyond what was experienced as excessive surveillance. Those who perpetrate violence against transgender populations often target their gender nonconformity or gender expression (Wirtz et al, 2018), a finding also reflected in research examining police violence against trans sex workers (Nichols, 2010). Just as Wilton's (2018) trans participants described, examples of harassment by the police prior to decriminalisation included the deadnaming[5] and misgendering of participants:

> 'They'd always refer to us, no matter what as ... "he" ... They'd always say that. And it was just ... You'd stand there constantly going "she, she, she". And they're like: "You're a bloody he. Stop kidding yourself." They were quite rude really.' (Gabriella)

Gabriella specifically articulated that she felt police harassment was repeatedly aimed at her because she was trans: "I don't think it's so much that the police were disrespectful to me for being a sex worker. I think they were disrespectful to me for being transgender".

However, this harassment cannot be understood as solely related to the pre-decriminalisation environment; several participants who had only entered the sex industry after decriminalisation also reported harassment from the police that specifically targeted their gender identity:

> 'I remember one night, I'm standing on Manchester Street, and the police have been assholes to me. They knew my real name, my born name, and they were driving past with their little megaphones yelling it out. I was like, that is so disrespectful and rude. I couldn't believe they were doing that.' (Faye)

> 'I've had one ... call me a freak. So that was quite, quite shocking really.' (Bonnie)

The failure of police to treat workers with respect obviously negatively impacts on police relationships with the trans sex work community. The specific attacks on gender identity also holds the potential to promote dysphoria and distress within a potentially vulnerable population. Some participants indicated that the police's poor treatment of them post decriminalisation was not only related to their gender identity, but also to stereotypes around sex workers and drug use:

> 'They look down upon prostitution. They look down upon it and think that it's disgusting. They think that everyone's a junkie with no life. ... They're completely wrong if they think that everyone's junkies ... because they're not.' (Faye)

Armstrong (2010) notes that street-based sex workers are the most stigmatised group of sex workers, and may be doubly stigmatised through the conflation of street-based sex work with injecting drug use. In the quote just given, Faye, herself a former intravenous drug user, indicates this ongoing stereotype shapes police encounters. A shift from a mode of policing that sees sex workers as risky to seeing them as 'at risk' may be preferable, as there may be fewer overtly hostile interactions. Nonetheless, such a shift will not necessarily be perceived in a positive light, particularly when underlying stigmatising stereotypes shape police attitudes towards workers, and trans people may still experience overt harassment from police which targets their gender identity.

While several participants felt that relationships with law enforcement had improved with decriminalisation, there remained significant distrust, in particular the assumption that the police would be unhelpful if they were to be victimised. Gabriella's experience of the police was that if you called to say, "There's guys attacking me", then the police would respond with:

> '"What have you done? What have you stolen from them?" That's what they'd say ... They're like, "You cause it to yourself" ... They're not on your side. Even if they turned up to the site where the altercation is happening, they would take the client's side.' (Gabriella)

Faye, who, as mentioned earlier, was severely beaten by three men while working on the street, experienced an inadequate response from the police when she reported her victimisation:

> 'But then police went over the CCTV footage ... but they never followed it through. They just said, "Oh, we don't

know who they are, sorry". So they just kind of brushed it off. [with] "There's not much you can do about it". It took me three weeks to recover [from my injuries].' (Faye)

While research on the impacts of decriminalisation in New Zealand indicate improved police-worker relationships (Abel et al, 2007; Armstrong, 2016a), repeated accounts of inaction by the police suggest a normalisation of violence against trans sex workers by at least some law enforcement officers. Even in the absence of criminalisation, an assumption that sex work is inherently risky (rather than risky due to the web of social context and regulation that renders workers vulnerable) results in a failure to take sex worker victimisation seriously: sex workers can be seen as 'risky' subjects, who place themselves at risk by continuing to do sex work. Some members of the police thus tended to see sex workers as partially at fault for their own victimisation. As to whether interviewees would consider calling the police in the future, participants unsurprisingly had mixed responses. Some participants said they would be comfortable calling the police. Anahera said that she would, "Yep", while Dalia said, "Absolutely, absolutely. Yep, for sure." Other participants felt that it would depend on the situation. Esme said that she would call the police if she needed to but observed: "My threshold for 'need to' is very high. I wouldn't want their involvement. Unless it was absolutely necessary." Some participants articulated that they would be unlikely to contact law enforcement, either because they did not believe they would be seen as a priority for the police because of their worker status or work practices, or because of their existing discomfort with law enforcement:

> 'Um ... um, not really. I wouldn't expect them to sort of drop everything and come running out, sort of thing.' (Chloe)

> 'It would depend on the circumstances. I would say that if it was at home, or let's say a motel/hotel type situation, then probably. ... But street work ... you can be a bit wary of police cars; [it is] uncomfortable, and you feel like you are being questioned without cause.' (Bonnie)

Due to her past experiences of being harassed, as well as past police failures to respond appropriately to her experiences of victimisation, Faye said that there were no circumstances under which she would call the police. Although multiple participants did reference concerns around transmisogyny and sex work stigma on the part of law enforcement, these were not the only factors that impacted on their distrust of the police. Rather, concerns around police racism and drug laws also informed participants' views on policing as a potential resource they could call on:

> 'I wouldn't want to call them up because basically everyone in the scene has got something they don't want the police to know about going on that's nothing to do with the problem. That's why people don't ring. It's not because they think the police are going to screw them over the problem they're facing, it's because they're going to screw them over their work, screw them over the joint in the ashtray or whatever. I think that's probably the biggest factor in terms of the "war on drugs": that people can't call on the police for help when they need it. Because there's an empty point bag [a small plastic bag that previously contained methamphetamine] in the rubbish bin that might have some residue in it, so they won't call the cops. Just in case. ... I've just witnessed first hand so many times unequal treatment, you know? [A white person] can get away with murder ... but someone of colour doesn't. The bigotry is still rife in the police force.' (Esme)

Esme's quote here highlights the intersectional nature of structural violence and stigma. Perceptions of police racism and concerns around both the continued stigma of drug addiction and the ongoing criminalisation of drugs also impacted on participants' feelings about the police, particularly for those for whom street sex work and drug use were intertwined.

Conclusion

There have been significant shifts in policing efforts since decriminalisation – such as a collaboration between NZPC and the New Zealand Police on a booklet for people affected by sexual assault (NZPC, 2018) – and there was evidence of change and of increasingly positive relationships between law enforcement and trans sex workers in Christchurch. However, this should not be translated simplistically into the idea that trans sex workers are now safer because they can contact the police if they are victimised. For some participants this was true. For others, however, they simply felt safer from police harassment in the decriminalised era. Meanwhile, many participants had experienced negative interactions with the police, including in the post-decriminalisation context, and most participants continued to report that they would be hesitant to contact the police. Dwyer's (2014, p 149) analysis of LGBT-police histories cautions us from relying on the notion that what we can discern through the trajectory of recent history is 'a lineal progression from a painful past to a more productive present', and that we 'cannot just take away the history that emerged out of mistrust and pain'. Since many participants had experienced both police harassment, and a failure to take their reports of victimisation seriously, it is not surprising that there remains significant ongoing distrust.

Decriminalisation does not only impact on police-worker relationships but on societal attitudes. Participants certainly observed that stigma still remained. Armstrong (2019, p 1298) notes in her work with cisgender workers that, 'despite the fact that sex work has been decriminalised, changing attitudes is far from simple and requires undoing the patriarchal legacy that has constructed women who sell sex as deserving of violence'. The trans participants in this study reported sex work stigma, but also harassment specifically aimed at their gender identity. Their experiences reflect the intersection of multiple stigmatised identities. Participants nonetheless noted that decriminalisation made them more comfortable in an often-stressful work environment. They also observed that decriminalisation may have encouraged workers to feel more able to get in touch with organisations like NZPC, which provide ongoing support and resources for sex workers in New Zealand. And most importantly, perhaps, several participants felt that decriminalisation was important in terms of its broader societal impact, in that it was a step forward in reducing stigma. While this finding reflects the existing research on sex workers' perceptions of the impacts of decriminalisation in New Zealand, this reduction in stigma may be particularly important for the working conditions of trans women who work on the street, because of their visibility to the public and frequent interactions with law enforcement. Thus, while challenges remain in terms of combating stigmatising cultural narratives and addressing issues in worker-law enforcement interactions, the shift to decriminalisation in New Zealand is, as Esme put it, "a giant leap in the right direction".

Notes

[1] On 27 June 1969, the Stonewall rebellion occurred when bar patrons at the Stonewall Inn, a gay bar in Greenwich Village, New York, fought back against a police raid. While not the first time that the LGBT+ community fought back against police assaults and humiliating treatment, it is the most historically resonant,

and is now marked by an international commemorative ritual – the annual Gay Pride parade.
2   Takatāpui is a Māori term for Māori members of the rainbow community.
3   I would like to acknowledge NZPC, and in particular Bridie Sweetman from the Christchurch office, for their invaluable assistance in this research project.
4   Whanau is a Māori term which is often roughly translated as 'family' but which has a more complex meaning, incorporating emotional and spiritual dimensions. It is used by groups of unrelated people to signal connectedness, inclusivity and unity.
5   Deadnaming is a term that describes when a person refers to another person by the name they used before they transitioned.

References

Abel, G., Fitzgerald, L. & Brunton, C. (2007) *The Impact of the Prostitution Reform Act on the Health and Safety Practices of Sex Workers: Report to the Prostitution Law Review Committee,* Christchurch: University of Otago. Available at: https://www.otago.ac.nz/christchurch/otago018607.pdf.

Amnesty International (2005) *Stonewalled: Police abuse and misconduct against lesbian, gay, bisexual and transgender people in the U.S.* Available at: https://www.amnesty.org/en/documents/AMR51/122/2005/en/.

Armstrong, L. (2010) 'Out of the shadows (and into a bit of light): Decriminalisation, human rights and street-based sex work in New Zealand', in K. Hardy, S. Kingston & T. Sanders (eds) *New Sociologies of Sex Work,* Aldershot: Ashgate, pp 39–59.

Armstrong, L. (2011) 'Managing risk of violence in decriminalised street-based sex work: A feminist (sex worker rights) perspective', PhD thesis, Victoria University Wellington.

Armstrong, L. (2014) 'Screening clients in a decriminalised street-based sex industry: Insights into the experiences of New Zealand sex workers', *Australian and New Zealand Journal of Criminology,* 47(2): 207–22.

Armstrong, L. (2016a) 'From law enforcement to protection? Interactions between sex workers and police in a decriminalized street-based sex industry', *The British Journal of Criminology.* Available at: doi:10.1093/bjc/azw019.

Armstrong, L. (2016b) '"Who's the slut, who's the whore?": Street harassment in the workplace among female sex workers in New Zealand', *Feminist Criminology,* 11(3): 285–303.

Armstrong, L. (2019) 'Stigma, decriminalisation, and violence against street-based sex workers: Changing the narrative', *Sexualities,* 22(7–8): 1288–308.

Benoit, C., Jansson, M., Smith, M. & Flagg, J. (2018) 'Prostitution stigma and its effect on the working conditions, personal lives, and health of sex workers', *The Journal of Sex Research,* 55(4–5): 457–71.

Bernstein, E. (2007) *Temporarily Yours: Intimacy, authenticity, and the commerce of sex,* Chicago and London: The University of Chicago Press.

Carpenter, L. F. & Barrett Marshall, R. (2017) 'Walking while trans: Profiling of transgender women by law enforcement, and the problem of proof', *William & Mary Journal of Race, Gender, and Social Justice,* 24(1): 5–38.

Church, S., Henderson, M., Barnard, M. & Hart, G. (2001) 'Violence by clients towards female prostitutes in different work settings: Questionnaire survey', *British Medical Journal,* 322(No. 7285): 524–5.

Clements-Nolle, K., Marxi, R., Guzman, R. & Katz, M. (2001) 'HIV prevalence, risk behaviors, health care use, and mental health status of transgender persons: Implications for public health intervention', *American Journal of Public Health,* 91(6): 915–21.

Daum, C. W. (2015) 'The war on solicitation and intersectional subjection: Quality-of-life policing as a tool to control transgender populations', *New Political Science,* 37(4): 562–81.

Dwyer, A. (2011) 'Policing lesbian, gay, bisexual and transgender young people: A gap in the research literature', *Current Issues in Criminal Justice,* 22(3): 415–33.

Dwyer, A. (2014) 'Pleasures, perversities, and partnerships: The historical emergence of LGBT-police relationships', in D. Peterson & V. R. Panfil (eds) *Handbook of LGBT Communities, Crime and Justice,* New York: Springer, pp 149–64.

Dwyer, A. E. (2015) 'Teaching young queers a lesson: How police teach lessons about non-heteronormativity in public spaces', *Sexuality & Culture,* 19: 493–512.

Goffman, E. (1963) *Stigma: Notes on the management of a spoiled identity,* Englewood Cliffs, NJ: Prentice-Hall, Inc.

Groves, J., Newton, D. C., Chen, M. Y., Hocking, J., Bradshaw, C. S. & Fairley, C. K. (2008) 'Sex workers working with a legalised industry: Their side of the story', *Sexually Transmitted Infections,* 84(5): 393–4.

Harcourt, C. & Donovan, B. (2005) 'The many faces of sex work', *Sexually Transmitted Infections,* 81: 201–6.

Harcourt, C., Egger, S. & Donovan, B. (2005) 'Sex work and the law', *Sexual Health,* 2: 121–8.

Harcourt, C., van Beek, I., Heslop, J., McMahon, M. & Donovan, B. (2001) 'The health and welfare needs of female and transgender street sex workers in New South Wales', *Australian and New Zealand Journal of Public Health,* 25(1): 84–9.

Hill, B.J., Rosentel, K., Bak, T., Sliverman, M., Crosby, R., Salazar, L. & Kipke, M. (2017) 'Exploring individual and structural factors associated with employment among young transgender women of color using a no-cost transgender legal resource center', *Transgender Health,* 2(1): 29–34.

Hubbard, P., Matthews, R. & Scoular, J. (2008) 'Regulating sex work in the EU: Prostitute women and the new spaces of exclusion', *Gender, Place & Culture: A Journal of Feminist Geography,* 15(2): 137–52.

Jacobs, E., Finlayson, T., McKleroy, V., Neumann, M. & Crepaz, N. (2008) 'Estimating HIV prevalence and risk behaviors of transgender persons in the United States: A systematic review', *AIDS and Behavior,* 12(1): 1–17.

Jordan, J. (2005) *The Sex Industry in New Zealand: A literature review.* Available at: http://www.justice.govt.nz/pubs/reports/2005/sex-industry-in-nz-literature-review/index.html.

Krüsi, A., Kerr, T., Taylor, C., Rhodes, T. & Shannon, K. (2016) '"They won't change it back in their heads that we're trash": The intersection of sex-work related stigma and evolving police strategies', *Sociology of Health & Illness,* 38(7): 1137–50.

Lombardi, E., Wilchins, R., Priesing, D. & Malouf, D. (2002) 'Gender violence', *Journal of Homosexuality,* 42(1): 89–101.

Maher, J., Pickering, S. & Gerard, A. (2013) *Sex Work: Labour, mobility and sexual services*, London and New York: Routledge.

McCandless, S. (2018) 'LGBT homeless youth and policing', *Public Integrity,* 20(6): 558–70.

Miles-Johnson, T. (2015) '"They don't identify with us": Perceptions of police by Australian transgender people', *International Journal of Transgenderism,* 16(3): 169–89.

Miles-Johnson, T. (2016) 'Policing diversity: Examining police resistance to training reforms for transgender people in Australia', *Journal of Homosexuality,* 63(1): 1–34.

Nemoto, T., Bödeker, B. & Iwamoto, M. (2011) 'Social support, exposure to violence and transphobia, and correlates of depression among male-to-female transgender women with a history of sex work', *American Journal of Public Health,* 101(10): 1980–8.

Nichols, A. (2010) 'Dance Ponnaya, dance! Police abuses against transgender sex workers in Sri Lanka', *Feminist Criminology,* 5(2): 195–222.

NZPC & New Zealand Police (2018) *What To Do: A guide for sex workers who have experienced sexual assault*. Available at: http://www.nzpc.org.nz/pdfs/WHAT-TO-DO-A-guide-for-sex-workers-who-have-experienced-sexual-assault.pdf.

O'Neill, M., Campbell, R., Hubbard, P., Pitcher, J. & Scoular, J. (2008) 'Living with the other: Street sex work, contingent communities and degrees of tolerance', *Crime, Media, Culture,* 4(1): 73–93.

Pheterson, G. (1993) 'The whore stigma: Female dishonour and male unworthiness', *Social Text* 37, 39–64.

Pickering, S., Maher, J. & Gerard, A. (2009) *Working in Victorian Brothels*. Available at: www.consumer.vic.gov.au/library/publications/resources-and-education/research/working-in-victorian-brothels-2009.pdf.

Plumridge, L. & Abel, G. (2000) 'A "segmented" sex industry in New Zealand: Sexual and personal safety of female sex workers', *Australian and New Zealand Journal of Public Health,* 25(1): 78–83.

Praat, A. C. & Tuffin, K. F. (1996) 'Police discourses of homosexual men in New Zealand', *Journal of Homosexuality,* 31(4): 57–73.

Prostitution Law Review Committee (2008) *Report of the Prostitution Law Review Committee on the Operation of the Prostitution Reform Act 2003*. Available at: www.justice.govt.nz/policy/commercial-property-and-regulatory/prostitution/prostitution-law-review-committee/publications/plrc-report/report-of-the-prostitution-law-review-committee-on-the-operation-of-the-prostitution-reform-act-2003.

Russell, E. K. (2017) 'A "fair cop": Queer histories, affect and police image work in Pride March', *Crime, Media, Culture,* 13(3): 277–93.

Sabsay, L. (2011) 'The limits of democracy: Transgender sex work and citizenship', *Cultural Studies,* 25(2): 213–29.

Sanders, T. (2009) 'Controlling the "anti sexual" city: Sexual citizenship and the disciplining of female street sex workers', *Criminology & Criminal Justice,* 9(4): 507–25.

Sanders, T. & Campbell, R. (2007) 'Designing out vulnerability, building in respect: Violence, safety and sex work policy', *The British Journal of Sociology,* 58(1): 1–19.

Sausa, L.A., Keatley, J. & Operario, D. (2007) 'Perceived risks and benefits of sex work among transgender women of colour in San Francisco', *Archives of sexual behavior,* 36(6): 768–77.

Seib, C. (2007) 'Health, well-being and sexual violence among female sex workers: A comparative study', PhD thesis, Queensland University of Technology.

Shannon, K., Strathdee, S., Goldenberg, S., Duff, P., Mwangi, P., Rusakova, M., Paul, S.R., Lau, J., Deering, K., Pickles, M. & Boily, M-C. (2015) 'Global epidemiology of HIV among female sex workers: Influence of structural determinants', *The Lancet*, 385(9962): 55–71.

Stotzer, R. L. (2014) 'Law enforcement and criminal justice personnel interactions with transgender people in the United States: A literature review', *Aggression and Violent Behavior*, 19(3): 263–77.

Weitzer, R. (2007) 'Prostitution as a form of work', *Sociology Compass*, 1(1): 143–55.

Weldon, J. (2010) 'Show me the money: A sex worker reflects on research into the industry', in M. H. Ditmore, A. Levy & A. Willman (eds) *Sex Work Matters: Exploring money, power and intimacy in the sex industry*, London & New York: Zed Books, pp 147–54.

Whittaker, D. & Hart, G. (1996) 'Research note: Managing risks: The social organization of indoor sex work', *Sociology of Health & Illness*, 18(3): 399–414.

Wilton, C. (2018) *My Body, My Business: New Zealand sex workers in an era of change*, Dunedin: Otago University Press.

Wirtz, A., Poteat, T., Malik, M. & Glass, N. (2018) 'Gender-based violence against transgender people in the United States: A Call for research and programming', *Trauma, Violence & Abuse*, 21(2): 1–18.

Worth, H. (2000) 'Up on K road on a Saturday night: Sex, gender and sex work in Auckland', *Venereology*, 13(1): 15–24.

Zatz, N. (1997) 'Sex work / sex act: Law, labor and desire in constructions of prostitution', *Signs*, 22(2): 277–308.

5

Fear of Trafficking or Implicit Prejudice? Migrant Sex Workers and the Impacts of Section 19

Lynzi Armstrong, Gillian Abel and Michael Roguski

Introduction

The passing of the Prostitution Reform Act (PRA) 2003 was celebrated by sex workers in New Zealand as well as internationally. As outlined in previous chapters, the legislative change meant that all the laws which criminalised sex workers' activities were repealed and sex workers were then able to openly work without fear of arrest, and also able to exercise their human rights. Five years later, a review committee reported that the decriminalisation of sex work had been largely effective and that sex workers were better off in terms of their health, safety and access to human rights than they were prior to 2003 (Prostitution Law Review Committee, 2008). However, there was a missing group, whose experiences were not taken into account in the review – migrant sex workers.

While the PRA decriminalised sex work for permanent residents in New Zealand, temporary migrants were excluded due to a late amendment to the legislation. Shortly before the Act was passed, a Supplementary Order Paper was introduced by then Minister for Immigration, Lianne Dalziel, proposing to restrict the ability to freely work as a sex worker to permanent New Zealand residents and citizens. There had been little focus on fears of trafficking early in the law reform process, but towards the end of the parliamentary debate,

Dalziel was approached by the United Future party and the Ministry of Justice with concerns in this area (Dalziel, 2003). The rationale for the amendment was, in Dalziel's words, 'to ensure that in decriminalising the laws on prostitution, we do not unwittingly allow people to be brought into the country for the purposes of prostitution' (Dalziel, 2003). This resulted in the addition of Section 19 to the PRA. Section 19 relates to the Immigration Act 2009 (previously 1987), and states that no one who holds a temporary visa may provide commercial sexual services, or operate or invest in 'a business of prostitution'. The consequence of this is that anyone coming into the country on a temporary visa (whether visitor, student or work) cannot legally work as a sex worker. Thus, they can be refused entry to New Zealand if it is thought that they intend to work in the sex industry, or deported if they are found to be working in this area. This has created a two-tiered industry in which sex workers who are permanent residents or citizens have legal rights under the PRA to challenge exploitation, abuse and unfair treatment, while migrant sex workers work illegally, have no rights, and thus have heightened vulnerability to exploitation. The current policy framework is therefore contradictory, since some sex workers benefit from the protections of the PRA while others work in a precarious situation that places them at risk of harm. Given these circumstances, it cannot be argued that New Zealand has achieved 'full decriminalisation' (Armstrong, 2017).

Section 19 also exceptionalises sex work by prohibiting temporary migrants from working in the sex industry even if their permit allows them to work (Armstrong, 2017). This singling out of sex work infers that the sex industry is particularly vulnerable to trafficking, which merits further discussion. Immigration New Zealand claim that they are concerned about exploitation of all migrant workers but that the sex industry poses more concern as people in this industry are at higher risk of being trafficked (Gee, 2019). There is no evidence to suggest that trafficking into sex work is (or ever was) an issue in New Zealand (NZ Government, 2019). Meanwhile, a draft government report published in 2019 has stated that '[m]ost trafficking in New Zealand is linked to other industries (horticulture, construction, service)' (NZ Government, 2019). The report further states that:

> ... [t]here are occasional individual reports of exploitation of foreign sex workers, however, investigations showed no evidence of systemic exploitation. No instances of trafficking were confirmed and, in recent years, the Labour Inspectorate has received no complaints of exploitation.

Police also report there were no allegations of foreign sex worker exploitation or trafficking meeting the threshold for prosecution. 2018 independent research on the migrant sex industry in New Zealand commissioned by the relevant Ministry found no evidence of trafficking (NZ Government, 2019).

If trafficking occurs more commonly in industries other than sex work, then there is no sound justification for prohibiting temporary migrants from working in this area for this reason (Armstrong, 2017). Furthermore, if the decriminalisation of sex work was a genuine acknowledgement that sex work is an occupational choice, then this raises important questions about why Section 19 remains in place.

There is no evidence so far that indicates migrant sex workers are being forced to work in New Zealand. However, because of Section 19, there is ample opportunity for exploitative practices (Roguski, 2013; Abel and Roguski, 2018; Armstrong, 2018; Ting, 2018). Current research shows that migrant workers are vulnerable to blackmail, non-payment for services, coercion to provide certain services, and threats to expose them to authorities (Abel and Roguski, 2018). Migrant sex workers who are most disadvantaged are those who cannot speak English and who are working and living in informal brothels. These (most frequently) women are made vulnerable through poor practices by some brothel operators, who sometimes take their passports (although Roguski (2013) found that this was so for less than 5 per cent of migrant workers), do not allow them to refuse clients or certain services (Roguski, 2013; Abel and Roguski, 2018), and in extreme cases, some women have been raped by the operator (Abel and Roguski, 2018). In most cases, migrant sex workers are too afraid to report incidents to the police for fear that immigration will intervene and they would be deported (Abel and Roguski, 2018).

The enforcement of Section 19, as argued by Ting (2018), is both racialised and gendered, perpetuating long-held prejudices in New Zealand against Asian migrants. Asian women form the vast majority of migrants turned away at the border on suspicion that they are coming into New Zealand to enter into sex work, and they also constitute the bulk of those deported for engaging in sex work. Immigration New Zealand released numbers to the beginning of November 2019 which show that 207 'actual or suspected sex workers' had been refused entry to the country; 143 of these were from Asian countries and 56 were from Brazil (Gee, 2019). Additionally, many sex workers have been deported for working as a sex worker; all of these deportees have been from Asian countries (Ting, 2018).

Participants in Roguski's (2013) study on migrant workers argued that New Zealand was not upholding international obligations to grant migrant women the same rights as New Zealand women. Indeed, Roguski argues that Recommendation 26 of the Convention on the Elimination of All Forms of Discrimination Against Women (CEDAW) (2008), to which New Zealand is a signatory, states that countries need to 'ensure non-discrimination and the equal rights of women migrant workers'. CEDAW goes on to state in Article 26(a) that:

> State parties should repeal outright bans and discriminatory restrictions on women's immigration. They should ensure that their visa schemes do not directly discriminate against women by restricting permission to women migrant workers to be employed in certain job categories where men predominate, or by excluding certain female-dominated occupations from visa schemes. (CEDAW, 2018, p 11)

A small, qualitative case study, conducted in New Zealand in 2017 as part of a multi-country project coordinated by GAATW (Global Alliance Against Traffic in Women), found that participants from the New Zealand Prostitutes' Collective (NZPC) and sex workers who used their services were very concerned about the impacts that Section 19 was having on migrant sex workers (Armstrong, 2018). While no instances of trafficking were reported by participants, instances of exploitation were described and there was a concern that the prohibition of temporary migrants has created conditions that increase the risk of trafficking. The recommendations of the report included that Section 19 should be repealed, and at the very least there should be a guarantee that migrant sex workers can report instances of exploitation without the possibility of deportation (Armstrong, 2018).

While the negative implications of Section 19 have been highlighted through numerous academic studies, commentaries and media articles, temporary migrants continue to work in this precarious situation, and thus it is vital that researchers continue to explore the implications of their exclusion from the protections of the law. This chapter therefore adds to this evidence in examining the impacts of Section 19 from the perspective of both migrant sex workers and other sex workers working alongside them who have the right to work and are protected by the PRA.

Methods

This chapter draws its findings from two different studies. Abel and Roguski (2018) completed a study commissioned by the Ministry of Business, Innovation and Employment, which looked into the lived experiences of migrant sex workers in New Zealand. Ethics approval was granted from the University of Otago Human Ethics Committee (Ref: 18/084). In-depth interviews were carried out with 11 migrant sex workers, recruited with the help of NZPC, as well as nine key informants, who included two brothel operators, two sexual health specialists and five NZPC staff/outreach workers. Given the short period of time within which to carry out the research, it was only possible to recruit migrant workers who felt least vulnerable to deportation. Indeed, three of the sex worker participants had recently gained permanent residence in New Zealand and were no longer working illegally. Six participants were from Asian countries, three from Europe, and one each from North and South America. All sex worker participants received NZ$40 in recognition of their contribution to the research. Interviews included: discussion on their occupation before coming to New Zealand; what motivated them to come to New Zealand and what they knew about the country's sex work laws; their experiences and challenges in sex working in this country; how they looked after their health; their intentions for the future; and what trafficking meant to them. Interviews were recorded, transcribed and a thematic analysis was carried out.

Armstrong's study, conducted between 2017 and 2018, explored sex workers' perceptions of stigma and discrimination in New Zealand. The study involved 20 in-depth interviews with sex workers in Wellington, Auckland and Rotorua. Ethical approval for the study was granted by Victoria University of Wellington Human Ethics Committee (#0000025395). Interview participants were recruited via NZPC, through Twitter, and word of mouth. Participants included cisgender women (n=14), cisgender men (n=3) and transgender/gender diverse (n=3) sex workers. Half of participants identified as New Zealand European (n=10), while seven identified as Māori, one as Australian, and two were from other countries in the Global South. While two participants had previously been temporary migrants, both now had permanent residency and therefore were permitted by law to engage in sex work. All participants received a NZ$50 gift card as reciprocity for the time taken to participate in the project. Interviews focused on a broad range of issues relating to stigma and discrimination, including participants' views on existing laws, perceptions of other sex workers, awareness of Section 19 and their stance on this aspect of the law.

Migrant sex workers

All of the migrant sex workers interviewed in the Abel and Roguski (2018) study had come to New Zealand on either a temporary work visa with the intention of working as a sex worker or on a student or travel visa, subsequently making the decision to work as a sex worker during their stay. All migrant sex worker participants were legally allowed to be in New Zealand and were not illegal migrants. Most of them spoke of the anomaly of sex work being decriminalised and thus seen as work like any other employment, and yet it was not an option for them on their temporary visa. Faith argued that:

> '… [t]he law should be a little bit more humanitarian. Because … we're allowed to work, it says on my visa I'm allowed to work 20 hours or full-time, we're allowed to work. Okay, this is a job. It's legal in New Zealand, right? Yeah, so why that exception? And [why] only residents and permanent residents? Okay, they live here, but okay, I'm on a temporary visa. I'm here, so I'm independent. I have my feet on this land as any other person who [is] here. So why is it different? Because they say it's … to prevent human trafficking … You don't see that much in New Zealand. … but I'm not 100% sure if it is really the thing that they want to prevent. Maybe they just want to prevent people going to the industry because it's still seen as a dark side.' (Faith)

None of the participants saw themselves as trafficked. They defined trafficking as maybe pertinent to other people when "they don't have a choice to, you know, they just have to do what they tell them to do" (Chloe) or when "people are forced to do it, or they don't really want, like they're not forced, but they also don't really want to, but they go to that country specifically to do sex work because they feel like they have to" (Cynthia). Iris suggested that New Zealand was an unlikely target for traffickers: "I think it could happen in some countries. Yeah, it could happen in some countries, but I don't think so in New Zealand because I know that I do it willingly." Interviewees argued that they had freely chosen to work in sex work and they did not feel exploited. Instead, they argued that they felt exploited in other jobs that they were legally allowed to do in New Zealand. For example Chloe stated that she was grossly underpaid:

> 'I used to get paid like NZ$7 an hour, which is terrible. We had to work like literally our arses off, you know, working for 7 hours and getting paid for 5 hours, that kind of thing.' (Chloe)

A backpackers' guide lists New Zealand as a 'things are getting expensive' country requiring a budget of around US$60, €53 or £46 per day (MYFUNKYTRAVEL, 2019). Some backpackers subsidise their travels by working in horticulture, farming, hospitality or other occupations suitable for transient workers and are often paid below minimum wage, especially if they do not have a working holiday visa. Hope argued that she could have gone to work in a restaurant with her friends, but could work fewer hours for more money in sex work:

> 'Obviously you can get cash-in-hand jobs at restaurants and cafes, but they usually pay you under minimum wage because they feel like they're doing you a favour ... Oh my friends, they worked for a restaurant and they did so many hours a week and they'd just get paid like NZ$500, a set amount, regardless of how many hours they'd done ... they were completely underpaid and misused. ... They also offered me a job at that restaurant and I was like, "No, I'm not doing it". It would have been nicer to feel like I had a job that I could tell people about and feel like, "Oh yeah, I work for this restaurant" ... I study hospitality, it's something I want to go into. But ... the thing is I can make the amount that they made in a month in a night.' (Hope)

While Hope had made the decision to work in sex work instead of hospitality, she indicated that the stigma around sex work meant that she could not talk about what she did to her friends and family. Stigma and exploitation (in the form of low wages) were weighed up – the potential to be stigmatised was more manageable and thus acceptable than the potential for exploitation in a non-stigmatised occupation. While many non-migrant sex workers do not disclose their occupation to others because of the stigma associated with it, stigma is amplified for migrant sex workers as they risk deportation if they do disclose. Cynthia indicated that stigma created greater consequences for exposure of migrant workers than non-migrant sex workers.

> 'It's just that in general sex work still has a stigma which is already, you know, not a good feeling when it's your job. But if it's at least legal for you [non-migrants], it makes it better. But knowing that what you do is seen as wrong by other people, but you also know it's illegal … you're always a little bit worried what happens if you get caught. … it does make it harder.' (Cynthia)

A key issue to working in sex work for these migrant sex workers was the constant fear of being exposed as working and being deported from the country as a result.

> 'I do worry. … sometimes I come to work and I'm like, "Oh this is the day where someone's going to come in and hand me a deportation notice".' (Hope)

> '… you always have the fear inside you that someone might get to know and someone might inform against you. You have cameras around and, you know, it records, and tomorrow the Immigration guy can come up … you're scared about that … anything can happen. … So living in a fear, like I got used to it. … If you don't have a fear, you might end up exposing yourself to people. That's why I decided to have two different lives.' (Chloe)

> 'There's just always a bit of a fear what happens if someone finds out. I might get deported or whatever. It doesn't really change anything about how I'm living at the moment … yeah, it is a weird life, but it's because I'm a sex worker, not because it's illegal. But it would definitely make me feel better if it was legal.' (Cynthia)

As previously discussed, the way Section 19 has been enforced has arguably demonstrated racial discrimination, with most, if not all, deportations on the grounds of working as a sex worker on a temporary visa being of people of Asian descent (Ting, 2018). An outreach worker indicated that some migrant sex workers, who had minimal English, were not granted basic human rights through access to an interpreter or a lawyer when questioned by authorities:

> 'The [way the] legislation is written up, it looks at migrant sex workers from ethnic minorities as problematic, and

[that's] racial discrimination. And when I look at [police interview] transcripts from migrant sex workers from Asia, in particular, a lot of the times they haven't even offered that migrant worker an interpreter or a lawyer when there's been like an informal visit, and that's without a warrant.' (Outreach worker)

The probability that Asian migrant sex workers were more likely to be given deportation notices was also noted by European migrant workers: "from what I've heard in the news, it was all people from Asia that had been given deportation notices, but then also they were all like private workers …" (Hope).

The fear of deportation opens the door to exploitation of migrant workers. The participants were careful to not let clients become aware that they were working illegally. There was a fear that immigration agents might pose as clients to try and entrap them, as Faith argued:

'I was scared that when I get a client that is from Immigration … he could also take me and deport me. And I was always afraid, every single booking I'm afraid of saying too much, and always taking care … so said I've been in country for 100 years, like a lot, so that no one suspects. And it must be a very consistent story if they're going to believe it'. (Faith)

Migrant workers who worked privately were required by web hosts to include their nationality in their adverts online. While this is not a clear indication that someone is working illegally, as they may indeed have residency, it does provide some indication that they may be on a temporary visa – an opportunity not only for some clients looking to exploit the situation, but also for immigration officials to investigate further. Abbey thought that the latter was a possibility, but reasoned that there were so many adverts that immigration officials would be unlikely to trawl through them: "But there's a lot of other advertisements from all different countries, so … I just don't think that Immigration would check everyone".

Obviously, migrant sex workers' accents and physical appearance often provided an indication that they were foreign. This was mitigated by workers telling their clients that they had lived in New Zealand for a number of years.

'First thing is, "Oh she's got an accent or she's dark-skinned, [she is] obviously not European, there's no way she's Kiwi," and so you find some clients that will basically demand certain services, especially unprotected sex or natural oral, which I don't really do. I find that disgusting ... he's doing that because he thinks that he can get away with it because I don't have a voice in New Zealand because I don't have the right to work.' (Eva)

The majority of participants who worked privately, and therefore did not have a manager to screen clients, were afraid that clients would threaten them with deportation. Demands for unprotected sex and unwanted sexual activities, such as anal sex, non-payment, and other instances of blackmail, were experienced by other migrant workers, as Eva describes in this quote. Participants believed that the clients felt safe in doing so in the knowledge that sex workers working illegally would be unlikely to report these incidents to the authorities. Such unfair demands were not limited to clients. An outreach worker spoke of how the potential for deportation also created immense power differentials between brothel operators and migrant sex workers.

'I know of migrant sex workers who have got UK citizenship who are white and black, have worked in establishments and, just because they've got an English accent, the management or the sex workers there know that they're on a tourist visa or working tourist visa, ... those women were very vulnerable ... they would get deported if someone outed them. The management treats them differently because they're not working here legally. One worker told me that ... the boss will hold off paying her the money compared to the Kiwi workers ... she knows that she's been targeted because she's on a temporary visa. ... The brothel operator holds the power to pay out the money when they want, knowing that a migrant worker on a temporary visa has got no breaks [chance] because who is she going to talk to, who's going to believe her?' (Outreach worker)

Some non-migrant sex workers perceived migrant sex workers as a threat, arguing that migrant sex workers undercut prices and take business away from them. Consequently, some participants had received direct threats from non-migrant sex workers but, as Eva argued, clients were drawn to the "exotic"; because of this, she was actually charging more than non-migrant sex workers.

> 'I've gotten threats from places I've tried. ... It's basically that I'm taking away their business .... They feel, why are foreign girls allowed to come and work, "They're taking our money. They're taking our clients", you know, and some of them probably wouldn't charge that much because they would not be able to get away with it. But I'm exotic, I can charge whatever I want and I can still find clients because nobody is like me.' (Eva)

Eva's experience was not necessarily that of all migrant sex workers. Many formed friendships with non-migrant sex workers and enjoyed working alongside them. However, there have been some tensions expressed by a proportion of non-migrant workers and this is discussed in the following section.

Non-migrant sex workers

As highlighted in the previous section of this chapter, under the existing legal framework tensions may arise between migrant sex workers and non-migrant sex workers who see them as a threat to their business. The possibility of such tensions has also been highlighted in several media articles in recent years which have cited vocal sex worker, Lisa Lewis, arguing that migrants took work away from non-migrant workers and calling for harsher enforcement of the law against temporary migrants to reduce this perceived impact (Tan, 2018a, 2018b). Work in the sex industry has long been competitive, and in the contemporary context, sex workers form part of the broader precariously self-employed workforce that neoliberalism has given rise to (Simpson and Smith, 2019). It is inevitable that there is competitiveness between workers in this economic environment, which is certainly not unique to New Zealand. Nevertheless, even in such a context, the stigmatised nature of sex work and the legacy of oppressive laws and policies may also foster solidarity between workers that outweighs the need to compete to ensure economic survival. For example, a participant in a 2017 study described solidarity between migrants and permanently resident workers, illustrating this through a story of local workers helping a migrant worker to obtain her passport from a brothel operator who was retaining it (Armstrong, 2018). However, no research to date has explored relationships between temporary migrants and local workers from their perspectives.

To explore the possibility of divisions between groups of sex workers and discrimination within the sex industry, all interviewees were asked about how they felt about migrant sex workers coming to New Zealand. For a minority of participants, migrant sex workers were viewed as competition, but only one participant expressed what could be described as hostility towards migrant workers. Sasha cautioned that migrant workers should "Go back to your own country – stay back in your own country, we've got enough [sex workers] here, we barely have enough work". Amanda, by comparison, was conflicted. On the one hand she did not appreciate migrant workers coming to New Zealand specifically to do sex work, but as a sex worker she could understand why they came and would not be happy if she was singled out overseas. She explained:

> 'I can understand why they do it ... but I don't think it's right because they're not on a work visa, are they? I don't think so ... If they're coming here specifically to do sex work then I think that's quite rude ... However, in saying that - say I went to England ... I would be devastated if I got told, "No fuckhead, you can't come and work here, you're from New Zealand".' (Amanda)

Mark said that he could understand why some people felt threatened by temporary migrants but that conflict between sex workers was unhelpful, noting, "I don't see the point in attacking other workers". Bella strongly objected to the suggestion that temporary migrant sex workers took work away from local workers, explaining:

> 'I heard some people I know get indignant and be like "they're taking our work" which is just like fucking ridiculous ... There is that weird kind of competitive attitude sometimes with sex work, and racism comes into that ... If you're worried about those people taking your work then you shouldn't be in this profession, because if you're good at the job you're going to get clients.' (Bella)

Bobby felt similarly to Bella, that migrant sex workers had little impact on her and her work since they typically visited for short periods and clients had varied preferences anyway, noting, "we all look different and a guy wants different things". Elesei described having previously felt threatened by migrant workers but had discussed this with a friend who provided another perspective:

> 'I was very opinionated about this because I was like "they're coming to steal my jobs. What makes them think they have the right to come over here and take my clients?" And then someone said to me, "You know if your clients wants a particular thing and you're not it, they're not going to come to you, so what are you worried about?".' (Elesei)

From Amy's perspective migrant sex workers were "totally welcome". Clementine also felt this way, explaining, "I don't have an attitude of that they threaten my job or anything like that ... they're welcome to come and be here and make money".

Overall, while a handful of participants described feeling threatened by migrant sex workers, the majority were supportive and did not resent the presence of temporary migrants. Kate, in fact, described having a great deal of respect for migrant sex workers that she had worked with, explaining: "... there's a few [migrant sex workers] that used to work there ... and they just kick arse, they were awesome. They cleaned up, you know? They were smart, -making so much money". Bella described migrant co-workers as being "cool to work with". She also expressed admiration for those who travelled far and came from different cultural backgrounds, noting, "... if someone comes into a country, doesn't speak the language, doesn't understand a lot of the customs, it's incredibly brave of them to go into a job where you rely so heavily on communication". While several participants indicated that they admired and respected their migrant colleagues, there were also concerns about the possible vulnerability of migrants who were working in the sex industry. For example, Clementine explained:

> 'You know if you come to another country and you're not familiar with the law, you can't read or write or speak the language as well as you need to be able to, you're probably open to more coercion and things like that, which can be dangerous.' (Clementine)

Similarly, while Lucy had no objections to migrant sex workers coming to work in New Zealand, she felt it was essential that they had basic English language skills so that they could "communicate with the clients, give consent, things like that", otherwise they may be at risk. While Bella welcomed migrant sex workers, she also noted that migrant workers were sometimes unfamiliar with norms and standards in the New Zealand sex industry. On the one hand this meant that she and other sex workers were able to reassure them that abuse and violence towards them was unacceptable within New Zealand's legal framework. She explained:

> '... when I have met people coming from other countries to do sex work, a lot of the time they've experienced real horrific things doing sex work in their country and it's really nice to be able to be like, "That's totally not okay here" [in New Zealand]. You can kick a guy out, or come get someone and we'll kick him out kind of thing. You know it's really eye-opening.' (Bella)

Indeed, the overarching legal framework was described with pride by several participants and was seen as a factor which could attract migrant workers to New Zealand, since the labour conditions are known internationally to be better for sex workers than in other countries. However, Bella also felt that there could be problems for some migrant sex workers who were not familiar with New Zealand's laws and wider industry norms, and the importance of adapting – for example when it came to safer sex practices. She noted:

> 'A lot of the sex workers I've worked with, who are from other countries, there can be like a language barrier and understanding barrier which puts them in danger in terms of ... sometimes they will be used to breaking the rules – like breaking our rules in their country – so they push it, thinking the same laws don't exist. And so you have to be real kind of, "No, this is for your safety".' (Bella)

What Bella is referring to here is the use of condoms. The New Zealand sex industry has long had a strong culture of safer sex (see for example Plumridge and Abel, 2000). However, the PRA also mandates the use of condoms under Section 9, including for oral sex. This is a requirement that some sex workers who visit New Zealand temporarily may not be accustomed to, particularly if they have previously worked in countries where the sex industry operates underground due to criminalisation. Bella felt that the laws relating to migrant sex work in New Zealand contributed to such issues, since migrant sex workers were more isolated and reluctant to trust; this meant it was more difficult to connect them with services like NZPC. She explained:

'I think if it was easier for them to work here, then that wouldn't be as much of an issue. Like, if it was a more open thing and we could easily send them this way [to NZPC], then they wouldn't get spooked or worry about being sent home and stuff.' (Bella)

Other sex workers interviewed for the project also had opinions about the law relating to temporary migrants and its impacts, to which this chapter will now turn.

Perceptions of Section 19

Participants were asked what they knew about the law pertaining to temporary migrants working in the sex industry, and how they felt about this. While the majority of participants were aware of Section 19, a few of those interviewed were unaware and thus had not realised that temporary migrants were breaking the law by working in the sex industry. Harley, for example, thought that migrant sex workers were coming to New Zealand to work because they would "not get penalised for it like they would in their own country", unaware that migrants who were found working in New Zealand's sex industry can be deported. Lucy did not know the details but had a general idea of the situation, noting "I'm pretty sure it's illegal".

When asked about the possible reasons behind this aspect of the law, several participants referred to assumptions about trafficking. Jordan, for example, felt that the reason behind Section 19 was based on the "stereotype that if you're a nationality anything other than New Zealand European you must be trafficked". Kate was not aware of the law relating to migrant sex workers; when this was explained, she replied that it "didn't make sense" to her and wondered aloud in a sarcastic and mocking tone whether the purpose of this was to "stop the trafficking". Kate's reaction indicated that she did not think the perceived risk of trafficking into the sex industry was a sound rationale for prohibiting migrants from working in the sex industry. She continued, "I don't know if sex trafficking is even a problem?" and emphasised that the migrants she had worked with in the past had seemed "just, like, normal – definitely not sex trafficked". Sasha was worried about trafficking into sex work because of media portrayals she had seen, explaining, "You see all these things on TV, how they do people trafficking ... then you have these movies – *Taken* – how the daughter was taken, you know? Which make me scared to let my daughter out of my sight". However, Sasha felt that the decriminalisation of sex work in New Zealand provided an element of protection against such scenarios, noting "I don't know if we have that sort of stuff here ... the legislation kind of helps us stop from getting to that stage". These participants' comments regarding risks of trafficking in the sex industry echo those of sex workers interviewed for Roguski's (2013) study, as well as those interviewed for a 2017 study, who did not consider the risk of trafficking to be a sound rationale for prohibiting temporary migrants from working in the sex industry (Armstrong, 2018), and also the migrant sex workers quoted earlier in this chapter – none of whom considered themselves to be victims of trafficking.

While three participants were not initially aware of Section 19, the majority were, and all participants felt that there were problems with the policy. Several described it as discriminatory, such as Clementine who felt that it was "pretty unfair", Amber who thought it was "nonsense", and Amy who reflected "if I come from overseas I can be a plumber ... Why can I not be a sex worker? ... I should have this right". Similarly, Sophie felt that setting migrant workers apart was discriminatory, since people who hold temporary visas can often work in other occupations – a sentiment also expressed by participants in previous studies undertaken in New Zealand (Roguski, 2013; Armstrong, 2018). Sophie explained:

> 'They should have the same rights and same protections because anything else just makes sex work into some sort of special category, because people with lots of different types of visas can work here in other jobs. So not allowing them to work in jobs where they are involved in sexual services is just discriminatory, I think, against sex work'. (Sophie)

Like Sophie, Bella also felt that Section 19 represented a form of discrimination against sex workers and that this meant that the policy was not only problematic for migrant workers but for all sex workers:

> 'It's bullshit ... apart from being bad for them [migrant sex workers], it's bad for us as well. It's bad for sex workers in general because it creates the idea that this isn't like any other job. Anything that separates us from other workplaces is bullshit ... You know if they're [temporary migrants] allowed to work retail they should be allowed to work sex work – it's customer service.' (Bella)

As noted earlier, the enforcement of Section 19 appears to be profoundly discriminatory, with Asian sex workers particularly targeted. Lucy alluded to this by explaining that she assumed that "non-white sex workers who come to New Zealand would be targeted more".

Several participants also raised concerns about Section 19 on the basis that it could render sex workers more vulnerable to experiencing violence and exploitation; this aligns with the experiences of migrant sex workers and reflections of key informants relayed earlier in this chapter, along with the findings of previous studies (Roguski, 2013; Armstrong, 2018). Amy felt that this aspect of the law made migrant workers more vulnerable to being mistreated by exploitative third parties, predicting that such individuals would say, "Oh I see you're illegal – you have to pay us this money, and then we protect you". Bella felt that Section 19 meant migrant workers could not access information as readily and were at an increased risk as a result:

> '… it's upsetting that it's kind of more dangerous for them you know? … I wish there was more support for those people … If you're saying "you're not allowed to do this" and not giving them support and the same kind of access to information, then you're just making it more dangerous for them to do the job. You're not going to stop them doing the job, you're just going to make it less safe.' (Bella)

Kayla felt that it was important for migrant workers to "respect who's working there first" – referring to the importance of migrant sex workers aligning themselves and their marketing with the local workers so to not "undercut" anyone else. However, she was unequivocal that migrant sex workers should have the same rights and protections as local workers. She thought that migrant sex workers should feel safe reporting violence and unfair treatment to the police, regardless of their immigration status because of New Zealand's policy framework, noting: "They don't pay you, sweetheart, let the cops know. You can take them to court whether you're a foreigner or not". As Kayla has alluded, given New Zealand's legal framework, it is likely that police would in many cases help a migrant worker who had experienced violence. However, reluctance to report violence among migrant workers described earlier in this chapter is understandable given the serious consequences if police did provide information to Immigration New Zealand.

Almost all participants felt that the policy needed to change so that migrant workers had access to the same rights as other sex workers.

As Kayla passionately stated, "Sex workers ... throughout the world should be entitled to the same rules of protection and rights". The exception was Elesei, who was not sure that migrant sex workers should have access to the same rights as permanent residents explaining, "I think they should have those rights in their own country first". He was concerned that provision of the same rights would mean that New Zealand would "become that country to go to", which he felt could impact negatively on sex workers who lived in New Zealand permanently – reflecting the anxiety discussed earlier in the chapter that migrant workers represented unwanted competition. However, despite Elesei's concerns, the overwhelming sentiment among participants was that temporary migrant sex workers are welcome in New Zealand's sex industry and that they should be protected by the same law that benefits permanent residents.

Conclusion

This chapter has discussed the implications of Section 19 of the PRA, which prohibits temporary migrants from working in the sex industry, and has outlined perceptions of it among participants of two studies, including migrant sex workers and their permanent resident co-workers, along with key informants who interact with sex workers regularly. The findings clearly indicate that Section 19 is impacting negatively on temporary migrant sex workers.

The existence of Section 19 is also peculiar given the extensive involvement of sex workers in the law reform. In a global policy landscape in which sex workers are often not listened to, the fact that sex workers in New Zealand were heard in the process of law reform is (sadly) very unique. However, the existence of Section 19 illustrates that, while NZPC spearheaded the decriminalisation of sex work, politicians remained in control of the process. As outlined in Chapter 2, the introduction of Section 19 in the final months of the law reform process caught NZPC unawares and, despite their opposition, it was implemented. NZPC has subsequently spent years mitigating the negative impact of Section 19 on migrant workers. Thus, while the passing of the PRA was a significant victory for sex workers, it was not a perfect law that remained untouched by the agendas of politicians and the global politics of migration and trafficking.

There is a strong possibility that the annual report issued by the US State Department, the Trafficking in Persons (TiP) Report, may have some impact on New Zealand's decision to retain the status quo regarding Section 19. This report ranks countries on their perceived efforts to combat human trafficking. New Zealand is listed as a 'tier one' country, as they deem it as fully meeting minimum standards to eliminate trafficking. However, their 2019 report on New Zealand states:

> Foreign women from Asia and South America are at risk of sex trafficking. Some international students and temporary visa holders are vulnerable to forced labor or prostitution.
> (p 349)

No New Zealand studies in this area have found any evidence of 'sex trafficking' or 'forced labor' involving migrants but all have found potential for the exploitation of migrant sex workers as a consequence of Section 19 (Roguski, 2013; Abel and Roguski, 2018; Armstrong, 2018; Ting, 2018). The question that begs answering is whether or not the New Zealand government feels compelled to act, regardless of evidence, to maintain their 'tier one' status in the TiP Report. The Ministry for Business, Innovation and Employment has recently put out a call for submissions on its proposals to reduce exploitation of all migrant workers (sex working and non-sex working) (MBIE, 2019). The proposals are divided into three categories, which cover prevention, protection and enforcement measures (all category headings discussed in the TiP report). In none of these is the repeal of Section 19 mentioned as a possibility for preventing exploitation of migrant sex workers, despite the research evidence. There is thus a rhetoric of wanting to reduce exploitation and protect migrant workers, but no real commitment to see this happen for migrant sex workers.

Numerous studies have highlighted the problems of conflating sex work and trafficking and have critiqued anti-trafficking policies globally for their impacts on sex workers and their mobility (see, for example: Butcher, 2003; Pong, 2003; Sanghera, 2005; Weitzer, 2007; Musto, 2009; Coghlan, 2011; Maher et al, 2015). Section 19 is therefore far from unique as an example of state action taken with the intention of curbing trafficking with no evidence for its occurrence. However, what does differ is the wider policy context of New Zealand. In a context in which sex work remains criminalised and the focus is one of eradicating sex work rather than minimising harms, placing sex workers in dangerous situations and deporting migrant workers is par for the course. However New Zealand's decriminalised framework is based upon a commitment to providing safe and fair working conditions, and thus Section 19 is incongruous with this. New Zealand needs to live up to its ethos of fairness (Abel, 2017) and properly engage in providing prevention of, and protection from, exploitation of migrant sex workers.

References

Abel, G. (2017) 'In search of a free and fair society: The regulation of sex work in New Zealand', in E. Ward & G. Wylie (eds) *Feminism, Prostitution and the State,* Abingdon: Routledge, pp 140–54.

Abel, G. & Roguski, M. (2018) *Migrant Sex Workers in New Zealand: Report for MBIE.* Christchurch: University of Otago.

Armstrong, L. (2017) 'Commentary: Decriminalisation and the rights of migrant sex workers in Aotearoa/New Zealand: Making a case for change', *Women's Studies Journal,* 31: 69–76.

Armstrong, L. (2018) 'New Zealand', in Global Alliance Against Trafficking in Women, *Sex Workers Organising for Change: Self-representation, community mobilisation, and working conditions,* Thailand: GAATW, pp 73–107.

Butcher, K. (2003) 'Confusion between prostitution and sex trafficking', *The Lancet,* 361: 1983.

CEDAW (2008) General Recommendation No. 26 on women migrant workers. Available at: https://www2.ohchr.org/english/bodies/cedaw/docs/GR_26_on_women_migrant_workers_en.pdf.

Coghlan, D. (2011) 'Defining trafficking/denying justice? Forced labour in Ireland and the consequences of trafficking discourse', *Journal of Ethnic and Migration Studies,* 37: 1513–26.

Dalziel, L. (2003) *Prostitution Reform Bill – In Committee,* Hansard Debates. Available at: https://www.parliament.nz/en/pb/hansard-debates/rhr/document/47HansD_20030514_00001525/prostitution-reform-bill-in-committee.

Gee, S. (2019) 'Migrant sex workers in top of the south deported', Stuff, 11 November. Available at: https://www.stuff.co.nz/national/crime/117188869/migrant-sex-workers-in-top-of-the-south-deported.

Maher, L., Dixon, T., Phlong, P., Mooney-Somers, J., Stein, E. & Page, K. (2015) 'Conflicting rights: How the prohibition of human trafficking and sexual exploitation infringes the right to health of female sex workers in Phnom Penh, Cambodia', *Health & Human Rights: An International Journal,* 17.

MBIE (2019) 'Addressing temporary migrant worker exploitation: Consultation Document', Wellington: New Zealand Government. Available at: https://www.mbie.govt.nz/dmsdocument/7056-addressing-temporary-migrant-worker-exploitation-consultation-document.

Musto, J. (2009) 'What's in a name? Conflations and contradictions in contemporary US discourses of human trafficking', *Women's Studies International Forum,* 32(4): 281–7.

MYFUNKYTRAVEL (2019) 'World budget travel table 2019 - Backpacking costs in different countries', MYFUNKYTRAVEL. Available at: https://myfunkytravel.com/budgettraveltable.html.

NZ Government (2019) 'New Zealand's seventh periodic report under the Convention against Torture and Other Cruel, Inhuman or Degrading Treatment or Punishment: Draft report for public consultation'. Available at: https://consultations.justice.govt.nz/policy/cat-2019/.

Plumridge, L. & Abel, G. (2000) 'Services and information utilised by female sex workers for sexual and physical safety', *New Zealand Medical Journal,* 113: 370–2.

Pong, P. (2003) '"We don't want rescue, we want our rights!": Experiences on anti-trafficking efforts in Thailand', *Research for Sex Work,* 6: 8–9.

Prostitution Law Review Committee (2008) *Report of the Prostitution Law Review Committee on the Operation of the Prostitution Reform Act 2003.* Available at: http://www.justice.govt.nz/policy/commercial-property-and-regulatory/prostitution/prostitution-law-review-committee/publications/plrc-report/report-of-the-prostitution-law-review-committee-on-the-operation-of-the-prostitution-reform-act-2003.

Roguski, M. (2013) 'Occupational health and safety of migrant sex workers in New Zealand', Kaitiaki Research and Evaluation. Available at: https://www.nswp.org/resource/occupational-health-and-safety-migrant-sex-workers-new-zealand.

Sanghera, J. (2005) 'Unpacking the trafficking discourse', in K. Kempadoo, J. Sanghera & P. B. Pattanaik (eds) *Trafficking and Prostitution Reconsidered: New perspectives on migration, sex work, and human rights,* London: Paradigm Publishers, pp 3–24.

Simpson, J. & Smith, S. (2019) '"I'm not a bloody slave, I get paid and if I don't get paid then nothing happens": Sarah's experience of being a student sex worker', *Work, Employment and Society,* 33: 709–18.

Tan, L. (2018a) 'NZ sex workers lodge complaint over foreigm prostitute website advertisements', *New Zealand Herald,* 22 April. Available at: https://www.nzherald.co.nz/nz/news/article.cfm?c_id=1&objectid=12037429.

Tan, L. (2018b) 'NZ sex workers write open letter to Government asking for a Minister of Prostitution', *New Zealand Herald,* 11 June. Available at: https://www.nzherald.co.nz/nz/news/article.cfm?c_id=1&objectid=12068493.

Ting, D. (2018) 'Understanding the experiences of migrant Asian sex workers in New Zealand: An exploratory study', MA thesis, University of Auckland.

US Department of State (2019) *Trafficking in Persons Report*. Available at: https://www.state.gov/reports/2019-trafficking-in-persons-report/

Weitzer, R. (2007) 'The social construction of sex trafficking: Ideology and institutionalization of a moral crusade', *Politics and Society*, 35: 447–75.

6

"My Dollar Doesn't Mean I've Got Any Power or Control over Them": Clients Speak About Purchasing Sex

Shannon Mower

Introduction

Within contemporary global debates on sex work laws, clients of sex workers are a central focus. While punitive legislation used to regulate the sex industry has a long history of targeting sex workers, policy makers are now increasingly directing their attention to clients as the targets of criminalisation. As Sanders (2008) explains, 'there has been a repositioning of men who buy sex as the problem' (p 135). That is, clients of sex workers are increasingly being depicted as sexual abusers, and the abolitionist feminist perspective that sex work is a form of male violence against women appears to have gained more support (Bernstein, 2007; Coy et al, 2019). As such, policy makers in many countries have opted to enact new laws which criminalise the purchase of sex, including Sweden in 1999, Norway and Iceland in 2009, Canada in 2014, France in 2016, Northern Ireland in 2015, and the Republic of Ireland in 2017 (Serughetti, 2012; Arisman, 2019; Calderaro and Giametta, 2019; Coy et al, 2019; McMenzie et al, 2019). This approach is often referred to as 'the Swedish model' – owing to its initial adoption in Sweden – and also 'the Nordic model' since versions of it have now been adopted in several countries in the Nordic region. As noted by McMenzie et al, (2019), between

2012 and 2014, Northern Ireland's Democratic Unionist Party campaigned to introduce client criminalisation through drawing on Sweden as a source of inspiration and as a country to be learnt from and emulated. Likewise, when sex work regulation was debated in France during 2011, a key report presented to the National Assembly for parliamentary debate argued that the onus for sex work should be located with clients, as their demand for paid sexual services fosters exploitation and trafficking (Calderaro and Giametta, 2019). Sanders and Campbell (2014) have further noted that the political agenda in the United Kingdom is beginning to mirror this trend, with some politicians clearly influenced by the Swedish model and the discourse of client criminalisation.

Sanders (2008) proposes that there are separate processes contributing to the increased popularity of client criminalisation. Most central to this is the abolitionist feminist commitment to eradicating sex work through the criminalisation of clients and the related growth of activism fuelled by stereotypes of clients as 'sexual predators and perverts warranting increased police attention and official policy response' (Sanders, 2008, p 136). In the context of this policy focus on clients internationally, increased attention has in recent years been directed towards New Zealand's sex work model and there has subsequently been speculation as to how this has impacted on client conduct. For example, critics of decriminalisation have alleged that decriminalising sex work increases the power and control clients hold over sex workers, allowing them free rein to act violently and coercively when purchasing sex (see, for example: Raymond, 2003; Farley, 2004; Bindel, 2014, 2017; Coy and Molisa, 2016). However, clients remain a relatively under-researched population – particularly where more liberal legislative frameworks are in place. While there is a growing body of research on the experiences of clients from diverse ideological vantage points, none of these studies have examined the experiences of clients within a decriminalised context (see, for example: Michael et al, 1994; Sanders, 2008; Milrod and Weitzer, 2012; Birch, 2015; Farley et al, 2015). The lack of research on the experiences of clients in New Zealand's decriminalised context is a significant gap, since the conduct of clients has important implications for the experiences of sex workers.

Research conducted post decriminalisation has uncovered significant improvements in the working conditions of sex workers, with findings indicating that sex workers feel legally empowered in their interactions with clients (see, for example: Abel, 2010, 2014; Armstrong, 2010, 2014). Nevertheless, as previously noted, the lack of research with clients in this context has enabled speculation among opponents of decriminalisation. For example, Raymond (2004, p 1163) has suggested that 'more men go to more and bigger brothels because decriminalisation is out of control and, quite simply, impossible to control'. Similarly, Coy and Molisa (2016) claim that, since the law reform, men now demand cheaper prices and more 'extras' from sex workers. Moreover, Farley (2004, p 1118) describes clients under decriminalisation as 'socially tolerated sexual predators' and Bindel (2017, p 199) argues that 'rape, beatings and stabbings' and 'having sex with distressed, terrified women ... and being violent' defines typical client behaviour since decriminalisation. Accordingly, Molisa (2015) argues that decriminalisation gives power and control to clients, noting that 'it's the buyers of prostituted people who are the ones being empowered – to use and abuse sex workers as they please'.

While there is no evidence to support these claims, the increasing global popularity of client criminalisation means that such conjecture about the situation in New Zealand is appealing to those who oppose decriminalisation regardless of the lack of evidence. Thus, given the focus on clients in international policy debates and these assumptions regarding client conduct under New Zealand's decriminalised framework, it is particularly important that research is conducted to provide insights into how clients navigate and experience purchasing sex within this unique context. This chapter provides a starting point to address this gap in presenting insights into the experiences of 12 clients in New Zealand, considering the significance of their experiences in the context of decriminalisation and the broader policy landscape.

Methods

The research that forms the basis of this chapter was conducted between March 2018 and May 2019 for an MA thesis in criminology. The overall aim of the research was to explore the experiences of clients purchasing sex within the context of decriminalisation in New Zealand. In-depth, face-to-face interviews were conducted with 12 clients in New Zealand. The purpose of these interviews was to explore how clients experienced and navigated paying for sex in this context. The overarching objective was to explore client's lived experiences in order to better understand their perspectives on purchasing sex in New Zealand. Interviews were also conducted with three key informants, who included a brothel operator, a medical practitioner and the National Coordinator of the New Zealand Prostitutes' Collective

(NZPC), Dame Catherine Healy. Given their diverse positions across the New Zealand sex industry, the key informants were interviewed in order to provide broader insights on decriminalisation and their perceptions of client conduct in this context. Prior to commencing the fieldwork, ethical approval to conduct the research was granted by Victoria University of Wellington Human Ethics Committee (#26055).

Of the 12 participants who were clients of sex workers, 11 were male and one was female. All clients who were interviewed for the project were Caucasian, though seven identified their nationality as New Zealand European, two as Scottish, two as American (US), and one as South African. Their average age at the time of the interview was 41, with an age range of 23–65 across the sample. Most participants were employed full-time at the time of the interviews and worked across a range of sectors. Nine of the participants were actively purchasing sex at the time of the interviews, while three were no longer paying for sex. The frequency of visiting sex workers varied considerably between participants: two clients saw sex workers weekly, three fortnightly or monthly, two monthly, four bi-monthly, while one client had only purchased sex once in his life. While nine of the participants solely purchased sex from cisgender women, three had also been clients of male and transgender sex workers. All participants had only purchased sex indoors, through brothels, independent sex workers, and escort agencies. Half of the participants had also purchased sex in places where sex work is not decriminalised, including in New Zealand prior to the 2003 law reform, and in various contexts internationally.

Clients who participated in the project were primarily recruited online through a popular local Facebook group and online client forum, while a few were recruited via hard copy recruitment posters that were placed in public bathrooms on a university campus. Interviews with clients were conducted between May and July 2018. Interviews were conducted in private meeting rooms in public locations. The duration of interviews ranged from 56 to 93 minutes, with an average of approximately one hour. All interviews were recorded and transcribed verbatim. Participants were given the opportunity to select their own pseudonym to protect their identity. The interviews explored the participants' introduction to the sex industry; how they experienced purchasing sex in New Zealand and elsewhere; their preferences and motivations; their perceptions of sex workers and impacts of spending time with them; and their understanding of the laws surrounding sex work. As such, the interviews produced incredibly rich and personal insights, which offer detailed accounts of each participant's experiences of purchasing sex.

Findings

Speculation regarding the conduct of clients of sex workers in New Zealand, as noted earlier in this chapter, is based on the belief that power has been skewed in favour of clients and managers, to the detriment of sex workers. This is based on an assumption that all clients are motivated by a desire for power and control. However, the experiences described in interviews with clients strongly challenged this, with participants indicating an acute awareness of the power dynamics involved in commercial sex, with sex workers considered to be in control of the encounter. This awareness was exemplified by Eddie, who explained he "knew straight away that it's not real, I know they are not into me, I know that. And I know that my dollar doesn't mean I've got any power or control over them or anything". Likewise, Katie expressed a desire for sex workers to maintain control over the booking process when noting "I always like to check that before I contact anyone, I don't want to ask for things that people might feel pressured to give". Adam also located control over the direction of the booking with sex workers, explaining sex workers "have the power ... in terms of the social dynamic of the booking, they can kind of dictate how it goes". Thus, for these clients, the sex worker was very much in charge in the context of decriminalisation. However, it is important to also explore how their perceptions and expectations of power and control were enacted during their interactions with sex workers. Central to the Prostitution Reform Act 2003 (PRA) is a requirement that sex workers can refuse to see clients or to continue with a service; thus, exploring how clients navigate sex worker's boundaries is particularly important.

Client recognition of sex worker boundaries

All clients interviewed acknowledged that there are legal boundaries surrounding the purchase of sex in New Zealand. However, half the participants expanded on this to acknowledge that, in addition to legal boundaries, sex workers have personal boundaries that must be respected. For example, when discussing his conceptualisation of the different boundaries clients must observe, JC explained that:

> 'There are two separate boundaries, one is the legal boundary and one is her comfort boundary. You know one to start with because that's what is legally set down, but you also know the second one by ensuring that the service being provided is something she is comfortable with'. (JC)

Underlying JC's understanding of boundaries was a recognition that sex workers are people and, thus, the letter of the law was not the only consideration in the encounter. This was evident when JC noted: "the girls' boundaries are probably more important than the legal boundaries, because they are unique to the individual". Soothill and Sanders (2005) note that some clients concede that sex workers are experts in their work and, hence, prices and rules must be respected. Arthur echoed this sentiment when acknowledging the importance of respecting individual boundaries, explaining: "Sometimes they will refuse to kiss you or allow you to give them oral. That's just the rules they have for themselves, that's just the service that they provide. They have their boundaries so that's the way it is." Likewise, while Kevin considered purchasing sex as a personal indulgence, he acknowledged this was to be enjoyed according to the sex worker's boundaries:

> 'I guess sex work to me is quite similar to counselling – it's an hour about you. You paid for the time, so you get to indulge in it, within the boundaries the sex worker has set, within those boundaries you can indulge in it.' (Kevin)

Thus participants were, overall, cognisant and respectful of sex worker's boundaries, aligning with findings of research conducted with sex workers in New Zealand, which indicates that they have considerable power both to dictate the services they wish to offer and to enforce their boundaries in the context of decriminalisation (Abel et al, 2010; Armstrong, 2014, 2016). This also applies to instances of clients attempting to push sex workers' boundaries. Accounts from sex workers in New Zealand indicate that clients sometimes request oral and penetrative sex without a condom (Abel et al, 2007; Laverack and Whipple, 2010). The experiences of two participants further illustrated this. For example, Alex and Victor noted that they had requested unprotected oral sex from sex workers. In doing so, these clients attempted to push sex workers' boundaries for the sake of their own pleasure. For example, while he was "embarrassed to say", Alex explained:

> 'I have asked for unprotected oral sex, and they've said no. Not in a coercive way, but I've just asked if it's something they offer. I don't do it now, but there was an escort I was seeing for quite some time that was quite happy to do it if I paid more.' (Alex)

Likewise, Victor admitted to receiving "unprotected oral sex by a lady within the last 12 months". However, Alex noted that while he "did ask other escorts if they would do it, one or two others said yes, but most declined". Existing research aligns with Alex's experience of being denied unprotected oral sex. Abel et al (2007) found that just over 10 per cent of the 772 surveyed sex workers reported not using condoms or dental dams for oral sex with clients. While some clients may successfully pressure sex workers to engage in unprotected sex, participants interviewed for this study who made such requests were typically rejected. This further highlights the legal power that decriminalisation has provided to sex workers in enabling them to dictate the services they are comfortable offering and to enforce their boundaries if clients attempt to push them (Jordan, 2005; Fitzharris and Taylor, 2010; Abel, 2010, 2014).

However, it is equally important to acknowledge that, while two participants admitted that they had made requests for unprotected oral sex, the remaining ten participants did not indicate that they had pushed a sex worker's boundaries in this way. In fact, several of those interviewed stressed that sexual health was also a personal priority for them. Seven clients indicated a strong aversion to "natural" services and felt that not using condoms when purchasing sex was crossing a boundary. For example, Mark noted he had "never asked for any natural services or stupid shit like that", while Steve explained he "would never go to a woman who wanted to go without a condom. That's really important to me." Likewise, Alex expressed that he would "never purchase it unprotected" and had "never asked for it either". Furthermore, while Riaan noted that purchasing sex is "safe in New Zealand", this was only relevant "as long as you wear a condom, as long as you're safe and have certain boundaries ... wearing condoms and protective gear is a must". The perspectives of these clients strongly challenge the claims made by those who allege that decriminalising sex work encourages a culture of requesting unprotected full-service sex among clients (see, for example: Coy and Molisa, 2016; Geddes, 2018).

The boundaries established under the PRA were further perceived by the participants as enabling safer interactions with sex workers. For example, JC believed that "the PRA sets the boundaries of where you can and cannot go. To me they are actually very sensible boundaries which keep you safe ... it's a great environment." Sullivan (2004) argues that, through enforcing these legal standards within the sex industry, decriminalisation increases the recognition of a sex worker's capacity for consent and this ensures that non-consensual activity is more effectively recognised and legally responded to. This is well exemplified by a 2015 court case in New Zealand which saw a sex worker successfully prosecute their client for attempting to remove a condom without their consent (Shadwell, 2015). On the successful prosecution, Dame Catherine Healy commented that it was 'certainly indicative of a different relationship where a sex worker feels that they have rights and can access justice and so forth if they feel a crime has been committed against them' (Shadwell, 2015). Reflecting this, the participants' recognition of sex worker boundaries suggests that they are aware their payment does not revoke a sex worker's capacity for consent and, further, that consent must be actively sought. Hence, these participants understood that in purchasing the services of a sex worker, they are not paying for unbridled access to their body, but, rather, conditional access that is restricted by the sex worker's boundaries. Through discussing this conditional access with the participants, it became evident that clear communication was integral to establishing boundaries and comfort in interactions with sex workers.

Communication and accessibility under decriminalisation

Effective communication with clients is a priority for sex workers as it is part of the screening process where they communicate their boundaries to clients and set the terms of the encounter (Sanders, 2005; Armstrong, 2014). This process allows sex workers to set boundaries which protect themselves not only physically but also mentally, through separating their professional and personal lives (Day, 2007). Further, Sanders (2001) has explained that these initial conversations provide an opportunity to evaluate the extent to which clients may bargain and attempt to push these boundaries. Communication, and how it was navigated, was a key theme that emerged in this research. For example, JC felt that communication within the sex industry should be "unrestrained and unrestricted", something he felt the decriminalised context allows for, since sex workers can have open conversations with clients without fearing legal repercussions. Likewise, Adam felt that communication was important to establish the expectations of clients:

> 'I think it's important to negotiate and figure out what the experiences of the customer are and then agree on, at least loosely, what they want to get out of it ... "Have you done this before?" Yes ok, "What do you enjoy and what are you here for?" This, this and this.' (Adam)

In doing so, Adam felt that sex workers could respond in turn and clarify their boundaries when noting "Ok, these are all services I offer" or "Ok, I can offer this and not that". Through this process, Adam perceived that sex workers could dictate "the social dynamic of the booking ... and how it goes". Katie also felt that communication was important to establish comfort and consent at all stages of purchasing sex. When describing conversations prior to having sex with a sex worker, Katie noted:

> 'It's nice to just sit and have a chat, it doesn't have to be anything serious, just talk to them for a little so you can get a feel for that person ... Sit down, chill, make sure that they're comfortable and you're comfortable, make sure that everyone is good with what's going on and no one feels like they want to walk out.' (Katie)

Katie further explained the importance of communicating after bookings: "It's good to have established that you're both good with one another and there's no unfinished business or anything left unsaid". Similarly, JC linked clear communication to consensual commercial sex and argued that, to effectively gauge a sex worker's boundaries and the services they are comfortable providing, clear communication is essential: "You don't just go in there and start poking around unless she has told you that you can do that. You've got to be very clear at the start before the booking commences and make clear the expectations on both sides."

The experiences these clients describe indicate they were able to communicate openly with sex workers under decriminalisation. However, achieving this prior to decriminalisation would have been difficult, as sex workers risked entrapment on soliciting charges if they attempted to explicitly negotiate with clients (Abel and Fitzgerald, 2010). Sanders (2004) argues that the process of screening clients is complicated by the criminalisation of sex work, as in many criminalised contexts sex workers must manage the risk of arrest both for themselves and their client. While clients were not risking criminalisation when they paid for sex prior to decriminalisation, the experiences of the six participants who had purchased sex in New Zealand prior to the PRA still indicated a significant shift in how they communicated with sex workers after the law changed. When reflecting on his experiences paying for sex during the 1980s and 1990s in massage parlours, Alex described awkward interactions with sex workers:

> 'You would walk in and pay for a massage ... The girl would start massaging you and then after a while they would have to come up with something like "Is there anything else I can do for you?", or "Can I help you with anything else?" They couldn't offer it directly, they would have to get you to ask for the sex.' (Alex)

Expanding on this, Alex explained that "you were going in blind" and had to endure "awkward conversations about having sex even though both people knew why you were there". Jordan (2005) has noted that the duplicity criminalisation caused within massage parlours hindered sex workers from openly communicating with clients. These disjointed exchanges are the quintessential opposite of sex work under decriminalisation, which Alex felt was significantly more straightforward and accessible, explaining: "Now, you just pay up front at the beginning ... you make an appointment and just turn up". Alex's experience in different legal contexts suggests that decriminalisation has enabled an environment in which sex workers can transparently communicate their services and expectations, which aligns with the findings of research with sex workers in New Zealand (see, for example: Abel et al, 2007; Armstrong, 2014). Victor's experiences further illustrate this. He noted that:

> 'The ladies are more open to being upfront about what they do and what they offer, as opposed to you having to wait until you've committed to the massage before you find out what they do or don't do ... which might not have been the understanding that the front desk gave you. ... It's quite upfront now.' (Victor)

Similarly, Arthur described purchasing sex in New Zealand as a straightforward transaction that was "totally different" from purchasing sex overseas. He explained, "Here, everything is already settled ... Here, it's 'Ok, this is the amount you pay and this is what you get' ... Here is way better". The difference participants observed across contexts are well summarised by JC, who argued that decriminalisation meant "dealing with the known rather than the unknown". These experiences further reflect accounts provided by sex workers in New Zealand, which also indicate they can more easily negotiate services with clients under decriminalisation (Abel, 2010, 2014). As decriminalisation fosters transparency, the participants perceived sex work in New Zealand to be more accessible. As Alex explained, "Pre-decriminalisation, you really had to look around and see where the massage parlours were". Likewise, Victor felt that sex work in New Zealand was "more out in the open and upfront" since decriminalisation, as "there's no secrecy about it anymore".

Participants who had experience purchasing sex in alternative legal contexts further connected this accessibility to improved safety. For example, Riaan felt that sex work in New Zealand is "more visible and user-friendly" than in the criminalised sex industry in South Africa, where he relied on "behind the scenes activity" and informal social networks of "men that get together over weekends or Friday nights" to access sex workers. Riaan's experience highlights the underground and informal structure of the sex industry when it is criminalised (Mac, 2016). For example, when considering how clients engage with commercial sex in these differing legal climates, Riaan noted: "There are so many choices here ... Whereas in South Africa you could go to a place and it would be hidden away ... It's not in the central CBD [city] area, it's in a suburb". Criminalising sex work inevitably impacts on its accessibility – as demonstrated by Riaan, Alex, and Victor, criminalisation forces sex work to operate under secrecy and at the fringes of society, which has been widely noted to place sex workers at increased risk (Sallmann, 2010; Krüsi et al, 2014). Riaan, JC and Arthur further connected this to a perception of their own risk as clients. As Riaan observed, "There is always that factor of you might get caught out or the place might get raided". Likewise, Arthur was concerned about "all the baggage that comes with it being criminal" and, accordingly, felt that to purchase sex internationally, you had to "take the risk ... you wouldn't even consider going over to America ... There's no point because you have the criminal part. Why take the risk?"

While proponents of client criminalisation may see this reluctance to pay for sex in such contexts as positive, it is important to consider this in the context of what such environments mean for sex workers. As discussed in previous chapters, the harms criminalisation imposes on sex workers have been well documented, including contexts in which clients are criminalised. For example, research conducted by Krüsi et al (2014) found that sex workers in Canada hurried or abandoned screening practices and got into clients' cars more quickly in order to avoid law enforcement officers, and that clients also requested bookings in areas away from police presence, often in isolated locations. Such approaches, therefore, force sex workers to prioritise the client's safety over their own. Thus, a reluctance among these clients to pay for sex in such contexts only contributes to this situation by forcing sex workers to work under increased financial pressure and in isolation.

In comparison to such contexts, JC felt that the New Zealand sex industry was much safer for both sex workers and their clients, noting: "I know that there will be measures in place to make sure that it's safe. The law is pretty good in this respect, as it protects both the sex worker and client." The way the participants described interacting with sex workers clearly indicates that they consider open communication important: it facilitated the negotiation of services with sex workers, established boundaries, improved safety, and allowed both parties to feel comfortable during their interactions. The comparisons participants drew between purchasing sex across legal contexts further highlights how influential sex work legislation is in shaping client interactions with sex workers – while criminalisation led to cumbersome, inaccurate, and rushed communication of services, decriminalisation enabled clear and transparent communication between the participants and sex workers, leading to safer and more straightforward exchanges. These findings challenge speculation regarding the conduct of clients in the decriminalised context: first, the suggestion that sex workers lose control over client encounters under decriminalisation; and second, the claim that clients cannot, or do not, want to look beyond their own experiences and extend consideration to the circumstances for sex workers (Bindel, 2017). These arguments were further challenged by the ethical considerations the participants described when interacting with sex workers.

Ethical considerations when purchasing sex

When discussing how, where and with whom they purchased sex, the participants described several ethical considerations. These ethical considerations presented in a variety of ways and were concerned with different stages of interacting with sex workers, be that during the booking process or while having sex. Through these considerations, the participants indicated an awareness of the sex workers' experience and a desire to improve this. This is demonstrated by Kevin:

> 'What I hope from their point of view is that they have a good day at work, that's all I hope for. If they have a fantastic day at work and if they have really good sex with me, or a genuine orgasm, that's great! But I don't pretend that's going to happen. If they have a good day at work, then I'm happy, that's all I need.' (Kevin)

When discussing bookings with sex workers, many participants mentioned strategies they used in an attempt to ensure that sex workers were comfortable with them. Prior research has found similar behaviour evident in chat rooms and message boards organised by clients, where men engage in discussions about what they perceive to be appropriate and inappropriate behaviour when interacting with sex workers (Soothill and Sanders, 2005). For example, Alex recognised that there were some sex acts that may be experienced as demeaning by some sex workers, such as "cumming on someone's face". To ensure he was treating sex workers with respect, he drew comparisons between his engagements with sex workers and his wife, noting: "I've never done anal with my wife, so I wouldn't do it with a sex worker either … At least I can say that I'm not treating her any different to how I treat my wife."

Similarly, JC recognised that sex workers often have numerous clients and, hence, felt that it was important to "try to make their hour with you as least stressful as possible and, at times, to make it as enjoyable as possible". To reduce the stress sex workers may encounter when engaging with clients, JC felt that clients should uphold certain standards, including being "polite, respectful, don't walk in drunk or anything like that, always be clean. Be there as a person, rather than someone who is just there to take what you can from them." Likewise, Eddie understood that sex workers "must have good sessions but also bad sessions" and so, in a bid to make the sex workers he saw more comfortable, Eddie made the hotel room welcoming when booking an outcall. He explained: "I'd have music going or the TV going … I'd always offer them a wine, or a beer, or a coffee, or orange juice, never straight into it … I wanted to make it a nice setting for them."

The effort these participants extended to create a comfortable environment for sex workers and the emphasis participants placed on workers' humanity outside of their identities as sex workers contradicts two core abolitionist claims about clients – first, that clients are incapable of perceiving sex workers as more than their occupation, and second, that clients seek to dehumanise sex workers when purchasing sex (Jacobson, 2002; Julián, 2019). Alex evidenced this when explaining, "It's just the way you treat people really. I do look at them as people who deserve respect." Similarly, JC noted that, "people who have not experienced sex workers don't understand that they're human beings as well … some people I've met doing this have been some of the most wonderful human beings I've ever met" and he believed it was important to "not treat the girls as objects when you're discussing them".

Critics of decriminalisation have further argued that in the decriminalised context, clients are more likely to coerce and exploit sex workers (Bindel, 2014, 2017; Molisa, 2015; Coy and Molisa, 2016). However, three participants explained they specifically avoided circumstances that could be perceived as potentially exploitative. For example, Katie always talked to independent sex workers over the phone as this meant she could arrange the booking directly with them. She felt that booking independent sex workers and arranging bookings on the phone provided reassurance that the sex worker was in control rather than a third party, explaining "someone is not controlling their clients". Likewise, Katie perceived that migrant sex workers are at an increased risk of exploitation and, as such, she preferred to "see women who are from New Zealand purely because if they are from overseas it's more difficult to tell if they are here consensually". JC also identified migrant sex workers as being at an increased risk of exploitation, noting that "maybe they are being manipulated, being coerced, who knows. I don't want to put myself in that environment". Similarly, Kevin noted he "wouldn't feel terribly comfortable about street-based" sex workers and expressed concerns over their exploitation:

> 'I've tried to reorganise my thinking around street-based work away from the sort of conditioning that says it's all about horrific situations ... But I want it to be ethical, I don't want to be exploiting anyone. I don't want to be going to see anyone who is doing it for any other reason other than they are comfortable having sex with random people for money ... As long as it doesn't hurt them in any way emotionally or mentally, that's the main thing for me.' (Kevin)

Instead of purchasing through the street-based industry, Kevin preferred the context of a brothel or an independent worker, as he felt "like the sex workers themselves are in a better situation, or are safer, or surrounded by a more professional environment". This desire of Kevin, JC and Katie to avoid non-consensual sex work directly opposes the stereotypical image of an unattached consumer and those arguments which claim that purchasing sex raises no moral issues for clients (Sanders, 2008). Yet, it is important to note that, despite such concerns, research indicates that migrant and street-based sex workers are diverse populations and are entirely capable of consenting to sex work (Roguski, 2013; Armstrong, 2016). While JC and Katie reflect stereotypes of street-based and migrant workers, their concerns are well intentioned and indicate they consider the ethics of their conduct. The consideration that some New Zealand clients give to sex workers, particularly migrant workers, was also described by Dame Catherine Healy of NZPC, who noted that:

> 'We do have people ringing up about sex workers or … about migrant sex workers. I think it's a positive if they are moving through these communities and have a perception that is related to a concern. So, if they see somebody, and they are concerned about their welfare it is a very strong positive that they would take the extra act to contact us.' (Dame Catherine Healy, interview with author)

The ethical considerations discussed throughout this chapter demonstrate that the participants are aware of the rights of sex workers and wish to purchase sex ethically. As explained by Dame Catherine Healy in an interview with the author: "Clients must have a sense from sex workers, that the sex workers have rights now, and perhaps that contributes to better behaviour". As previously noted, a core argument mobilised by opponents of decriminalisation is that decriminalising sex work will embolden clients who wish to abuse, degrade and dehumanise sex workers (Farley, 2004). However, in this study, participants' interactions with sex workers indicated the opposite, in that they were defined by the recognition and respect of sex workers' boundaries, clear communication, and ethical conduct. This adds to the evidence that decriminalisation has achieved what it set out to do.

Conclusion

This chapter has explored how 12 clients of sex workers perceived and experienced purchasing sex in the context of decriminalisation in New Zealand. Three key themes underpinned these experiences. These included an acknowledgement of the boundaries that sex workers have, the ability for clear and effective communication with sex workers which fostered increased accessibility, and the ethical considerations of participants, which influenced how they chose to engage with sex workers. Such defining characteristics imply that the clients who were interviewed for this research prioritised whether their exchange with a sex worker could be considered 'ethical' and located power and control over the encounter with sex workers. When compared to the experiences of the six participants who had experienced criminalised sex industries, it became evident that the decriminalised environment enabled more open and transparent exchanges, which was conducive to the safety of both sex workers and clients.

These findings have important implications when considered in the context of the growth of client criminalisation and claims about client conduct in New Zealand's decriminalised industry by critics of decriminalisation. The push to criminalise clients in many parts of the world is based on the assumption that clients are dangerous to sex workers and also to wider communities (Birch, 2015). However, the findings of this research contradict such claims, since the clients who took part were 'ordinary' people and described interactions that placed sex workers in a position of power and in control of these encounters. These findings add to a growing literature base highlighting the benefits of decriminalising sex work, through offering insights into the perceptions and experiences of clients in the New Zealand context.

How participants conducted themselves in their interactions with sex workers appeared to be largely due to their understanding that purchasing sex represents a business transaction and that a sex worker's consent is not 'bought' with a client's payment. Thus, in defining sex work as work, the New Zealand model may influence clients to conduct themselves similarly to how they may in other customer service industries, but with an additional understanding that sex with a sex worker is a privilege. As such, those interviewed clearly demonstrated a desire to treat sex workers with respect, through employing open communication, acknowledging boundaries, and considering the ethical implications of their behaviour. Thus, from the perspective of the clients interviewed, it appears that rather than creating an environment which empowers clients to harm and exploit sex workers, the decriminalisation of sex work in New Zealand may have created an environment that fosters greater respect among clients for sex workers and their rights.

It should be noted that there are limitations to this study. The small sample means that the findings cannot be extrapolated to the broader client population of New Zealand. For the research to be manageable within the scope of a Masters' thesis, participants needed to live within the wider Wellington region, meaning that the experiences of clients in other areas of New Zealand were not represented in the study. It is also possible that those who participated presented themselves from a positive perspective, and there are undoubtedly clients who do not behave as ethically as the clients who participated in the study (Kinnell, 2013). However, despite these limitations, these findings provide important and novel in-depth insights into the perspectives and experiences of the 12 clients who participated and so may pave the way for further research.

While the fact that the clients interviewed spoke positively about the decriminalised framework and how it impacted their experience is interesting, it is critical to stress that decriminalisation is not *for* clients. As outlined in previous sections of this book, the overarching rationale for decriminalising sex work in New Zealand was to improve the occupational health and safety of sex workers. Furthermore, sex workers globally have campaigned for decades for decriminalisation, not to improve the experiences of their clients but for the sake of their own human rights. Thus, the significance of these findings is not whether or not the clients interviewed felt they had benefited from decriminalisation, but how they interpreted the legal framework and interacted with sex workers in this context. These findings clearly indicate that participants were acutely aware that sex workers had rights under the PRA that must be upheld. Furthermore, sex workers were not seen as objects by participants but as people who were deserving of respect. Thus, overall, the clients who were interviewed described conducting themselves in a manner that aligns with what the PRA intended. Such findings should be of significant interest to policy makers seeking to better protect sex workers. However, this requires looking beyond ideologically driven stereotypes and conjecture about clients promoted by those who seek to abolish the sex industry. This research contributes novel insights which help to further complicate such portrayals, enabling more nuanced insights into what decriminalisation means for clients and how it shapes their interactions with sex workers.

References

Abel, G. (2010) 'Decriminalisation: A harm minimisation and human rights approach to regulating sex work', PhD thesis, University of Otago.

Abel, G. (2014) 'A decade of decriminalization: Sex work "down under" but not underground', *Criminology & Criminal Justice*, 14(5): 580–92.

Abel, G. & Fitzgerald, L. (2010) 'Risk and risk management in sex work post-Prostitution Reform Act: A public health perspective', in G. Abel, L. Fitzgerald, C. Healy & A. Taylor (eds) *Taking the Crime Out of Sex Work: New Zealand sex workers' fight for decriminalisation*, Bristol: Policy Press, pp 217–37.

Abel, G., Fitzgerald, L. & Brunton, C. (2007) *The Impact of the Prostitution Reform Act on the Health and Safety Practices of Sex Workers: Report to the Prostitution Law Review Committee*, Christchurch: University of Otago.

Abel, G., Fitzgerald, L. & Brunton, C. (2009) 'The impact of decriminalisation on the number of sex workers in New Zealand', *Journal of Social Policy*, 38(3): 515–31.

Arisman, K. (2019) 'Let's talk about sex', *University of Saskatchewan Undergraduate Research Journal*, 5(2): 1–10.

Armstrong, L. (2010) 'Out of the shadows (and into a bit of light): Decriminalisation, human rights and street-based sex work in New Zealand', in T. Sanders, S. Kingston & K. Hardy (eds) *New Sociologies of Sex Work*, Surrey: Ashgate, pp 39–59.

Armstrong, L. (2014) 'Screening clients in a decriminalised street-based sex industry: Insights into the experiences of New Zealand sex workers', *Australian & New Zealand Journal of Criminology*, 47(2): 207–22.

Armstrong, L. (2016) 'From law enforcement to protection? Interactions between sex workers and police in a decriminalized street-based sex industry', *British Journal of Criminology*, 57(3): 570–88.

Bernstein, E. (2007) *Temporarily Yours: Intimacy, authenticity, and the commerce of sex*, Chicago: University of Chicago Press.

Bindel, J. (2014) 'Decriminalising the sex trade will not protect its workers from abuse', *The Guardian*. Available at: https://www.theguardian.com/commentisfree/2016/jul/13/decriminalising-sex-trade-protect-workers-abuse.

Bindel, J. (2017) *The Pimping of Prostitution: Abolishing the sex work myth*, Basingstoke: Palgrave Macmillan.

Birch, P. (2015) *Why Men Buy Sex: Examining sex worker clients*, London: Routledge.

Calderaro, C. & Giametta, C. (2019) ' "The problem of prostitution": Repressive policies in the name of migration control, public order, and women's rights in France', *Anti-Trafficking Review*, (12): 155–71.

Coy, M. & Molisa, P. (2016) 'What lies beneath prostitution policy in New Zealand?', OpenDemocracy. Available at: https://www.opendemocracy.net/en/5050/what-lies-beneath-prostitution-and-policy-in-new-zealand/.

Coy, M., Smiley, C. & Tyler, M. (2019) 'Challenging the "prostitution problem": Dissenting voices, sex buyers, and the myth of neutrality in prostitution research', *Archives of Sexual Behavior*, 1–5.

Day, S. (2007) *On the Game*, London: Pluto Press.

Farley, M. (2004) '"Bad for the body, bad for the heart": Prostitution harms women even if legalized or decriminalized', *Violence Against Women*, 10(10): 1087–125.

Farley, M., Golding, J. M., Matthews, E. S., Malamuth, N.M. & Jarrett, L. (2015) 'Comparing sex buyers with men who do not buy sex: New data on prostitution and trafficking', *Journal of Interpersonal Violence*, 32(23): 3601–25.

Geddes, C. (2018) 'No, decriminalisation of johns and pimps has not improved our safety or lives', NordicModelNow. Available at: https://nordicmodelnow.org/2018/08/26/no-decriminalisation-of-johns-and-pimps-has-not-improved-our-safety-or-lives/.

Jacobson, M. (2002) 'Why do men buy sex. The interview: Professor Sven-Axel Månsson, Sweden', *Nordic Institute for Women's Studies and Gender Research*, 1: 22–5.

Jordan, J. (2005) *The Sex Industry in New Zealand: A literature review*. Available at: https://www.justice.govt.nz/assets/Documents/Publications/sex-industry-in-nz.pdf.

Julián, S. (2019) 'Tensions between feminist principles and the demand for prostitution in the neoliberal age: A critical analysis of sex buyer's discourse', *Recerca. Revista de pensament I anàlisi*, 24(2): 109–28.

Kinnell, H. (2013) *Violence and Sex Work in Britain*, Cullompton: Willan Publishing.

Krusi, A., Pacey, K., Bird, L., Taylor, C., Chettiar, J., Allan, S., Bennett, D., Montaner, J. S., Kerr, T. & Shannon, K. (2014) 'Criminalisation of clients: reproducing vulnerabilities for violence and poor health among street-based sex workers in Canada - a qualitative study', *BMJ Open*, 4(6): e005191–e005191.

Laverack, G. & Whipple, A. (2010) 'The sirens' song of empowerment: A case study of health promotion and the New Zealand Prostitutes' Collective', *Global Health Promotion*, 17(1): 33–8.

Mac, J. (2016) 'The laws that sex workers really want | Juno Mac', TED. Available at: https://www.ted.com/talks/juno_mac_the_laws_that_sex_workers_really_want.

McMenzie, L., Cook, I. R. & Laing, M. (2019) 'Criminological policy mobilities and sex work: Understanding the movement of the "Swedish Model" to Northern Ireland', *The British Journal of Criminology*, 59(5): 1199–216.

Michael, T., Gagnon, H., Laumann, O. & Kolata, G. (1994) *Sex in America: A definitive survey*, New York: Warner Books.

Milrod, C. & Weitzer, R. (2012) 'The intimacy prism', *Men and Masculinities*, 15(5): 447–67.

Molisa, P. (2015) 'Breaking the silence on prostitution and rape culture', e-tangata. Available at: https://e-tangata.co.nz/comment-and-analysis/breaking-the-silence-on-prostitution-and-rape-culture/.

Raymond, J. (2003) 'Ten reasons for not legalizing prostitution and a legal response to the demand for prostitution', *Journal of Trauma Practice*, 2: 315–32.

Raymond, J. (2004) 'Prostitution on demand: Legalizing the buyers as sexual consumers', *Violence Against Women*, 10(10): 1156–86.

Roguski, M. (2013) 'Occupational health and safety of migrant sex workers in New Zealand', NSWP. Available at: https://www.nswp.org/resource/occupational-health-and-safety-migrant-sex-workers-new-zealand.

Sallmann, J. (2010) 'Living with stigma: Women's experiences of prostitution and substance use', *Affilia*, 25(2): 146–59.

Sanders, T. (2001) 'Female street sex workers, sexual violence, and protection strategies', *Journal of Sexual Aggression*, 7(1): 5–18.

Sanders, T. (2004) 'The risks of street prostitution: Punters, police and protesters', *Urban Studies*, 41(9): 1703–17.

Sanders, T. (2005) '"It's just acting": Sex workers' strategies for capitalizing on sexuality', *Gender, Work and Organization*, 12(4): 319–42.

Sanders, T. (2008) *Paying for Pleasure: Men who buy sex*, Abingdon: Routledge.

Sanders, T. & Campbell, R. (2014) 'Criminalization, protection and rights: Global tensions in the governance of commercial sex', *Criminology & Criminal Justice*, 14(5): 535–548.

Serughetti, G. (2012) 'Prostitution and clients' responsibility', *Men and Masculinities*, 16(1): 35–48.

Shadwell, T. (2015) 'Man charged with failing to use condom with prostitute', Stuff. Available at: https://www.stuff.co.nz/national/crime/67464897/null.

Soothill, K. & Sanders, T. (2005) 'The geographical mobility, preferences and pleasures of prolific punters: A demonstration study of the activities of prostitutes' clients', *Sociological Research Online*, 10(1): 17–30.

Sullivan, B. (2004) 'Prostitution and Consent: Beyond the Liberal Dichotomy of "Free and Forced"', in M. Crowling & P. Reynolds (eds) *Making Sense of Sexual Consent*, London: Ashgate Publishing.

Sullivan, B. (2010) 'When (some) prostitution is legal: The impact of law reform on sex work in Australia', *Journal of Law and Society*, 37(1): 85–104.

PART III

Perceptions of Sex Workers in New Zealand

7

"Genuinely Keen to Work": Sex Work, Emotional Labour, and the News Media

Gwyn Easterbrook-Smith

Introduction

Media representations are key texts where knowledge and understandings of sex work and sex workers are produced and reproduced for the general public. Existing literature has identified that media coverage of sex work often acts as a proxy for 'lived interaction with the sex industry', (Hallgrimsdottir et al, 2006) and that media produced by sex workers for clients, such as advertising copy or social media postings, is sometimes misunderstood as an authentic representation of their jobs (Grant, 2014). Prior research into media coverage of the sex industry in New Zealand following the passing of the Prostitution Reform Act (PRA) found that sex workers often felt that the media sensationalised or misrepresented the industry, or that media coverage perpetuated stereotypes about sex workers (Fitzgerald and Abel, 2010, p 204). Research internationally has identified narratives within media accounts which position sex work as a social problem in need of a solution (Van Brunschot et al, 2000; Hallgrimsdottir et al, 2006). In the case of coverage immediately following the passing of the PRA in New Zealand, reporting focused on politicians' voices, rather than those of experts with specific knowledge of the industry, and also utilised moral frameworks to underpin discourses about sex work (Fitzgerald and Abel, 2010). In-house/indoor sex workers are more likely to be allowed to speak about their lives than street-based sex workers, and media representations of indoor sex work sometimes frame it as offering financial advantages and as the 'lesser of two evils' within the industry (Farvid and Glass, 2014, pp 57–8). This chapter expands on existing research into media coverage of the sex industry by investigating discourses of indoor sex work, based on the examination of different types of media coverage ('texts') aired or published between 2010 and 2016, that is 7–13 years after decriminalisation.

Van Brunschot et al (2000) argue that the ways that sex work is produced in the media reflects prevailing social attitudes, as well as serving a claims-making role in producing activities which may be understood as social problems. Media portrayals serve a particular role in persuading an audience towards particular understandings of activities, like sex work, which may be understood as social problems, as they are one of the trusted sources on this issue. This chapter investigates news media discourses about low-volume indoor sex workers in order to establish if and how, after decriminalisation, the image of an 'acceptable' sex worker has been constructed in the news media. Bernstein (2007) has identified that a side effect (or, arguably, a secondary but intentional effect) of other legal models for regulating sex work is first to make it clear that the 'desirable' kind of sex worker is a white, indoor worker and second to attempt to force out migrant workers, underage workers and drug-using workers, thus removing the most visible parts of the sex industry from the public eye. Attempts to supplant the public notion of 'sex worker' with 'acceptable' indoor workers may reduce stigma for some, but risk instead shifting stigma more heavily onto workers who cannot so easily make themselves and the labour they engage in disappear. Abel (2014, p 587) has discussed this with specific reference to New Zealand sex workers under decriminalisation, identifying that indoor workers are largely unseen and therefore 'able to fly under the radar of moral indignation'. Scoular (2010, pp 33–4), discussing sex work in Sweden, echoes this, noting that acceptability is available to sex workers who are able to 'perform the rituals of middle class society'.

Hallgrimsdottir et al (2006, p 268) additionally note that the production and interpretation of media texts (such as newspaper articles) are contextually and culturally specific, and that the location and scope of stigma placed upon sex workers relates to 'the moral and social location of stigmatized subjects'. Fairclough (1992, pp 271–2) uses the term 'manifest intertextuality' to describe the condition of texts being reliant on external knowledge to be made fully comprehensible. Approaching analysis of the media through this framework suggests that this image of the 'acceptable' sex worker only functions effectively if it is understood to be in opposition to existing tropes. That is, the audience are expected to have a familiarity with negative stereotypes about sex workers, against which the acceptable sex worker is measured. Prior research into media representations of the sex industry has identified recurring narratives which include: the sex worker as a vector of disease and contagion, the victimisation and exploitation of sex workers, and the visible sex worker as a public nuisance (Van Brunschot et al, 2000; Hallgrimsdottir et al, 2006; Farvid and Glass, 2014). This chapter aims to articulate some of the ways in which the acceptability of sex work is mediated and conveyed, and what conditions are attached to it, through an analysis of news media texts (such as TV broadcasts, radio interviews, and online articles). In many cases, the acceptability of (some) sex workers is heavily dependent on their ability to distance themselves from other sectors of the industry, including through signalling their class position.

Methods

As part of a three-year doctoral project, news texts published or broadcast in New Zealand on sex work between 2010–16 were examined, including texts discussing street-based sex workers in South Auckland, migrant sex workers, and low-volume indoor sex workers (Easterbrook-Smith, 2018). The selected timeframe encompassed the period from 7–13 years post decriminalisation, and included several media 'events', including a push to pass bylaws to restrict street-based sex work, and increased coverage of migrant workers around the time of the Rugby World Cup, hosted by New Zealand in 2011. The corpus of texts used to assess the dominant narratives within coverage of low-volume indoor workers included 14 in total: two television/ video texts – a news segment, and a video accompanying an online news article, one radio interview , and 11 written texts from both print and online sources. The texts primarily discussed workers in Auckland and Wellington. Searches for relevant texts were conducted via the Newztext database, the Victoria University of Wellington Te Waharoa search portal, and the Australia/New Zealand Reference Centre Database, as well as the host websites of New Zealand news outlets such as Stuff.co.nz, nzherald.co.nz and tvnz.co.nz. Search terms used included 'sex work', 'sex worker', and 'prostitute'. Collection of articles ceased when new texts being found contained narratives and themes which had already been identified in the previously collected articles and broadcasts, indicating that collecting additional data had reached a point of diminishing returns.

This chapter discusses and expands upon the findings from the doctoral project about recurrent narratives in coverage of low-volume[1] indoor sex workers. A key aim of the full project was to determine if some sex workers had been rendered discursively 'acceptable' after decriminalisation, and to identify the conditions attached to this acceptability. This chapter aims to explain how intertwined discourses – of invisibility and normality, of authentic enjoyment of the work, and of neoliberal empowerment – function to establish one kind of sex worker as less stigmatised under decriminalisation.

The selected texts were analysed to ascertain who was interviewed and positioned as an expert in the texts, applying Fairclough's model of 'discourse representation' (1992, pp 272–4). Following the methodological approach of prior work on this topic, the texts were also examined to identify recurrent themes and narratives for closer analysis (Van Brunschot et al, 2000; Hallgrimsdottir et al, 2006). Fairclough's model of critical discourse analysis includes a consideration of intertextuality, and the analysis of the texts included here was carried out simultaneously with analysis of texts concerning different groups of sex workers. Conducting these analyses in parallel allowed for a heightened awareness of, for example, how texts about indoor workers often implicitly compared them to other sectors of the sex industry, allowing for a consideration of the existing stereotypes which discourses about indoor workers anticipated and responded to. Existing work on media representations of sex workers has also identified the existence of an advertorial framing; in some instances language in the analysed media texts was compared to the marketing copy of the agencies being discussed to establish commonalities in the terminology used. (Fitzgerald and Abel, 2010; Grant, 2014).

Several key narratives were identified in the 14 analysed texts; these contribute to the reasons some workers may become considered 'acceptable', and also indicate the commonalities in how the image of low-volume indoor workers was constructed in these discussions. These linked narratives or themes include: an ability to be functionally invisible as a sex worker due to adherence to other normative identity categories, such as 'student' or 'business owner'; the obfuscation of the actual *work* of sex work and the associated emotional labour which both the work and obscuring it requires; and, comparisons between indoor workers who see relatively few clients and those who see more clients and/or charge less for their services. When compared to other groups of sex workers, low-volume indoor workers were most likely to be described as 'sex workers' or 'escorts', instead of 'prostitutes' or 'hookers', and more likely to have positive modifiers attached to these descriptors.[2] The final thematic trope discussed in this chapter is the ability and willingness of workers to frame their job in an advertorial manner, emphasising their enjoyment of the work. This final narrative has links to the others: performing enjoyment in this way normalises the sexual labour carried out, and also minimises the labour more generally by making the work seem effortless or incidental.

Analysis of the texts

Visibility

Existing literature on sex work has identified visibility as a contributing factor in the degree of social stigma faced by sex workers both in New Zealand and elsewhere (O'Neill et al, 2008; Scoular, 2010; Abel, 2014; Armstrong, 2016). Within the analysed texts, those discussing agency workers emphasise that they do not conform to stereotypical ideas about what a sex worker looks like, with one describing the brothel décor and appearance of the worker, then observing '[i]t's not what you would expect from a woman who sells her body' (*Dominion Post*, 2012). Many of the texts that were analysed also emphasise the private and discreet nature of the premises the profiled workers use (Cooke, 2012; Meadows, 2014; Chang, 2015). In one case, an agency owner highlights the secluded nature of her business by comparing it implicitly to higher volume brothels, mentioning 'strip bars, neon lights' (Meadows, 2014).

Such an emphasis on privacy and discretion, and the discussion of workers not looking 'like a sex worker', is arguably intended to place this engagement in sex work in opposition to street-based sex work, the most visible but smallest part of the industry (Abel et al, 2007). Bernstein (2007) and Grant (2014) both identify that signifiers associated with street-based sex work, such as fishnets and stilettos, are often used as a visual shorthand for the sex industry as a whole. In one article, a brothel owner explicitly makes this comparison, saying people expect her to be more 'hard arse and in your face' because street-based sex workers are 'all they see' (Hewitson, 2015). The reassurance that the workers being interviewed and profiled are entirely distinct from street-based sex workers is one of the mechanisms by which their acceptability is established, and by extension one of the ways in which stigma against more visible workers is entrenched.

The repeated emphasis on indoor workers not 'looking like' a sex worker and of agency premises being hidden, combined with the normalising details about the workers which are often included in the texts studied, implies that the most appropriate way to engage in sex work is to do it in as close to total secrecy as possible. For example, one worker is quoted as stating that she takes a 'long lunch' from her office job when she has an appointment, indicating that she hides her second job, while an owner comments that many of her workers might say they are employed as a receptionist or nanny to hide the nature of their work (Cooke, 2012; Meadows, 2014). Abel (2014) identifies that one of the anticipated outcomes of the Prostitution Reform Act (PRA) was that street-based workers would move indoors, making sex work functionally invisible to the wider public. Ham and Gerard (2014) refer to 'strategic invisibility', in which sex workers carefully manage their own visibility as a mechanism to reduce the stigma they are subjected to, from institutions and from individuals. This appears to be a tactic employed by many of the agency workers featured in the analysed texts. One worker notes that many sex workers are wary of reporting labour rights violations or assaults because of the fear of being treated poorly as sex workers, indicating the structural as well as interpersonal invisibility which sex workers occupy (Trengrove, 2014).

Normalising identities

Assisting with this framing of agency workers as being able to make their jobs functionally invisible to the wider community, and therefore more acceptable, are the other normalising details provided about them. Over half of the analysed texts present sex workers' tertiary education, previous or parallel careers, or goals to own a small business or buy property as mechanisms through which to understand them as not 'just' a sex worker (Cooke, 2012; *Dominion Post*, 2012; Trengrove, 2014; Bones, 2015; Chang, 2015; McCarthy, 2015; Meadows, 2014; Olds, 2016). In some cases, this is done with an evident intention to reduce the stigma against sex workers, concurrent with arguing for more respect to be afforded the job, as in Trengrove (2014) which opens with descriptions of the activities and identities of the profiled workers aside from their employment in the sex industry. However, even in these instances the texts still rely upon the other identities which sex workers can claim as a way of justifying their work as worthy of respect. Describing these sex workers' adherence to middle- or upper-class socioeconomic status markers together with approving descriptions of their appearance and demeanour (going to pains to point out they are 'articulate', for example (Cooke, 2012)) further highlights that, in many cases, sex work is these workers' only deviation from modes of normative acceptability. Their right to have their work afforded dignity is made contingent, requiring an appropriate performance of respectability in other areas of their lives.

In addition to being permitted a modicum of acceptability, the way that agency sex workers are framed within the analysed corpus of texts also permitted them to speak more frequently than either migrant workers or street-based sex workers. Sex workers were quoted or paraphrased in 57 per cent of the analysed texts discussing indoor workers, compared with 20 per cent in texts discussing street-based sex workers, and 27 per cent discussing migrant workers. Fairclough (1992) has identified that indirect speech within texts can be ambivalent in meaning, therefore according some sex workers the ability to have their comments reported more directly further privileges them over others. Hallgrimsdottir et al (2006, p 267) writes: '[e]ssentially, in the absence of any lived interaction with the sex industry, media texts are key cultural sites at which the stigmas of sex work are produced and consumed by the majority of citizens'. In this instance, media texts simultaneously function to shore up stigma against sex workers not able to make themselves invisible (street-based sex workers, for example), but also permit a degree of mitigation for agency and independent workers. Their ability to shape media discourses about sex work, even if to a small degree, are often possible precisely *because* media coverage will remain the only interaction most of the general public will have with their work personas. Indoor workers are not speaking into a vacuum of ideas about what their work entails, but nor are they seeking to establish a public profile in competition with a more *literally* public profile.

The 'making invisible' of low-volume, indoor sex workers is frequently buttressed by descriptions of their surroundings which explicitly draw similarities between paid sex and personal sexual encounters, obscuring the labour carried out by erasing the nature of brothels as workplaces. One of the analysed texts describes a newly opened agency as having 'luxurious bed linen' and being designed to feel, for clients, 'like their mistress's bedroom', while another compares the premises of an agency to an expensive hotel room (*Dominion Post*, 2012; TVNZ, 2015). With media texts being a key site at which notions of sex work are established and contested, particularly under a model of decriminalisation where the power to determine 'acceptable' and 'unacceptable' forms of sex work no longer resides with the courts, these descriptions serve to normalise small sectors of the industry through comparisons with domestic settings. These scene-setting elements may establish a new or alternate visual language of sex work – one which, as much as possible, is stripped of associations with labour.

Embedded in these descriptions of agency workers is an emphasis on the perceived exclusivity of their services; this further functions both to make their work appear as close as possible to the sexual behaviour of non-sex workers and to distinguish them from other sectors of the industry. Descriptions of the physical environment of brothels describe them looking untouched, or like a hotel room; this creates a discursive linkage to the workers who use them, suggesting a link between a smaller volume of clients and 'cleanliness' (Cooke, 2012; TVNZ, 2015). Scoular (2004) writes that many representations of sex workers, in attempting to represent the worker as an acceptable subject, may go to significant lengths to emphasise the normative aspects of their lives. The consequence of this is to inadvertently reinforce normative ideas about sexuality and desire. Even discourses that aim to normalise sex work and make it more acceptable still presume that a form which results in workers seeing fewer clients or having less actual sexual contact with them is preferable. Disguising the nature and frequency of the work is critical to producing the acceptability of agency and independent sex workers.

While most of the analysed texts are content to leave the audience to infer the intended linkage between 'clean linen' and the sex workers profiled, one claimed that:

> 'In most high-end agencies, women who have previously worked as escorts in "low class" establishments or on the street will be turned away. The aim in doing this is to ensure the safety of everyone involved by further removing the risk of STI [sexually transmitted infection].' (Bones, 2015)

The 'everyone' referred to in the text clearly does not include women who have worked in other sectors of the industry (or their clients), and the implication here is that they do not deserve the safety presumed to be afforded by working for a low-volume agency. Additionally, the phrasing here situates some sectors of the industry as unclean, a discursive linkage back to the 'clean linen' discussed in other texts. The phrasing also suggests a permanent stain caused by working in higher volume settings – STIs are spoken of as though they are all incurable, leaving the worker as a permanent risk to acceptable (respectable) workers and clients.

Later in this text the author refers to high-volume workplaces as 'low class'. In the first occurrence the phrase is located inside quotation marks, but without attributing this descriptor to any of the interviewees in the text. The author also claims that 'lower-class agencies tend to accept anyone', indicating that a sense of financial and moral value is attached to agency workers (Bones, 2015). Working for an agency, it is suggested, puts a worker in a position of having been carefully selected based on undefined (but explicitly classed) criteria, and therefore less likely to have an STI. This also positions a worker's STI status as a moral judgement about their character and value, further stigmatising STI infection. This is reflective of Hallgrimsdottir et al's (2006) work, which identifies sex workers as frequently being portrayed as a vector of literal or moral contagion, although in this case there is evidence that the moral and literal senses are collapsed together, with each standing in for the other in discourse.

Financial justifications

One way that low-volume work is further justified as a 'correct' or 'logical' choice is through financial comparisons between sectors. Two of the analysed articles give a specific financial comparison between agency and high-volume work, with Catherine Healy, the National Coordinator of NZPC, quoted as saying that sex workers earn between NZ$60 and NZ$300 for an hour of work and an independent sex worker describing brothel workers getting 'about half' of a fee of NZ$160-NZ$220 (*Dominion Post*, 2012; Meadows, 2014). The earnings (real or potential) of agency workers are highlighted by owners and managers in five of the analysed texts, and mentioned by the writer or by interviewed sex workers in a further four. Sarah, the owner of The Bedroom, explains that sex workers keep 60 per cent of what a client pays, and Brennan, owner of Funhouse and in one text described as the 'highest paid dominatrix in the country', says that her staff made half of the hourly fee of NZ$320 – NZ$380, adding 'the girls have no outgoings apart from tax and ACC'[3] and 'if you broke it down, actually the girls are probably getting 70%' (Meadows, 2014; Hewitson, 2015). Brennan's comments elide the other outgoings associated with being an independently contracted sex worker: clothing, make-up, grooming expenses, maintaining a business phone, and in some cases paying for an accountant. Her comment disguises the effortful labour required to market oneself as a successful, professional sex worker: the clothing and grooming required in order to deliver the correct impression of heteronormative femininity to appeal to male clients, and the literal and emotional labour involved in performing beauty (Sanders, 2005; Rivers-Moore, 2013).

Financial success (or the appearance thereof) here is used as a stand-in for respectability and class position. The extensive justification of sex work through the financial benefits gained by sex workers suggests that the work can only be made acceptable by the material gains made, and this is often accented by characterising sex workers as funding their tertiary studies with sex work. This is similar to the trend identified by Rivers-Moore (2010, p 276) of sex work being made acceptable by stressing the 'ideally short term' tenure of workers in the industry. This emphasis on the high prices commanded by agency and independent workers may also constitute a perceived distancing from the moral and literal contagion discourses attached to higher volume workers, with a key site of stigma being the notion of services which are supplied indiscriminately (Pheterson, 1993). The implicit, and in some cases explicit, message in these texts is that agency workers' services are accessed by relatively few clients.

This appeal to the scarcity value of their services positions them as a luxury 'product', but must also be considered within the context of perceptions of promiscuity as defiling, as seen in the presumption, reported by Bones (2015), that workers who have engaged in high-volume work are permanently unsuitable for work in higher priced agencies. In one text the owner of Bon Ton, an agency which at the time charged NZ$500 per hour, compares 'lower-end' brothels where 'anyone can walk in off the streets' to 'a zoo', claiming she can tell when 'coarse' clients who call Bon Ton are used to these brothels. She adds that workers who do not respect themselves will not be respected by clients, and concludes by noting that the sexual labour of any given hour with a client is likely to be around ten minutes (McAllen, 2015).

The owner's comments here, again, position the acceptability of agency workers through explicit comparison with higher-volume workers with a high degree of specificity. The implication is that workers who offer services to 'anyone' do not respect themselves. This line of commentary is echoed in a text where Funhouse workers are described as 'high class escorts' who can 'pick and choose' which client to see, unlike street-based sex workers (McCarthy, 2015). This comment also carries the uncomfortable suggestion that a sex worker who does not 'respect [herself]', by working at the 'wrong kind' of brothel or on the street, should expect clients to behave poorly. Research carried out post decriminalisation has indicated that violence is still an issue for sex workers, although indoor workers, both managed and private, are more likely to be able to decline a particular client than they were before the law change (Abel et al, 2007). There are also indications that, in some instances, police may understand disputes with clients – including refusal to pay for services or to leave when asked – as breaches of contract, not criminal acts (Armstrong, 2017). Framing of disrespectful, violent or abusive behaviour by clients as virtually certain to occur in some sectors of the industry reproduces a narrative in which violence against sex workers is unfortunate but inevitable, and in which sex workers are considered partially to blame (Farvid and Glass, 2014).

Bon Ton's owner goes on to suggest that clients in higher-volume brothels treat sex workers like a 'piece of meat' (McCarthy, 2015). This language dehumanises brothel workers by suggesting their humanity is stripped via their interactions with 'coarse' clientele. Finally, the owner's comments about the small fraction of client-facing time spent engaged in sex acts functions to reify workers at her agency as being more respectable than other workers – a reassurance to clients reading this text that they do not have to 'share' their provider with (too many) other men, and particularly not men of a lower class bracket – indicated here by the use of 'anyone' and 'coarse'.

Advertorial frames

The use of the class position of their clientele as a means of distinguishing who is a respectable or acceptable sex worker has been identified elsewhere, although this has been documented primarily as being carried out by workers in their own identity formation. Carrier-Moisan (2015, p 500) reports Brazilian sex workers using foreign clients 'in their self-making process', to support claims about what sort of sex worker they were, leveraging clients' respectability and class position to support their own. While this is one function of this discursive theme within the analysed texts, this narrative contributes to at least two further tasks (which will be discussed in this chapter). One is to allow for potential clients to self-identify with the descriptions of the men who use the services of agency and independent workers. The other is to carry out some of the scaffolding work of allowing workers to express their occupation as an enthusiastic choice, and to further embed discourses of acceptability through it being genuinely enjoyable.

These two purposes function synergistically: the descriptions of what constitutes an ideal (or actual) client of an agency interpellate men who consider themselves discerning, considerate and respectful and suggests to them the possibility of their being a client-type man. Simultaneously, the emphasis on the respectability of workers and their enthusiastic choice to engage in sex work bolster these identifications for potential clients, as they are constituted as considerate of workers' feelings by choosing workers who have, or sufficiently perform, enthusiasm for their work. The PRA restricts where commercial sexual services may be advertised to clients: Section 11 prohibits advertising on television, radio, or in newspapers (except in classified ads). Brothels, agencies, and independent workers are therefore restricted in how they can market themselves to potential clientele who are not specifically seeking their services. The use of mass media interviews as a form of advertising by sex workers in New Zealand has been identified before (Fitzgerald and Abel, 2010). Grant (2014) has specifically argued that there is a frequent misunderstanding of advertorial media as being an accurate depiction of the sex industry.

An advertorial framing is prominent in the analysed texts, and occurs in multiple ways. As mentioned earlier, many texts specifically mention the discreet nature of the workplaces. A total of six include descriptions of the surroundings of the physical work spaces, emphasising their distance from visual markers of sex work more associated with street-based sex workers and normalising them through comparisons to private bedrooms and hotels (Cooke, 2012; *Dominion Post*, 2012; Meadows, 2014; Chang, 2015; Bones, 2015; TVNZ, 2015). Workers are also described in ways that highlight their adherence to conventional forms of femininity, which Carrier-Moisan (2015, p 502) describes as a 'cultural resource and form of embodied capital' that must be considered in the context of class and race. Although it is seldom addressed directly – a notable exception being where an interviewer on Radio New Zealand points out to Brennan that her workers 'fit a media ideal' of a dress size six to eight – the form of femininity presented by workers in the most frequently profiled agencies is materially unattainable to many workers (McCarthy, 2015; Budgeon, 2015). It emphasises thinness, youth, whiteness (or the ability to market oneself as Pākehā/white), and class privilege (or, again, the ability to successfully produce the impression of belonging to a middle- or upper-class background). Sanders (2005, p 323) explains this deliberate creation of a manufactured work persona by sex workers as 'exploiting the male customers' desire for a stereotypical display of female sexuality' and 'a calculated response made by sex workers to capitalize on their own sexuality and the cultural ideals of the client'.

Sanders' description was based largely on manufactured identity as it occurred in direct interactions with clients, while the manufactured identities outlined here suggest very similar creation occurs in media discourses, intended to attract clients (and establish a profile for the agencies mentioned). Given the legal environment at play this approach may be more feasible under a model of decriminalisation – the agencies can be named, and to a degree so can individual workers, along with specific descriptions of services offered, without fear of police attention as a result. Grant (2014, p 9) discusses the ways in which prostitution is criminalised as a 'talking crime', where soliciting or negotiating specific acts or sums is a behaviour that is made illegal. Decriminalisation removes that concern, potentially making space for the advertorial function of media coverage to be realised more explicitly.

Carrier-Moisan (2015) has identified the duality of workers in Brazil performing both hypersexuality and respectability concurrently to distinguish themselves from other sex workers. This production is frequently accomplished in part by emphasising that they experience an authentic connection with their clients. In addition to describing workers adhering to hyperfemininity, many of the analysed media texts also position workers as empowered by their choice to engage in sex work, which is done, in part, to further advertorial ends behind such coverage.

Bones (2015) writes: '… women get to work in safe, respectful workplaces where they can feel comfortable. And the best part? The girls call the shots' and elsewhere in the text says '[t]here is no shame in embracing your own sexuality, and in the world of sex workers, this is respected'. An interview with Bella, a worker at Bon Ton, describes her sitting 'on a couch in the tiled office of Bon Ton founder, Jennifer Souness. The two sip rosé. A large mood board with pinned images and buzzwords takes up one wall' and later quotes her saying 'with confidence' that '"I earn good money in my daytime job. I don't need to do this; I choose to do this"' (Olds, 2016). The advertorial function here is positioning the workers as motivated by deriving pleasure from their work as much, or more, than by the financial rewards. This has the potential to be viewed by clients, or prospective clients, as an indicator that the authentic connection promised by advertising copy is, indeed, *authentic*.

Enjoyment and authenticity

An emphasis on the enjoyment of the work is a common theme throughout news media coverage of agencies, often coupled with a comment that the work (and, by extension, the specific work conditions) has been deliberately chosen. The owner of Funhouse describes her workers as "genuinely keen to work" in one interview, and tells another journalist that her staff "really, really enjoy it. And it's not obviously just about the sex but they all enjoy sex" (Meadows, 2014; McCarthy, 2015). In a third text, she speaks both for herself as a dominatrix and for her staff, saying "we love what we do" (Cooke, 2012). In a fourth text, a worker is described as feeling a 'thrill of anticipation' when a client arrives, while another characterises her job as involving 'intimate encounters with nice men' (*Dominion Post*, 2012). Elsewhere a dominatrix emphasises "the love of actually doing it" as being a key contributor to what makes her good at her job, and in yet another text the author says 'a man can be treated to a woman who enjoys his deepest fantasies', and adds that women tend to work at agencies which 'reflect their own areas of interest' (McCarthy, 2015; Bones, 2015). Such constructions of the interactions with clients as enjoyable may have the effect of positioning work-sex as pleasurable, normalising it by implicitly drawing comparisons with the sexual contact workers have in their private lives, and possibly pre-emptively addressing stereotypes of sex work as psychologically risky (Farvid and Glass, 2014). Combined with the identified emphasis on the limited number of clients seen by agency workers, this narrative functions to normalise the sexualities and desires of sex workers (Scoular, 2004).

Maher et al (2012)[4] have noted that indoor sex workers in a regulated environment repeatedly emphasised that the sex they had at work was unrelated to their personal sexual desires and wants. They additionally noted that, within regulatory spaces, an excessive focus on intimacy and heterosexual sex can diminish an ability to discuss working rights and conditions. In the analysed texts, a focus on genuine enjoyment of work-sex and comparisons being drawn between personal life and work, as in the explicit linkage of 'areas of interest', foreclose the possibility of discussing dissatisfaction or bad experiences at work as a labour issue. In this framing it is a question of sexual compatibility, or a lack of 'fit', magnifying the relationship between client and worker, and minimising the one between a worker and their manager. Positioning work-sex as analogous to private sexual contact suggests the solutions are those that would be appropriate in a relationship, rather than in a workplace, and imply the existence of non-fiscal rewards.

Conclusion

This chapter has discussed the recurring narratives which exist in news media coverage of low-volume indoor sex work in New Zealand under decriminalisation. The narratives are indicative of the kind of conditions which are attached to acceptability as a sex worker, in particular a convincing performance of choice and enjoyment, and a combination of financial success and class position presented as evidence of respectability by workers and brothel management. McRobbie (2009) discusses how, within a neoliberal framework, women's earning potential and success are presented as though based on a meritocracy: pushing the ideal of individual exceptionalism, rather than considering the structural inequalities that feminism sought to change. This framework posits that the onus is on the individual to make the 'right choice', ignoring the structural inequalities which make such choices materially accessible. McRobbie (2009, pp 57–8) also notes that '… [n]owadays the young woman's success seems to promise economic prosperity on the basis of her enthusiasm for work'. This is exemplified in the presentation of agency sex workers as exceptional and acceptable through their active choice to engage in the work because of the pleasure they derive from it, with the economic benefits presented as a further justification but an almost incidental reward.

Workers are rewarded with acceptability for a successful and seemingly enthusiastic performance of heterosexual femininity – this performance is monitored by external forces, both closely by their managers (who denigrate other workers as lacking in self-respect) and more broadly by media coverage. Gill (2007a) identified the role which media coverage plays in surveilling femininity, and the ways that such surveillance is aided by other women. While McRobbie (2009) discusses enthusiasm for work, and Gill (2007a) analyses adherence to conventional modes of bodily femininity being communicated in language of choice and empowerment, the acceptable sex worker is obliged to perform both of these simultaneously. The enthusiasm for one is enthusiasm for the other, a sleight of hand achieved by making the work invisible as effortful labour and instead conflated with heterosexual femininity put to work in a way which delivers financial and confidence-boosting benefits to the workers. The correct 'choice' to adhere to conventional femininities (here meaning also being most or all of young, white, thin, cisgender and therefore able to secure employment with an agency) in this instance is rewarded with greater tolerance, but only insofar as the choice is foregrounded and any labour is incidental.

This performance of choice seeks to sanitise the transactional nature of the work by minimising the labour involved, particularly the emotional labour. In identifying evidence of emotional labour within the analysed texts, Hochschild's (1979/2012) seminal text, *The Managed Heart*, is used. Emotional labour, as it is used here, is the work of managing one's own emotional state or display, carried out for or in expectation of payment. Hochschild (2012) notes that in roles which involve direct contact with clients '[s]eeming to 'love the job' becomes part of the job itself' (p 5). Although it is not carried out in direct contact with clients, the work of presenting a seemingly authentic enjoyment of client-interactions *does* constitute emotional labour, in the sense that it is work done in expectation of being paid. This is not, to be clear, to suggest that all comments from sex workers about their enjoyment or satisfaction with the work are false or constructed, but rather that their comments are made with a self-conscious knowledge of the likely audience (Agustín, 2004).

As well as potential clients, the majority of this audience will be the general public, many of whom will (as noted earlier in this chapter) otherwise have little to no contact with the sex industry. As discussed earlier, the acceptability and respectability of agency work is often established through comparisons with other sectors of the industry. The differences between agency work and existing negative narratives and stereotypes about sex workers are highlighted. This is frequently achieved through discussions of the visual differences between their workplaces and street-based sex work, and by focusing on aspects of high-volume work presumed to be unpleasant or demeaning which agency work dispenses with. Emphasising the sincere enjoyment of the work also serves this purpose: it distinguishes the work, by making it not-work. The acceptability of workers is contingent on their willingness to obscure the labour they do – sex work is made palatable by eliding the transaction. This, however, is its own form of effortful labour, carried out for an audience as well as for individual clients and conducted with the kind of self-monitoring of acceptably feminine behaviour which Gill (2007b) characterises as a hallmark of neoliberal post-feminism.

This performance of choice is self-conscious of presenting sex work as the 'right' choice, rather than as a choice without an inherent moral value attached to it, and as particular ways of doing sex work as more correct and defensible. The comment from Bon Ton's owner, that workers in high-volume brothels lack self-respect, is one example of what this can look like in discourse. Sex work is made exceptional through the requirement that workers enjoy their work. Grant (2014, pp 93–4) writes: '[s]ex workers, more than any other, are expected to justify their labor as a choice, as if the choice to engage in a form of labor is what makes that labor legitimate'.

The advertorial nature of the texts is certainly not the only function they serve, and there is evidence that the analysed coverage does also aim to destigmatise the industry, but this is often done at the expense of other sectors. The most stigmatised workers are usually those with fewer options about where or how to work. The 'choice' to work at low-volume agencies is limited to a relatively small proportion of workers – there are structural issues which restrict the ability of many people to make this choice, if they do not fit the aesthetic and class conditions necessary to fulfil the stipulations of these agencies (McRobbie, 2009; Budgeon, 2015). Additionally, this mode of working (on call, with a high degree of emotional work and payments for periods of time, not per act) may not be the preferred mode of working for all workers.

The exceptionalising of the work in this way may make it more difficult for sex workers to publicly speak about sex work as labour and discuss labour rights issues, even within a decriminalised industry. If sex work can only be accepted when it is enjoyed, this creates a bind in which workers risk what acceptability they have by expressing dissatisfaction with their work conditions. Voicing such complaints may also, though it may not be expressed so bluntly, prompt questions about why they have not made a better 'choice' about where to work. Further, the advertorial nature of coverage of agency workers creates a slippage between a version of the industry designed for the eyes of clients and a version which reflects the realities of the work. The advertorial possibilities allowed by decriminalisation potentially heighten the conflation of these two forms of representation. While decriminalisation creates the conditions for sex work as a socially acceptable profession, the treatment of it in media coverage, by turns sanitised and titillating, indicates acceptance is still conditional at best.

Notes

[1] Within this chapter, the terms 'low-volume' and 'high-volume' are used to distinguish between the number of clients an individual worker could potentially see during a day or week. Many higher priced agencies emphasise the low-volume nature of their business, as explored elsewhere in this chapter; meanwhile the terminology high-volume refers more to brothel or parlour-style environments where there is the potential for a worker to see more clients during a shift, although, depending on the relative busyness of an establishment, this may not always be the reality.
[2] Many of the street-based sex workers discussed in the texts were transgender women and some of the analysed texts misgendered them, used transphobic slurs, or described them using modifiers like 'bullying' (Easterbrook-Smith, 2018). Coverage of migrant sex workers often described them as 'illegal', as in 'illegal prostitutes'.
[3] ACC is the Accident Compensation Commission, a government run workers' compensation scheme into which all workers are required to pay a proportion of their earnings in exchange for cover for accidental injury.
[4] Maher et al's research related to workers in Australia.

References

Abel, G. (2014) 'A decade of decriminalization: Sex work "down under" but not underground', *Criminology and Criminal Justice*, 14(5): 580–92.

Abel, G., Fitzgerald, L. & Brunton, C. (2007) *The Impact of the Prostitution Reform Act on the Health and Safety Practices of Sex Workers: Report to the Prostitution Law Review Committee,* Christchurch: University of Otago. Available at: https://www.otago.ac.nz/christchurch/otago018607.pdf.

Agustín, L. (2004) 'Alternate ethics, or: Telling lies to researchers', *Research for Sex Work*, 6–7.

Armstrong, L. (2016) '"Who's the slut, who's the whore?": Street harassment in the workplace among female sex workers in New Zealand', *Feminist Criminology*, 11(3): 285–303.

Armstrong, L. (2017) 'From law enforcement to protection? Interactions between Sex workers and police in a decriminalised street-based sex industry', *British Journal of Criminology*, 57(3): 570–88.

Bernstein, E. (2007) *Temporarily Yours: Intimacy, authenticity, and the commerce of sex*, Chicago: University of Chicago Press.

Bones, B. (2015) 'The working girls class', Salient. Available at: http://salient.org.nz/2015/08/the-working-girls-class/.

Budgeon, S. (2015) 'Individualized femininity and feminist politics of choice', *European Journal of Women's Studies*, 22(3): 303–18.

Carrier-Moisan, M-E. (2015) '"Putting femininity to work": Negotiating hypersexuality and respectability in sex tourism, Brazil', *Sexualities*, 18(4): 499–518.

Chang, J. (2015) 'Trick or tweet - How the NZ sex industry is embracing hi-tech', Idealog. Available at: http://idealog.co.nz/tech/2015/07/trick-or-tweet.

Cooke, M. (2012) 'Sex, conditions safer but prostitute stigma remains', *The Dominion Post*. Available at: http://www.stuff.co.nz/national/6292753/Sex-conditions-safer-but-prostitute-stigma-remains.

Dominion Post (2011) 'School's cash went on sex and high living', *The Dominion Post*. Available at: http://www.stuff.co.nz/dominion-post/news/5972521/Schools-cash-went-on-sex-and-high-living.

Dominion Post (2012) 'High-fliers who turn to escorting', Capital Life. Available at: http://www.stuff.co.nz/dominion-post/capital-life/7677129/High-fliers-who-turn-to-escorting.

Easterbrook-Smith, G. (2018) '"Illicit drive-through sex", "migrant prostitutes", and "highly educated escorts": Productions of "acceptable" sex work in New Zealand news media 2010–2016', PhD thesis, Victoria University of Wellington.

Fairclough, N. (1992) 'Intertextuality in critical discourse analysis', *Linguistics and Education*, 4(3): 269–93.

Farvid, P. & Glass, L. (2014) '"It isn't prostitution as you normally think of it. It's survival sex": Media representations of adult and child prostitution in New Zealand', *Women's Studies Journal*, 28(1): 47–67.

Fitzgerald, L. & Abel, G. (2010) 'The media and the Prostitution Reform Act', in G. Abel, L. Fitzgerald, C. Healy & A. Taylor (eds) *Taking the Crime Out of Sex Work: New Zealand sex workers' fight for decriminalisation*, Bristol: Policy Press, pp 197–216.

Gill, R. (2007a) 'Postfeminist media culture: Elements of a sensibility', *European Journal of Cultural Studies*, 10(2): 147–66.

Gill, R. (2007b) *Gender and the media*, Cambridge: Polity Press.

Grant, M. (2014) *Playing the Whore: The work of sex work*, London & New York: Verso Books.

Hallgrimsdottir, H. K., Phillips, R. & Benoit, C. (2006) 'Fallen women and rescued girls: Social stigma and media narratives of the sex industry in Victoria, B.C., from 1980 to 2005', *Canadian Review of Sociology/Revue Canadienne de Sociologie*, 43(3): 265–80.

Ham, J. & Gerard, A. (2014) 'Strategic in/visibility: Does agency make sex workers invisible?', *Criminology & Criminal Justice*, 14(3): 298–313.

Henry, P. (2014) 'Sex industry's revolutionary madam?', The Paul Henry Show, Newshub. Available at: http://www.newshub.co.nz/tvshows/paulhenryshow/sex-industrys-revolutionary-madam-2014100110#ixzz3z67eBdcB.

Hewitson, M. (2015) 'Michele Hewitson interview: Mary Brennan', *New Zealand Herald*. Available at: http://www.nzherald.co.nz/lifestyle/news/article.cfm?c_id=6&objectid=11478963.

Hochschild, A. (2012) *The Managed Heart: Commercialization of human feeling* (1st ed), Berkeley: University of California Press.

Maher, J., Pickering, S. & Gerard, A. (2012) 'Privileging work not sex: Flexibility and employment in the sexual services industry', *The Sociological Review*, 60(4): 654–75.

McAllen, J. (2015) 'Behind the red lights of New Zealand's brothels', *Sunday Star Times*. Available at: http://www.stuff.co.nz/life-style/love-sex/68565738/Behind-the-red-lights-of-New-Zealands-brothels.

McCarthy, N. (2015) 'Mary Brennan: Domination and submission', Saturday Morning, Radio NZ. Available at: http://www.radionz.co.nz/audio/player?audio_id=201762029.

McRobbie, A. (2009) *The Aftermath of Feminism: Gender, culture and social change*, Los Angeles/London: Sage.

Meadows, R. (2014) 'Sex industry doing it tough', *Stuff.* Available at: http://www.stuff.co.nz/business/small-business/10665008/Sex-industry-doing-it-tough.

Olds, J. (2016) 'The rules of the game', *Stuff.* Available at: http://www.stuff.co.nz/business/77300913/The-rules-of-the-game-Did-New-Zealand-get-its-prostitution-laws-right.

O'Neill, M., Campbell, R., Hubbard, P., Pitcher, J. & Scoular, J. (2008) 'Living with the other: Street sex work, contingent communities and degrees of tolerance', *Crime, Media, Culture: An international journal*, 4(1): 73–93.

Pheterson, G. (1993) 'The whore stigma: Female dishonor and male unworthiness', *Social Text*, (37): 39–64.

Rivers-Moore, M. (2010) 'But the kids are okay: motherhood, consumption and sex work in neo-liberal Latin America', *The British Journal of Sociology*, 61(4): 716–36.

Rivers-Moore, M. (2013) 'Affective sex: Beauty, race and nation in the sex industry', *Feminist Theory*, 14(2): 153–69.

Sanders, T. (2005) ' "It's just acting": Sex workers' strategies for capitalizing on sexuality', *Gender, Work & Organization*, 12(4): 319–42.

Scoular, J. (2004) 'The "subject" of prostitution: Interpreting the discursive, symbolic and material position of sex/work in feminist theory', *Feminist Theory*, 5(3): 343–56.

Scoular, J. (2010) 'What's law got to do with it? How and why law matters in the regulation of sex work', *Journal of Law and Society*, 37(1): 12–39.

Trengrove, S. (2014) 'On the job', *Salient.* Available at: http://salient.org.nz/2014/04/on-the-job/.

TVNZ (2015) 'Meet the pro dominatrix', *Seven Sharp.* Available at: http://tvnz.co.nz/seven-sharp/meet-pro-dominatrix-i-provide-stress-relief-s-simple-video-6356411.

Van Brunschot, E. G., Sydie, R. A. & Krull, C. (2000) 'Images of prostitution', *Women & Criminal Justice*, 10(4): 47–72.

8

The Disclosure Dilemma: Stigma and Talking About Sex Work in the Decriminalised Context

Lynzi Armstrong and Cherida Fraser

Introduction

Sex workers are widely regarded as a population subject to considerable stigma (Sanders, 2016; Weitzer, 2018; Benoit et al, 2018). Sex work stigma is complex and multifaceted and, while it is rooted in patriarchal history, it is also deeply connected to prostitution laws. The laws surrounding sex work influence stigma by reflecting and reproducing a distinct moral message about the sale and purchase of sexual services. For example, when sex workers are criminalised, the societal message is that sex workers are 'bad' people, who must be punished for their behaviour – criminalisation is therefore widely considered to fuel stigma (Vanwesenbeeck, 2017). On the other hand, when their clients are criminalised, sex workers are defined as passive victims of gendered violence who must be saved by eliminating demand for their services (Levy and Jakobsson, 2014). In defining sex workers as passive victims who have no agency and their clients as dangerous predators, legislative models which focus explicitly on the criminalisation of clients also exacerbate stigma by positioning sex work as a form of exploitation. Thus, in order to make inroads into eroding sex work stigma, it is reasonable to suggest that sex work must be recognised as a form of labour. The decriminalised framework in New Zealand offers a useful case study through which to explore this, since sex workers can work without the threat of either they or their clients being criminalised.

Measuring stigma in any context is challenging, since stigma is a nebulous concept and can manifest in a multitude of ways. One very telling indicator of stigma, however, is the extent to which sex workers feel they can be open about talking about their work with others in their lives, and their experiences of this. It is well-documented that stigma and criminalisation combined mean that sex workers often live 'double lives' and manage an ongoing dilemma of restricting who knows about their work (Benoit et al, 2019). But to what extent does decriminalisation impact the disclosure dilemma, and the responses sex workers receive when telling others about their work?

Drawing on in-depth interviews with 20 sex workers in New Zealand, in this chapter we explore the experiences of sex workers telling close friends and family about their work, the emotional labour of deciding who to tell, and managing responses to these disclosures. We consider the extent to which the decriminalisation of sex work may help to foster an environment in which it is easier and more comfortable for sex workers to talk about their work with people in their lives. To conclude, we discuss the significance of participants' experiences in New Zealand's decriminalised context, and how this contributes to existing knowledge on stigma and sex work.

Stigma and sex work

It is commonly accepted that sex workers manage stigma in the course of their work, though only a small number of published studies have examined this in-depth (Koken et al, 2004; Fick, 2005; Scambler, 2007; Sallmann, 2010; Wong et al, 2011; Bruckert, 2012; Benoit et al, 2018). The concept of 'stigma' was famously explored by Erving Goffman (1963); he described the 'spoiled identities' of the stigmatised. Such individuals, Goffman argued, possessed attributes that were considered deviant and deeply discrediting by the majority population, whom he termed 'normals'. Since Goffman's seminal work in this area, stigma theory and research has evolved to envisage stigma beyond the individual level, conceptualising it as a social, cultural and structural process. Link and Phelan (2014), for example, define stigma as a form of power used by dominant groups to repress minority groups. As such, stigma may be understood, not as something that is necessarily internalised by stigmatised people, but as something that is imposed on them through societal structures in the form of laws and policies.

The stigma associated with sex workers has a long history and is a legacy of patriarchal norms that defined women who flaunted their sexuality as deviant and 'bad' (Armstrong, 2018). The legacy of patriarchy has ensured that, in the present day, sex work remains highly stigmatised and is often associated with criminality and vulnerability (Putnis and Burr, 2019). The stigma associated with sex work means that there are significant barriers to sex workers talking about their work, both to those they are close to and to external agencies, such as police and medical professionals along with landlords, accountants and employers outside the sex industry.

Stigma, sex work and the law

The stigma that sex workers manage has been observed across diverse legislative contexts, particularly in jurisdictions where sex workers are subject to varying degrees of criminalisation. The laws which pertain to sex work both reflect and reproduce dominant attitudes towards the sex industry and those involved in it (Wong et al, 2011). Thus, as previously noted, it is thought that stigma is exacerbated by laws which criminalise sex workers, either directly or indirectly (Krüsi et al, 2014), through defining the sex industry as a shadowy underworld and those within it as deviant and problematic.

Thus, in the context of laws which criminalise either sex workers or third parties (such as clients or managers), sex workers are constructed as either deviant 'others' who threaten moral values or as hapless victims who must be 'saved'. Either way, sex workers are defined as being separate from the rest of society rather than existing within it. Criminalisation also provides a context in which stigma can be more easily enacted, since a criminal conviction leaves an imprint of stigma that has profound and long-lasting impacts. The potential consequences of criminalisation combined with stigma forces sex workers to live 'double lives', carefully compartmentalising their work to minimise risks. Thus, within such contexts, sex workers may be less inclined to tell others about their work due to fear of being judged, ostracised, outed to authorities, or pressured to stop working. For example, research commissioned in 2014 by the Department of Justice in Northern Ireland found that the top three factors about sex work that participants disliked were having to lie about what they did, having to hide their work, and the constant worry about friends and/or family members finding out about it. This was highlighted by over a third of participants and outnumbered those who worried about violence from clients (Huschke, 2017). The emotional labour that this identity and information management necessitates clearly takes a toll on sex workers and can be considered one of the harms of the legislative framework in place.

The relationship between stigma and sex work laws is arguably cyclical in nature. The laws which criminalise sex workers or their clients and/or other third parties are a consequence of stigma and a contributor to it. As Altink et al (2017) note:

> Stigma, deliberately and surreptitiously, shapes laws, regulations, practices, institutions and policies, it undermines the effectiveness and fairness of the regulation of prostitution, and, in general, it results in the social marginalisation of sex workers. (Altink et al, 2017, p 29)

The law is therefore an important tool for those who oppose sex work and are invested in the maintenance of stigma. Specifically, criminalisation enables stigma to be weaponised by those who wish to eradicate the sex industry. As such, Sanders argues that to reduce stigma there must be an undoing of the laws that criminalise sex work (Sanders, 2016).

The question of whether decriminalisation can help to break the cycle of stigma is therefore an important one, particularly since stigma is widely recognised as a social determinant of health (Hatzenbuehler, 2016). As discussed in earlier chapters, the rationale for passing the Prostitution Reform Act (PRA) 2003 was to better serve the occupational health and safety of sex workers – an explicit recognition that criminalisation was causing harm (Abel et al, 2007). If New Zealand is committed to reducing the harms that can occur in the context of sex work, then a desire to reduce stigma should logically follow decriminalisation. Research conducted in the immediate aftermath of the passing of the PRA indicated that sex workers continued to manage stigma (Abel and Fitzgerald, 2010). However, more than 15 years have now passed since sex work was decriminalised and it is important to continue to gauge how stigma is being experienced by sex workers in the context of decriminalisation. While an absence of published comparative studies means that comparisons across legislative frameworks are not possible, there is still much that can be learned about sex worker's experiences in the current context.

Methods

The research that forms the basis of this chapter was conducted between January and May 2018. The aim of the research was to explore, through qualitative interviews, sex worker's experiences and perceptions of stigma and discrimination in the context of decriminalisation in New Zealand. Ethical approval to conduct the research was granted by Victoria University of Wellington Human Ethics Committee. A total of 20 interviews were conducted with sex workers in Wellington (n=14), Auckland (n=4) and Rotorua (n=2). Fourteen participants were cisgender women, three were cisgender men and three were transgender or gender diverse. Most of the participants (n=17) worked indoors, either in managed brothels or independently. Most participants were born in New Zealand – ten identified their main ethnicity as New Zealand European, seven as Māori, one was Australian and two were from other countries in the Global South. Most of the participants had begun sex work after decriminalisation, though five participants had worked in the industry before the law changed in 2003.

Interviews were conducted in a private location – either in the offices of NZPC, the participant's home or their incall premises. The interviews lasted an average of approximately an hour, though the shortest interview was 32 minutes and two interviews were over two hours. The interviews explored the participants' experience of getting into sex work, their perceptions of media depictions of sex workers, experiences of telling others about their work, how they felt about different types of sex work and sex workers, and their perceptions of the status of sex workers in the context of decriminalisation. The interviews were recorded with the participants' consent, transcribed verbatim and participants who requested a copy of their transcript had the opportunity to comment on and request edits to it. Three participants requested amendments to their transcript to remove or disguise information that they were concerned could be potentially identifying. All names used in the research are pseudonyms and participants were given the opportunity to select their own pseudonym so that they could recognise themselves in the project and have ownership over how they were identified.

Findings

Talking about sex work: an ongoing dilemma

It has long been understood that people who experience stigma for a multitude of reasons are regularly engaged in managing information about their identity which could be used to discredit them (Corrigan and Matthews, 2003; Flett, 2012; Quinn and Earnshaw, 2013; Itzhaky and Kissil, 2015; Capell et al, 2016; Lynch and Rodell, 2018). In his famous 1963 text, Goffman reflected on this noting 'to tell or not to tell; to let on or not to let on; to lie or not to lie; and in each case to whom, how and where', describing the thought process that people grapple with when deciding whether or not to be open about who they are (Goffman, 1963, p 42). Goffman describes the process of concealing a stigmatised identity as 'passing' and 'covering', where individuals at risk of being stigmatised either present in ways which enables them to 'pass' or develop strategies to disguise stigmatising physical attributes. Previous research has demonstrated how sex workers employ numerous strategies to conceal their sex worker identity (Wong et al, 2011). As such, in common with other stigmatised populations, they face complex decisions about how to manage their level of 'outness' (Chaudoir and Quinn, 2010).

The issue of outness was discussed at length in interviews and all participants managed an ongoing dilemma of who they told about their work, varying in their degree of openness in their everyday lives. Elesei, for example, said that he had chosen to be completely open about his sex work because he preferred to "cut the head off the snake" instead of having to worry about the possibility of people inadvertently finding out. He explained:

> 'Everyone knows that I work. I made a point when I became an escort ... I just said, "Well, I don't want my mum to hear from anyone else that I'm doing it, so I'm going to tell her myself" ... I was very open about what I did at art school because I knew that gossip got around and eventually they'd find out. So, I just thought, "Well, let's just cut the head off the snake and get straight down to it" and just let them all know ... because once they know what can they do?' (Elesei)

Elesei's decision to be open about his work therefore appeared to represent a resistance strategy through which he refused to be impacted by stigma by hiding his work from others. Instead, he confronted the possibility that others would gossip about his work and judge him for it by taking control of the information and proactively sharing it with others. Like Elesei, Lucy explained that being "super open" about her work with most people in her life was important to her because she did not want people to find out indirectly and more generally because she described herself as an open person and felt it was "important to talk about stuff and [I] don't want to have secrets".

While Elesei and Lucy described being very open about their work with others, most participants were very selective of who they told about their work. These decisions were not generally driven by shame about being a sex worker but by an awareness of the need to protect oneself from the consequences of stigma. Sophie explained that she wanted to be able to talk openly about her work and was frustrated that she could not:

> 'I'm immensely proud to be a sex worker and I just want to tell everyone. I want to like scream it from the roof tops, you know, but you can't, you just can't talk about it in the way – oh, I can't talk about it in the way that I want to.' (Sophie)

There was clearly an awareness among participants that, once they told someone, there was no going back and there could be consequences. Amy explained that she was aware that some people would not accept her work and "you don't want [them to] gossip behind your back especially when you have a family – you don't want them to say too much in front of your kids". Protecting children from stigma was also prioritised by other participants like Amanda, who explained that she was not ashamed of her work but was "protecting the little people" by containing who knew about it.

Decisions about who to tell were often driven by two factors – having some awareness of the other person's views relating to gender and sexuality (which may indicate how they feel about sex work) and being able to trust that they would keep the information to themselves. Bella explained that her knowledge of her mother's world views and, specifically, her brother's derogatory views on sex work confirmed to her that telling them was not an option, noting:

> 'So my mother's quite mentally ill and has very dysfunctional ideas towards women ... My older brother's actually a doctor ... he's the one who said we're human toilets ... and that, so I haven't told him ... I went to stay at his house and I hadn't seen him for a couple of years and then he launched into this big kind of diatribe against sex workers, and I thought "I won't tell you".' (Bella)

Aroha, a street-based sex worker, explained that she had boundaries around whom she told and where she did this, and an expectation that the people she told would respect her privacy. She explained:

> 'Depending on the situation, depending on who I'm with, I don't mind if I'm asked but I just say, "Don't tell everybody". Just don't go out there and ... start talking about my life. If I'm doing peer support work, I prefer not to talk about it in a café because it's an environment where everybody listens to everybody's business. And everybody likes to twist that business ... However, if I'm approached and asked questions, by all means yes. If I'm comfortable with a person ... like with you, I'm happy to share what I have ... it's knowledge that I've got for you.' (Aroha)

In agreement with Aroha, Bobby noted that trust was important, in addition to her having a sense of the motivation of the person, explaining that she did not want to tell people she felt would just be "nosey". Mark said that he "hummed and haa'd" for a very long time before telling his sister, not because he felt she would have any problem with his work but because he needed to be able to trust that she would "shut up and not tell our mother". Trust and respect were therefore important factors in making decisions about who to tell about their work. For many of those who were interviewed, the process of deciding who to tell was emotionally fraught. Jordan explained:

> 'So, it's what are going to be the unknown consequences? Will this be used against me? ... when telling people [thinking], "Oh my god, what's their reaction going to be?" You just dread them turning around going, "Oh my god, why did you do this, you're so immoral" or just making you feel so small so quickly.' (Jordan)

Similarly, Harley noted:

> 'I guess anxiety comes over you and you start sweating, and you're thinking "Oh no" and your heart's racing, and you're thinking "Oh, is this a good idea or is this not a good idea?" and then, all of a sudden, you just say it, and I guess you expect the worst to come from that person because of the stigma around it.' (Harley)

While telling people was usually planned and emotionally laborious, sometimes it was spontaneous and unexpected. Jordan, for example described how she had ended up telling her mother:

'So, six months into becoming a sex worker my mum rings me up and says she's got something to tell me and she says, "Sit down ... don't get upset" ... and then she says, "Your sister's become a hooker". And I said, "Well, mum, I've been a hooker for six months". And she went "fabulous" and that's how I told my mum.' (Jordan)

While participants almost uniformly resisted the stigma associated with their work and felt they should be able to talk about their work more openly, Kate had a quite different view. She felt it was positive that some people could talk openly with their families about their work, but she explained that this did not apply to her:

'I think it's cool when people do tell their families – that's great – but they're obviously in very different families. You know [their families are] people that will accept that ... my parents would just like freak out, be disgusted, be upset just like, "What did we do wrong? Oh my god, you're on drugs again" ... I think that's a natural thing ... You know like when it comes to sex ... I mean I do agree with the rights ... but ... I don't think that it should be that accepted.' (Kate)

Thus, all participants were clearly impacted by stigma and the issue of whether or not to tell friends and family about their work was, for most, an ongoing dilemma. However, this emotional labour did not cease once this decision was made and the telling had occurred – responding to reactions from those they told required further, extensive, emotional work.

Managing reactions from others

When telling friends and family about their work, participants frequently described having expectations of how the other person would respond, though as discussed earlier in this chapter this was usually accompanied by a degree of uncertainty, which made it a nerve-wracking experience. Elesei explained that his mother's very positive reaction was surprising to him, because he assumed that she would endorse stigmatising ideas. Instead, she felt that what he was doing was an "honest" way of living. He explained:

'"Hey mum, guess what I'm doing?" And [after I told her] she was like, "Oh well, that's more like it". And I was shocked, because I was like, "That's not what you're meant to say". What you're meant to say is, "You shouldn't be doing that work" and all these other things. She was just like, "Oh well, you know, at least you're being honest".' (Elesei)

Conversely, Jordan told a close friend who she had expected would have no problem with her work, but who was shocked. Jordan explained:

'... she was speechless and she threw her hand over her mouth. Like I had just said that I was becoming a Nazi or something. She was horrified at the thought that I was a sex worker, and that's not the reaction I expected her to have. I expected her, you know, to laugh and ... make some sort of cock joke at me, but I didn't expect her to be in such shock.' (Jordan)

Shock and surprise were reactions that several participants described and this was sometimes accompanied by stigmatising ideas about sex workers, couched in 'concern' for their wellbeing. Amanda for example explained that, at first, her father wanted to make sure she was not being "abused by pimps" and Olivia's parents wanted to check that she was not "doing drugs", while Jordan had to reassure her panicking aunt that she was not being "abused" and was doing sex work of her "own will". This meant that they had to engage in yet more emotional labour to reassure the person of their wellbeing. It also meant that they had to tailor the way that they spoke about sex work to these people, lest those they had told deploy 'rescue' mode. For example, Bella explained:

'... you have a day which sucks and then you can't tell people that, because you know that there's already that stigma and they're just waiting to rescue you. So, like in retail you can come home and be like "had a shit day", but if you come home and [say] "I've had a shit day. I had this client who was a dick", people are horrified and see that as trauma. And so it can be exhausting, if you're not in the mood to be this bubbly positive superb sex worker, super great!' (Bella)

The reactions of extreme concern and shock that some participants received meant they, or others, felt that it was easier to address the situation by lying to the person, telling them they had stopped working so that they did not have to deal with the other's emotions. Kate, for example, described feeling "shit" and "no good" when a close friend reacted in this way, and that she had then lied that she had stopped doing sex work, while Jordan recalled her mother having to pretend to her aunt that Jordan had stopped working, because the aunt was not coping with the "thought of her brilliant niece doing sex work". These sex workers therefore had additional emotional labour imposed on them by people who could not cope with the idea of their work because of stigma. And, rather than the other person having to do the emotional labour of working through these ideas, instead the sex worker (or others) felt responsible for protecting them from these emotions.

While shock was in some instances paired with concern, in others it was accompanied by intrigue. Several participants described being subject to many questions after they had told someone about their job. Jordan, for example, described telling a colleague and friend at her bar job that she intended to start working as a sex worker, recalling:

> '... she was all giggly about it and asking lots of questions, and it was more a curiosity thing ... her bouncing questions off me like, "Well, what are you going to do if you don't like it?" Or, "What are you going to do if your vagina gets sore?" ... All these things that I couldn't answer yet because I hadn't started it. I didn't know what I was going to say.' (Jordan)

For Jordan, this instance was not emotionally laborious, but several other participants described the exhaustion of constantly being an educator of others. Bella, for example, described her frustration with people's curiosity, explaining, " I can't be bothered kind of being the provider of all that information and knowledge over sex work". However, fortunately, this was not always the case. Olivia, for instance, described telling two friends who were at first "kind of shocked" and found the information "a bit exciting", asking her lots of questions. But Olivia explained that over time the excitement and intrigue wore off, and her friends did not tend to ask about it any more frequently than they would "any other job".

Although several participants described the challenges that they had encountered when disclosing their work, Clementine – a student in her early 20s – described particularly positive and enthusiastic responses, which she attributed to her social circle being "really liberal" and the fact that "a lot of people do it". Interestingly, she also felt that this acceptance was because she is part of a younger generation and subsequently having "more knowledge of the law and what it does", referring to the PRA. She described her interaction with her flatmates shortly before she began working:

> 'I had my profile put up on the website and they knew that I was going to a photo shoot, they knew when I was doing my training ... I was waiting the whole day for my photos to go up on the website, and then they did. And I was like, "Guys, it's happening, everyone come and have a look!" and we all went through my profile together and looked at my photos and my friends were just like, "Oh my god, you look so good!", like screaming and really happy for me, and it was really great.' (Clementine)

Given that internalised sexism can often mean women compete with and shame each other for their sexuality, the support Clementine received from her flatmates is heartening. However, for other participants, such 'positive' responses were accompanied by overcompensating, manifested in overt reassurances that their friends had no problem with sex work. Bella, for example, described an interaction with a friend she attended art school with:

> 'I was like, "I do sex work now" and [she replied] "You know what, I'm actually okay with that" ... She's younger than me, unemployed ... but she still feels ... she has to validate that. And I wanted to be like, "I'm not asking if you're okay with that, *I'm* okay with it" ... I don't say, "I'm okay that you work for retail" ... then [she] proceeded to list all the sex workers she had met ... And I was like, "Oh, great".' (Bella)

Thus, while in this instance the person was presumably trying to respond to Bella in a helpful way, they inadvertently reinforced stigma through this assumption that their approval was needed. Furthermore, in emphasising that sex work is something that they approved of, they set it apart from other forms of work: such assurances would not be deemed appropriate if Bella were working in another legal industry.

As the responses from sex workers quoted so far show, while initial reactions from those they told about their work were not ideal, this usually improved over time, once the shock, concern and intrigue had subsided. However, not all participants had this experience, and a minority described profoundly negative and often abusive reactions. Making sense of how stigma is experienced requires using an intersectional lens that takes account of a range of factors which may influence an individual's experience, such as race, class, sexual orientation and gender identity. In the case of sex work this also requires taking into account the location and type of work, since sex work stigma is more pronounced for those who work more visibly, namely those who work on the street. The identities of those who experienced the most negative and traumatic reactions from those they told about their work highlighted this. For example, Bobbie, a Māori sex worker in a provincial town, said that several people she had told about her work over the years now "don't want to know me". Kayla, a Māori transgender street-based sex worker described being met with abuse when she told people about her sex work. However, she did not passively accept these reactions and resisted these attempts to belittle her. She explained:

> 'I've been spat at … I've been barred from seeing my nephews and nieces … but I have a unique way of confronting that … the way I communicate with people, I make them know that there's nothing they're going to say out of their mouth that's going to bring me down a level, because it's what comes out of my mouth which makes me go up a level.' (Kayla)

Elesei, a queer Māori male sex worker, described being ostracised by several of his peers at art school when he told them about his sex work: "as soon as they found out that I was doing sex work, there were probably about one or two people that were able to look past that and treat me like a person. So that told me a lot about them".

Like Kayla, Elesei did not internalise these responses and instead explained that this confirmed to him that these people were "not really friends" and that their reactions were simply evidence of their "boring lives". The responses to these sex workers' disclosures indicate that, in the decriminalised context, some sex workers are considered more palatable that others, and the experience of sex work stigma must be understood in the context of other types of discrimination. This echoes what Easterbrook-Smith discusses in Chapter 7, in which they argue that the 'acceptability' of sex workers is conditional, with those sex workers who are considered 'high class' and 'exclusive' more likely to be afforded respect.

As the experiences outlined in this chapter demonstrate, reactions to sex workers who were open about their work required emotional labour of the sex worker, both when the response appeared to have positive intent and when it was explicitly negative. However, participants also described responses which were refreshingly mundane and did not require emotional labour of them. These responses were described as being truly positive and affirming. Jordan, for example, described her ex-boyfriend's reaction when she told him:

> '… the second person I told was actually my ex-boyfriend … I met up with him … and I said to him, "What would you think of me if I became an escort?" And he smiled and said, "Hey, if I had a vagina I'd do it", which was fantastic! I felt really comfortable talking to him about it.' (Jordan)

Jordan also talked about her mother's reaction, characterised not by shock, concern or intrigue but by an assurance that her mother could be included in this part of her life. This, Jordan explained, was "really good" and meant that she could share aspects of her working life with her mother and "now … mum and I go lingerie shopping together and all sorts of shit". Similarly, while it was not safe for Bella to tell her own mother about her work, she described telling the mother of her close friend (also a sex worker) and described her "incredibly supportive" response as having been a "liberating" experience. Bella also demonstrated how it is possible to express concern for a sex worker without entering 'rescue mode', noting that close friends she had told were very supportive but also let her know that it was ok to talk about negative experiences, explaining, "They were like, 'If you ever don't feel good about it, don't be afraid to say', but didn't do the thing of trying to rescue me".

Amber described a similar reaction from a close friend, who responded in an open and supportive manner, one that did not 'other' her through shock, concern or intrigue. She explained:

> 'I had one close friend who I don't think it surprised her, you know, she was just like, "I want you to be safe and tell me how it goes and keep in contact about it and everything", and I went "yes absolutely". And she really helped me make the decision to leave the job I was currently doing [to just do] full-time sex working.' (Amber)

Similarly, Mark described a mundanely positive reaction from his sister, which meant that he was now able to be open with her about work, including talking about bad experiences:

'It's funny, my sister ... she's a socialist. So to her it was all very, "Oh yeah, whatever, I don't care". Well, no, that's not fair. I would say she was, you know, positive about it ... And she 'gets it', you know? It's quite good. If I have problems with clients and things, she's like, "Yeah ... they don't treat you right" or whatever it is. It's quite good, yes.' (Mark)

The responses that Amber and Mark experienced highlight how valuable it is to have friends who know about their work and 'get it'. For the same reason, several participants also noted the importance of their friendships with other sex workers. Jordan, for example, noted that her friendships with other sex workers were particularly important because they "understand you", while Bella felt it was easier to relax and talk candidly around other sex workers because there was reassurance in knowing that they are "an outsider too". However, the responses described here demonstrate how it is very much possible for non-sex workers to 'get it' and respond in a genuinely supportive way when they do not buy into stigmatising discourses and allow this to shape how they react. Furthermore, Harley's experience telling her friend further demonstrates how non-sex workers are entirely capable of respecting professional boundaries and the work of sex work. In response to Harley telling her that she had been working, her friend explained that she had known for three years. However, she had chosen to not say anything because she recognised that, "it's not her place to approach me [Harley] – when I was ready, I will tell her". Harley described her friend's response as "awesome", in that her friend recognised her success in her work and quietly expressed admiration for what she had achieved in her business. What these experiences highlight is that, while it remains pervasive, stigma does not inevitably determine reactions, and truly supportive responses are very much possible. The importance of being able to tell someone close was also emphasised in interviews, and it was clear that the pressure to conceal was a significant emotional burden for many participants.

The pressures of concealment

As noted in previous sections of this chapter, while all the sex workers interviewed for this project had told some of the people in their lives about their work, for most this was selective, meaning they were continually managing information about their work. The pressures of the emotional labour this necessitated were evident. For example, Amanda explained, "I think that it would be way easier if my kids knew, so I don't have to live ... the double life thing ... that gets exhausting". It was very common for participants to describe having to conceal their work as "tiring"; being able to be open was described as much easier emotionally. Clementine, for example, noted, "There's always that feeling of relief when you do tell someone". Jordan explained this further:

> 'Not having to lie is a lot more freeing and being able to not censor what you're talking about. Like when somebody says to you, "How was your day?" I have to automatically think, 'Right, do I tell you some made-up mundane story about how my day was because you don't know I'm a sex worker, or can I say, "Yeah, I shoved my finger up a guy's arse today, it was fantastic, what did you do?"' And so you're constantly filtering that out ... what's my lie, what's my preparation, what's my story? And it's really tiring having to think beforehand, crap, where in the lie am I? What kind of a story have I told? ... You don't want it to be a lie.' (Jordan)

Several participants also described experiencing guilt and regret that they did not feel that they could share this part of their life with some of the people they were close to. Clementine, for example, described wishing she could tell her mother because she spoke to her frequently and "that's going to get harder and harder, because I like to tell [her] stuff about what I'm doing here". However, while Mark found it difficult not telling his mother about his sex work, he was also pragmatic about this, noting that, "There's lots of other things about my life she probably doesn't know ... she doesn't need to know everything".

Furthermore, while managing information about their work required emotional labour, a few participants also noted that there were positive sides to this too. Bella, for example, explained that being able to selectively hide her work provided an important form of protection from stigma, explaining: "I like being able to escape the stigma and pass as a non-sex worker as shitty as it is ... I like not everyone knowing". Mark described a contradictory experience in which managing a secret part of his life was stressful but also, to some extent, exciting. He explained:

> '... in terms of secrecy and deception ... it does feel weird sometimes where you're living this double life, where I get up in the morning, put my suit on and go to work ... and then, after work, I'm this other person. Well, I'm still me

but you're different and the two things cannot cross over ... sometimes I have to remember what my name is. Who am I today? Who am I at the moment? ... In some ways I wonder if I get a sort of a thrill out of that. I mean the danger of it. In that sense, it's almost as if you're being in a Bond movie, you've got that sort of secret spy double life happening ... In a small town, you're going to run across people ... sometimes it's a bit of a buzz when you get away with it – Woohoo! you know? ... I'm always aware that every day ... it is risky what I am doing, leading this double life ... You've got these two very disparate worlds that you're trying to keep hermetically sealed but ... you've got both of them within you, you know? ... You've got to be on your toes. But, as I said, sometimes I find that exciting [that] I'm playing with danger.' (Mark)

However, overall, it was clear that the pressure to manage information about their work was a significant emotional burden for most participants. Interestingly though, two of the participants who had worked prior to decriminalisation felt that this burden had been lifted to some extent since the law had changed. Jeff, for example, said that he felt able to talk openly about work with his co-workers without worrying about people overhearing and that the "shield, that cocoon" had gone, which he described as "so liberating". Sasha said that prior to the law change she used to lie to her family and "tell them I was in an office job" but it was difficult to justify the money she was making, which was evident from her lack of debt and fully stocked cupboards. Sasha explained that she had lied to her family because she was "ashamed" and that she was "scared of being hurt ... hurting others, perceptions of me". However, she felt that since the law had changed it was "a lot easier" and that she was less likely to experience abusive "commentary" about her work, particularly from intimate partners. Thus, while further research is needed to explore this more fully, these experiences suggest that the decriminalisation of sex work may help to remove at least some of the barriers to sex workers talking about their work and, in doing so, alleviate at least some of the emotional burden of stigma.

Conclusion

The overall objective of this chapter was to explore how 20 sex workers in New Zealand felt about telling friends and family about their work, and their experiences of doing so. In exploring these experiences, we aimed to shed further light on how stigma operates in the decriminalised environment.

Levels of outness to friends and family regarding work varied considerably among participants. While a few participants described being completely open about their work to most of their friends and family members, the majority employed selective disclosure, choosing to tell only those they trusted and/or who they felt confident would be comfortable with the information. However, these participants were able to fly under the radar relatively easily, since their 'otherness' was not immediately apparent to potential stigmatisers. Thus, what Goffman termed 'passing' was not, overall, a challenge for them making them individuals who were potentially "discreditable" rather than being immediately discredited (Goffman, 1963: p 41). These participants, therefore, managed concealable stigmatised identities; this is widely associated with emotional stress, such as guilt due to hiding information from others (Chaudoir and Quinn, 2010). The risk of being discriminated against, ostracised and/or shamed underpinned motivations to keep sex work private. However, for almost all of the participants, this was a form of protection for themselves and their loved ones, not because they felt ashamed. This echoes the findings of studies on information management among other stigmatised populations (Itzhaky and Kissil, 2015). While for sex workers in New Zealand such social disapproval cannot translate into criminalisation, fear of the consequences of stigma was still evident in the accounts of participants.

While the interviews clearly highlighted an ongoing need to manage information about sex work, it was evident that almost all of those interviewed had no internalised stigma. Indeed, several participants explicitly stated that not only were they not ashamed, they felt proud to be sex workers. The pride in their work that these participants described may speak to the increased legitimacy that sex workers have post decriminalisation. This was further bolstered in 2018 when the founder of NZPC, Catherine Healy, was made a Dame in recognition of her services to the rights of sex workers (Davison, 2018). While Goffman's work has been hugely influential in the development of stigma scholarship, the experiences of the sex workers interviewed for this project are better understood within the context of more recent theorising, which focuses on structural stigma rather than Goffman's more individualised framing. Structural stigma, according to Hatzenbuehler (2016), refers to the societal level factors, norms and policies that function to limit the opportunities, resources and wellbeing of stigmatised populations. While the decriminalisation of sex work cannot reasonably be expected to eliminate stigma, it creates a societal context in which sex work is legally recognised as work, and as such it is possible for sex workers to be recognised for the valuable work that they do. Thus, decriminalisation may mitigate structural stigma at least to some extent, making it easier to resist and subsequently fostering more positive feelings about sex work, such as the pride that several participants described.

However, the accounts of these participants also highlight a need to consider experiences of disclosure through an intersectional lens, one which takes account of a range of stigmatised identity factors that may converge and result in more negative experiences (Turan et al, 2019). Those who most often described being able to selectively hide their work with relative ease, and who most commonly reported helpful and supportive responses from those they chose to disclose to, were typically white, middle-class, cisgender women who were either working independently or from a small appointment-only brothel. For those working in the street context, the visibility of their work meant that concealing it was not as straightforward. These participants also more commonly described judgemental reactions from those who were aware of their work. The two transgender participants also worked from the street, were Māori, and had struggled with addictions. Both described experiencing particularly negative reactions from some of those who knew about their work.

The importance of being able to tell others about their work without consequence was evident in participants' experiences. While managing information about work was an important protection strategy, it was also a significant emotional burden. That sex workers still carry this emotional burden, due to the ongoing risks posed by stigma, is particularly unjust in a decriminalised context. Link and Phelan (2014) define stigma as a form of power used by dominant groups to repress minority groups. While the law change may have disrupted the power of stigma to some extent, its oppressive impacts are clearly still being felt, evident in the need that several participants felt to closely guard information about their work. Attitudinal change is therefore particularly important going forward and public education to counter stigmatising narratives is crucial for this to occur. Decriminalisation has removed one of the fundamental building blocks of stigma, but there is much work still to be done to alleviate the burden of secrecy.

References

Abel, G. & Fitzgerald, L. (2010) 'Decriminalisation and stigma', in G. Abel, L. Fitzgerald, A. Taylor & C. Healy (eds) *Taking the Crime Out of Sex Work: New Zealand sex workers' fight for decriminalisation*, Bristol: Policy Press, pp 239–58.

Abel, G., Fitzgerald, L. & Brunton, C. (2007) *The Impact of the Prostitution Reform Act on the Health and Safety Practices of Sex Workers: Report to the Prostitution Law Review Committee*, Christchurch: University of Otago. Available at: https://www.otago.ac.nz/christchurch/otago018607.pdf.

Altink, S., Amesberger, H. & Wagenaar, H. (2017) *Designing Prostitution Policy: Intention and reality in regulating the sex trade*, Bristol: Policy Press.

Armstrong, L. (2018) 'Stigma, decriminalisation, and violence against street-based sex workers: Changing the narrative', *Sexualities*, DOI: 1363460718780216.

Benoit, C., Jansson, S., Smith, M. & Flagg, J. (2018) 'Prostitution stigma and its effect on the working conditions, personal lives, and health of sex workers', *The Journal of Sex Research*, 55: 457–71.

Benoit, C., Maurice, R., Abel, G., Smith, M., Jansson, M., Healey, P. & Magnuson, D. (2019) '"I dodged the stigma bullet": Canadian sex workers' situated responses to occupational stigma', *Culture, Health & Sexuality*, 1–15.

Bruckert, C. (2012) 'The mark of disreputable labour: Sex workers negotiate stigma', in S. Hannem & C. Bruckert (eds) *Stigma Revisited: Implications of the mark*, Ottawa: University of Ottawa Press.

Capell, B., Tzafrir, S. & Dolan, S. (2016) 'The disclosure of concealable stigmas: Analysis anchored in trust', *Cogent Psychology*, 3, DOI: 10.1080/23311908.2015.11210661121066.

Chaudoir, S. & Quinn, D. (2010) 'Revealing concealable stigmatized identities: The impact of disclosure motivations and positive first-disclosure experiences on fear of disclosure and well-being', *Journal of Social Issues*, 66: 570–84.

Corrigan, P. & Matthews, A. (2003) 'Stigma and disclosure: Implications for coming out of the closet', *Journal of Mental Health*, 12: 235–48.

Davison, I. (2018) 'Queen's Birthday Honours: Dame Catherine Healy–Sex workers "brought into the fold"', *New Zealand Herald*, https://www.nzherald.co.nz/nz/news/article.cfm?c_id=1&objectid=12062840.

Fick, N. (2005) 'Coping with stigma, discrimination and violence: Sex workers talk about their experiences', ChildHub. Available at: https://childhub.org/en/system/tdf/library/attachments/sweat_05_stigma_violence_0109.pdf?file=1&type=node&id=18601.

Flett, R. (2012) '"To tell or not to tell?" Managing a concealable identity in the workplace', *Vulnerable Groups & Inclusion,* 3, https://doi.org/10.3402/vgi.v3i0.16145.

Goffman, E. (1963) *Stigma: Notes on the management of spoiled identity,* Englewood Cliffs, NJ: Prentice-Hall.

Hatzenbuehler, M. (2016) 'Structural stigma: Research evidence and implications for psychological science', *American Psychologist,* 71: 742–51.

Huschke, S. (2017) 'Victims without a choice? A critical view on the debate about sex work in Northern Ireland', *Sexuality Research & Social Policy,* 14: 192–205.

Itzhaky, H. & Kissil, K. (2015) '"It's a horrible sin. If they find out, I will not be able to stay": Orthodox Jewish gay men's experiences living in secrecy', *Journal of Homosexuality,* 62: 621–43.

Koken, J., Bimbi, D., Parsons, J. & Halkitis, P. (2004) 'The experience of stigma in the lives of male internet escorts', *Journal of Psychology & Human Sexuality,* 16: 13–32.

Krüsi, A., Pacey, K., Bird, L., Taylor, C., Chettiar, J., Allan, S., Bennett, D., Montaner, J., Kerr, T. & Shannon, K. (2014) 'Criminalisation of clients: Reproducing vulnerabilities for violence and poor health among street-based sex workers in Canada—a qualitative study', *BMJ Open,* 4, DOI: 10.1136/bmjopen-2014-0051911.

Levy, J. & Jakobsson, P. (2014) 'Sweden's abolitionist discourse and law: Effects on the dynamics of Swedish sex work and on the lives of Sweden's sex workers', *Criminology & Criminal Justice,* 14: 593–607.

Link, B. & Phelan, J. (2014) 'Stigma power', *Social Science & Medicine (1982),* 103: 24–32.

Lynch, J. & Rodell, J. (2018) 'Blend in or stand out? Interpersonal outcomes of managing concealable stigmas at work', *Journal of Applied Psychology,* 103: 1307.

Putnis, N. & Burr, J. (2019) 'Evidence or stereotype? Health inequalities and representations of sex workers in health publications in England', *Health,* DOI: 1363459319833242.

Quinn, D. & Earnshaw, V. (2013) 'Concealable stigmatized identities and psychological well-being', *Social and Personality Psychology Compass,* 7: 40–51.

Sallmann, J. (2010) 'Living with stigma: Women's experiences of prostitution and substance use', *Affilia,* 25: 146–59.

Sanders, T. (2016) 'Inevitably violent? Dynamics of space, governance, and stigma in understanding violence against sex workers', *Studies in Law, Politics, and Society,* 71: 93–114.

Scambler, G. (2007) 'Sex work stigma: Opportunist migrants in London', *Sociology,* 41: 1079–96.

Turan, J., Elafros, M., Logie, C., Banik, S., Bulent, T., Crockett, K., Pescosolido, B. & Murry S. (2019) 'Challenges and opportunities in examining and addressing intersectional stigma and health', *BMC Medicine,* 17(7).

Vanwesenbeeck, I. (2017) 'Sex work criminalization is barking up the wrong tree', *Archives of Sexual Behavior,* 46: 1631–40.

Weitzer, R. (2018) 'Resistance to sex work stigma', *Sexualities,* 21: 717–29.

Wong, W., Holroyd, E. & Bingham, A. (2011) 'Stigma and sex work from the perspective of female sex workers in Hong Kong', *Sociology of Health & Illness,* 33: 50–65.

9

Contested Space: Street-based Sex Workers and Community Engagement

Gillian Abel

Introduction

Since sex work was decriminalised in New Zealand through the passing of the Prostitution Reform Act (PRA) 2003, all citizens have the right to work as a sex worker, and this right extends to those who work on the street. Sex workers are now able to exercise their rights as citizens through use of the legal system (Abel, 2018) and, because street-based sex workers have rights, some have a better relationship with the police and no longer fear arrest (Armstrong, 2017). In general, since the law change street-based sex workers are more likely to report violent acts committed against them to the police and to help police investigations of other crimes (Armstrong, 2017). But, while decriminalisation has been seen to be successful and is widely accepted in New Zealand (Prostitution Law Review Committee, 2008; Abel et al, 2010; Abel, 2014), there has still been some unease about street-based sex workers' presence within certain communities. Primarily, this unease has been linked to public nuisance associations with street-based sex work (Buckley, 2009; Boreham, 2012; Robinson, 2015; Law, 2017; Steele, 2018). Some community members have used these associations to argue that street-based sex workers' presence in some residential and mixed-use areas is not consistent with community values and therefore is out of place in a community environment (Boreham, 2012; Anon, 2017).

Place, in geographical terms, often refers to the physical environment. But the social relationships and activities that happen within any particular place make separating the social and geographical impossible (Cresswell, 1996). Spaces become places when people use them and make them meaningful (Chen et al, 2018). The city is made up of different places which are constructed through social processes into middle-class and working-class suburban spaces, industrial and commercial spaces, green spaces and entertainment spaces, each fulfilling particular social needs (Chen et al, 2018) and each having attachment and meaning to those who use or live in them (Holloway and Hubbard, 2001). It is important to understand social space because, although it is concealed, it plays a big part in the experiences minority cultures have in society (Sibley, 1995). Who is considered as belonging or not belonging to a community contributes to the shaping of a social space. Dominant groups in society, that is, those who have power or influence by virtue of their socioeconomic status, ethnicity, gender, age or sexuality, occupy the most desirable places, excluding the minority to less desirable places (Sibley, 1995). Some activities are deemed appropriate within a specific place but inappropriate elsewhere, which suggests that morals are an important component in defining whether individuals are included or excluded from community (Hubbard, 2001). This is highly relevant in the case of street-based sex work.

Globally, street-based sex workers receive a great deal of attention, primarily because they are visible and not in brothels or other indoor premises (O'Neill et al, 2008; Cook and Whowell, 2011). Their visibility is often seen as a threat to community values and efforts are made to exclude them through criminalising their practices or zoning them to non-residential places, usually in industrial settings (Van Doorninck and Campbell, 2006). As Campbell (2015, p 28) argues, such responses privilege 'a notion of community, within which sex workers have no lawful presence, [which has] ... the effect of depriving sex workers of social and political citizenship'. Zoning and criminalisation are negative reactions which more often than not lead to detrimental unintended consequences (Van Doorninck and Campbell, 2006; Sanders and Campbell, 2007). A more positive response of engaging with sex workers to arrive at solutions beneficial to all parties is less often used but far more effective (Newman, 2006; O'Neill and Campbell, 2006; Sanders et al, 2018).

In this chapter, street-based sex workers' (non)acceptance in the communities in which they work in New Zealand is explored. The chapter also outlines how community engagement worked effectively to counter proposed regulatory approaches to exclude street-based sex work from communities. To illustrate this, data are drawn from interviews conducted for a participatory study examining the relationships and tensions between community members and street-based sex workers in New Zealand's decriminalised context. The following section gives a brief overview of the study.

Methods

The study was funded by Lotteries Health and was carried out between 2017 and 2019 in Auckland, Christchurch and Wellington, the three cities in New Zealand in which most street-based sex work occurs. Over the last few years, however, numbers of street-based sex workers in Wellington, the capital city, have dwindled and there are few tensions between these street-based sex workers and community in this city. Thus, for the purposes of this chapter, Wellington is excluded and the focus is specifically on Christchurch and Auckland. Ethics approval was gained from the University of Otago Human Ethics Committee (Ref no: 17/039).

A community-based participatory approach was taken in this research with the author working in close partnership with New Zealand Prostitutes' Collective (NZPC). Consistent with a participatory approach, the research came about as a result of a concern expressed by NZPC, apprehensive that councils may respond to some communities' complaints about street-based sex workers by taking regulatory measures. Regulatory measures, such as zoning to other areas, have unintended effects. For instance, zoning would be unlikely to deter many street-based sex workers from working in their usual places of work, but a consequence of this would be that sex workers would be less likely to screen clients thoroughly before getting into a car, for fear of being spotted. It would also create a barrier to engagement with police if anything went wrong. Because of this, NZPC wanted the research to explore the existing tensions between community members and street-based sex workers in more depth, and also to explore the possibility of other non-regulatory approaches to dealing with these tensions.

The research involved in-depth, semi-structured interviews conducted in Auckland and Christchurch with 23 street-based sex workers, eight council representatives, nine outreach workers, and 18 residents/business owners who live or work in the areas where street-based sex work occurs. These interviews explored the meanings and interpretations the participants gave to their experiences, which provided a broad contextual understanding of the situation. Interviews were digitally recorded and a thematic analysis was undertaken. This analysis revealed that the way spaces were constructed had an important influence on whether sex workers were accepted or not accepted into the community.

One of the aims of the research was to develop a reference/interagency group consisting of a variety of interested parties, who would look at the findings of the research and work to develop solutions to any problems as a group. Serendipitously, an interagency group had just been formed in Christchurch around the time the research started, which consisted of representatives from NZPC and other street outreach organisations, police and Christchurch City Council. This group had formed as a result of problems some residents reported having with street-based workers in the area in which they lived. The author joined this group so that the research findings, as they emerged, could inform the discussions and in doing so, help inform effective intervention measures. Research which includes those involved at the grassroots level (such as outreach workers and community), as well as policy makers and those charged with enforcing the policies as fully engaged and equal participants in the research process, is more likely to produce effective outcomes (Stringer, 2013). It enhances all participants' understanding of the problem in a specific situation: they acquire information, reflect on this information, theorise on how to address the situation, and then put in place a plan of action. This methodological approach thus creates the conditions which lead 'to the formation of operational processes that are socially and culturally appropriate' (Stringer, 1996, p 37). As will be discussed later in this chapter, this proved to be the case in Christchurch.

Participants have been given pseudonyms in the analysis presented in the following sections to protect their anonymity. Two very different case studies are discussed in these sections. First, the context for sex work in Auckland is described, including the community engagement that had occurred there prior to the start of the research, before presenting the analysis of this heterogeneous inner city space where street-based sex workers were largely accepted. Secondly, the context for sex work in Christchurch immediately prior to the research is described, before analysing the homogeneous suburban space where there was resistance from many residents to the presence of sex workers on their street. This Christchurch analysis is concluded by returning to a discussion of how the interagency group, described earlier, worked to come to a mutually beneficial solution to the problem.

The Auckland case study

Auckland is the largest city in New Zealand and has the most street-based sex workers, predominantly located across five areas: in the central business district (CBD) in Karangahape (K) Road and its off-streets; and in South Auckland (Manukau) in several streets in the townships of Otahuhu, Papatoetoe, Manurewa and Onehunga. All areas are mixed-use areas, having both commercial and residential space. K Road has been undergoing some gentrification over recent years with some commercial buildings being converted to apartment blocks, bringing more residents into the area.

Following decriminalisation, residents and business owners in the South Auckland area of Manukau became increasingly vocal about the public nuisance impacts of street-based sex work in that area. The Manukau City Council made two attempts at getting a local bill through the New Zealand Parliament which would enable them to make it an offence to solicit in a public place, but in both cases were resoundingly defeated (NZPA, 2006; Scoop Media, 2015). As a consequence of the failure of these bills, a vigilante group of residents and business owners in the Papatoetoe area of South Auckland took the matter into their own hands; they went out in the evenings and filmed sex workers and their clients, took down car registration numbers of clients and sent warning letters to their homes (Buckley, 2009). Globally, and particularly in contexts in which street-based sex workers are criminalised, such vigilantism has been a common response of residents to street-based sex work in their neighbourhoods, and to a large extent these campaigns have been successful in driving street-based sex work out of a specific neighbourhood (Hubbard, 1998). However, in New Zealand, sex workers have the right to work without being intimidated and threatened by others and so this vigilante group was ultimately unsuccessful in disrupting street-based sex work to any great extent.

South Auckland was then subsumed within the Auckland City Council, and the Council then rejected a regulatory approach to managing the complaints of residents and business owners, instead embarking on a consultative process with NZPC to develop non-regulatory responses. NZPC initiated an education programme in Auckland to encourage street-based sex workers to keep noise levels down and pick up their litter. They began by trying to instil a sense of community 'responsibility' into the street-based sex worker population through the use of peer workers who were currently working on the street. Annah Pickering, the regional co-ordinator of Auckland NZPC, stated that:

> 'As a community we need to take responsibility and it affects all of us ... and when we had our regular street meetings, part of that strategy was about empowering the peer workers in that community, who ended up being the champions there. They're proud of their corner, and sort of saying, "No, we're not going to have this", you know, come up with solutions together.' (Annah, NZPC, interview with author)

NZPC then formed a working group comprising of sex workers, outreach workers, community members, police and Council to come up with options to improve relationships between street-based sex workers and other community members. Council representatives involved in this process saw this as being the most effective approach they could take. One Auckland City Council staff member (Ethan) argued that you had to 'get everybody around the table in some meaningful dialogue about how they can find a solution to the problems' and that in doing so they had to 'be able to actually work through those issues without judging the person or people that are involved'. Another Council staff member elaborated on the process:

> 'See, we had the police there. We had representatives of the community come in. These are both in favour and against, and so it's just getting people to sit down. They might not want to sit down with particular people, that's their business, but it's just getting people to talk, because once you've at least started a conversation, it's going to be hard upfront, but as long as people feel like they've got genuine input into a process, then you can make it happen .... Sure, it took time, hey, and I can't say we nailed it, but at least I think we provided a process, a place where everyone could sit and feel like, "I'm just as important as the person who's coming in a blue uniform. My voice matters just as much", and that was my interest in the discussions' (Alexander, council staff)

One of the solutions that the working group adopted was similar to the managed approach of street-based sex work in Leeds in the UK (Brown and Sanders, 2017). They promoted a 7am to 7pm informal curfew on street-based sex work in the area. Because sex work is decriminalised in New Zealand, it is not illegal to work outside of these designated times, but interviews conducted for the project indicated that most sex workers were happy to comply. This compromise recognised that sex work best fitted into the community at a particular time of the day and meant that sex workers had access to the night-time economy and other businesses to the daytime economy. In this scenario, place is temporally shared by sex workers and other members of the community. Annah explained that the curfew was monitored through a collaboration between police and outreach workers:

> 'So we had to monitor it as a community and as representatives of NZPC to ensure that that was put in place, and the police had the buy in. ... they sent out a patrol car and ... if there were workers working after 7am, be like, "Come on, girls, get off the street. You know the curfew". Even though they're not breaking the law, "we'll give you a ride home. Come on, you know the rules, or we're going to call Annah".' (Annah, NZPC)

Community engagement with residents and business owners allowed NZPC to build relationships and, through this, trust with other community members. Evelyn, a local business owner stated that 'you've got to collaborate, you know, work with Council, work with the police, work with the business owners, and then it's really just the humanity. ... establish a relationship with Annah and the Collective [NZPC], and then there was more trust'. Through collaboration, they were able to recognise the rights of all people in the community, and understand that sex workers were entitled to have their say in what happened in that space. William, who both lived and worked in the area where street-based sex work happened emphasised this: 'So any worker needs to be able to work alongside, collaborate with and find ways of working round anybody else, regardless of whether they're a sex worker or what their occupation is, it doesn't matter'. When issues arose between sex workers and other community members, these participants felt comfortable contacting NZPC and talking over how these could be dealt with. In recognising that this was vital to finding effective solutions, Elijah, a manager of a local business, stated that, 'You can't make that decision unilaterally ... It's not just, you know, "This is it. We don't want this". Yeah, it's never going to work that way because obviously the other party will just say no ... and that's how you get arguments erupting'.

Community members agreed that regulatory approaches were not the answer and were enthusiastic about the partnership they had with NZPC. This was the state of play when interviewing started in this study. It is thus probable that, largely as a result of the community engagement in Auckland, the tone of most of the interviews with all parties was positive. Most participants went along with their daily lives recognising that everyone had the right to occupy that space.

Recognition and respect in heterogeneous communities

Residents and business owners who lived and worked in Auckland's mixed-use, inner city areas focused on recognition and respect as key to harmonious relationships in a community. Sennett (2003, p 54), in thinking about the notion of respect in the context of exclusion, argued that recognition is a possible synonym for respect and cited John Rawls as proposing that 'recognition means respecting the needs of those who are unequal', and Jurgen Habermas, who suggests that 'recognition means respecting the views of those whose interests lead them to disagree'. However, Sennett (2003) argued that neither of these definitions 'encompass the awareness of mutual need' (p 55) and there is a necessity to explore 'ways to perform as equals [in order to] ... show mutual respect' (p 59).

There is no denying that there are inequalities between residents/business owners and street-based sex workers in inner-city communities. Many cities, including Auckland, have experienced gentrification, with expensive apartments attracting the middle class back into inner-city living. Yet despite this, decriminalisation and community engagement has enabled an acceptance of street-based sex workers in these spaces, as they are framed as contributing to the vibrancy of inner-city culture. The recognition of sex work as a legal occupation allows it place in vibrant spaces, where space is constructed as edgy and exciting, and sex workers are embraced as putting the place 'on the map'. Vibrant spaces attract people into the community, thereby strengthening the economy. In such instances, street-based sex workers become the exotic and needed 'others'. For example, one community member explained:

> 'I think generally speaking across the board in K Road that the population are quite supportive of a really diverse community ... Yeah, in fact many people choose to be here because of that diverse community .... We encourage people from all walks of life to be here and work together,

and it's what's given and made K Road a household name. So in many ways, you know, we just treat it as just another business …. It's what puts K Road on the map.' (William, resident)

To be accepted as part of a community one has to be recognised as a citizen in one's own right (Campbell, 2015). Being recognised as a community member carries with it obligations to respect other community members and to contribute within the community. This includes caring for the community environment. Public nuisance discourses in society reinforce the association between street-based sex work and littering (Kantola and Squires, 2004; Scoop Media, 2015). As mentioned earlier, NZPC engaged peer workers to reinforce the message that to counter such discourses, sex workers needed to take some responsibility and try to keep the space in which they worked clean. Many sex worker participants interviewed emphasised that they had taken this message on board and criticised those who had not. One street-based sex worker, who was homeless, complained about the litter other sex workers left in the vicinity of where she slept. She prided herself in contributing to keeping her space in the community clean: 'When I was homeless, I was sleeping in several car parks over here. … I've had to go and collect all the condoms and put them in the black bags before I went to sleep in the tent' (Addison). Some street-based sex workers also articulated how they contributed to the economy of the community through the use of service stations and other shops. For example, Luna explained:

> 'I feel like a lot of our money goes into the community, like a lot, because it's so easy to get, we spend a lot on crap, we really do. Like oh god, you know, a lot of the nights when I've made a lot of money, I literally go back to our 24/7 mart and buy everyone a feed, which ends up costing like NZ$300 total'. (Luna, sex worker)

Vibrant spaces function 24 hours a day and seven days a week. While residents and business owners were absent late at night and in the early hours of the morning, street-based sex workers were still using the space and many residents/business owners felt that this helped to keep the community safe. They fulfilled a neighbourhood watch-type role in that they 'look after our building after hours. … They keep an eye for us as well' (Benjamin). As sex workers are not criminalised, they can phone the police when they see criminal activity happening in the neighbourhood. Jacob argued that sex workers were thus valuable as witnesses to crime in the area:

> 'If the worst came to the worst, and someone got mugged over the road from the sex worker, or … if over the road from them someone breaks into our neighbour's, they are a very valuable source of witness …. Yeah, and having people on the street 24/7, that's the way you build the community.' (Jacob, resident)

To live in a heterogeneous space, you have to accept difference and be prepared to negotiate to arrive at a point where all parties feel heard. People's actions are a performance, and it is through performances done well that connections are made with others. This is measured in terms of respect (Sennett, 2003). In demonstrating respect, community members tried not to be rude or negative towards sex workers. Amelia argued that 'if you don't be rude to them or don't do things to upset them, then they give the same respect back'. Charlotte indicated that she was not confrontational with sex workers 'partly out of respect … they're working for a start, and I wouldn't want to anger them and create any kind of animosity or negativity for us or for the street'. Sex workers in turn appreciated the need to show respect to others in the community. Nora claimed that she knew how to interact with residents and business owners, which meant that 'they don't complain as long as we're respectful'. Layla condemned fellow sex workers who made a noise or littered as this indicated a lack of respect for others in the community:

> 'If everyone respected the community, I know that would play a big part. … Like at night time was rowdy, was really rowdy, and I think that's what would make it a lot better for street workers if they weren't rowdy and respected the space, cleaned up after themselves. I always cleaned up after myself'. (Layla, sex worker)

One business owner in K Road supplied food and other assistance to sex workers who worked near her restaurant and impressed on her staff that they should treat sex workers as they would any other customer:

> 'We're going to take ownership of this, of our little cut of K Road … and that means that if we have a message to be kind and however we would treat our guests in the restaurant,

we're going to extend that hospitality out to anyone in our kind of patch.' (Evelyn, business owner)

This business owner went on to state that mutual respect was easy to achieve if you recognised others as human beings by greeting them and paying attention to their needs: 'If you just say "hi" to people, you know, you get so much more back when there's a little bit of trust there, a little bit of recognition, I'm a person, you know ... they're totally respectful ... so it's just that mutual respect' (Evelyn).

A respectful city is one where difference is tolerated (Bannister et al, 2006). Respect is not looking for oneself, or elements of oneself, in another but in respecting the fact that everyone differs (Sennett, 2003). Sex working and non-sex working community members may not always understand things about each other, and this was certainly the case among the participants interviewed for this study. But there was an acceptance of each other by many, mostly as a result of community engagement. A commitment to getting along and making accommodations to achieve mutual recognition and respect was thus a dominant position in heterogeneous space. This contrasted with homogenous, suburban space in Christchurch, which is discussed in the following section.

The Christchurch case study

The main area for street-based sex work in Christchurch is Manchester Street, south of Bealey Avenue (hereafter referred to as Manchester South), which is considered as part of the inner city. It is a mixed-use area with shops, commercial businesses and some residences. It is heterogeneous space and so generally, street-based sex work has been accepted in this part of the city. However, following the 2011 earthquake in Christchurch, the inner city was cordoned off and street-based sex workers were displaced, with some moving to Manchester Street, north of Bealey Avenue (hereafter referred to as Manchester North) to work in an area which is purely residential. When the cordons moved back towards the city centre, most sex workers returned to work in Manchester South, but a few remained in the residential area, Manchester North, which created tensions with some community members (Law, 2017). Bealey Avenue is effectively the boundary line between inner city and suburb – on the one side sex work belongs and on the other side it does not.

When street-based sex workers moved into Manchester North following the earthquake, residents began complaining to the

Christchurch City Council and eventually engaged the services of a lawyer to explore options for banning street-based sex workers from the area. Their lawyer subsequently met with the police and the Council and agreed that the matter had reached a stage where Council intervention was required. The Councillors were then briefed by Council staff, who proposed that a bylaw be drafted to regulate the location of street-based sex work away from residential areas. This was vehemently opposed by other agencies who regularly work with street-based sex workers, namely, NZPC, the Salvation Army, and Youth and Cultural Development, who were concerned about the harms that might arise from such an approach. They argued that it was also unlikely to be effective and would be difficult to enforce. An interagency group (as mentioned earlier) was formed to discuss the issue. This was the state of play when the research began.

Rights and responsibilities in homogenous communities

In contrast to inner-city living, which embraces diversity, the suburb is constructed as family space and it is taken for granted that middle-class family space is not conducive to the presence of sex workers (Hubbard, 1999). Sibley (1995: 183) has argued that:

> ... [a] fear of mixing unlike things often signifies a reluctance to give ground and relinquish power. In all kinds of political, social and socio-spatial relationships, boundaries then assume considerable significance because they are simultaneously zones of uncertainty and security. ... The maintenance of secure borders is not always easy, however, because groups who are fearful of mixing and heterogeneity may lack the power to control entry to their space.

There are clear boundaries which demarcate homogeneous communities from the 'other'. When a street-based sex worker begins working on the peaceful streets of a suburb, it may create turmoil for some of those who regularly inhabit that space and consider it their home. It is an action out of place (Cresswell, 1996). The turmoil is heightened when sex workers have the right, in the eyes of the law, to have a presence in that space and they cannot, therefore, be easily excluded. Decriminalisation has effectively reduced the power of the middleclass to retain their suburban boundaries. Sex workers' presence in *their* space is seen as a threat to middle-class norms and values, and their anxieties are heightened by their inability to distance themselves from these unwanted intruders. This is the dynamic that was observed in the Manchester North area of Christchurch following the earthquake.

Sibley (1995, p 86) has suggested that '[p]ure spaces expose difference and facilitate the policing of boundaries'. People who see community as being family space see sex workers as being 'out of place' and therefore not-community. There is no room for noise, litter, human excrement and visible displays of sexuality (which some residents complain accompany sex work) in 'pure spaces'. The noise street-based sex workers made was a key issue highlighted by residents in Manchester North because, as one community member explained, 'that's most disruptive because it's mostly at night-time and so your sleep's getting disturbed and so that probably has the most effect on your day to day life' (Olivia).

Hubbard (1999) proposes that environmental nuisances (noise and litter) created by sex workers are not the issue that generates community groups' antipathy towards sex work. He instead argues that it is 'the idea that prostitution transforms a morally-ordered *family* space into an immoral and sexualised space that appears to underpin community protest' (Hubbard, 1999, p 163: original italics). However, residents in Christchurch, who were vocal that sex work did not fit the image of a family-orientated, residential community, argued that this was not based on moral judgements of whether selling sex was an acceptable practice or not. And it was not that they necessarily disagreed with decriminalisation. There was a tension in that on the one hand, they were supportive of sex workers' right to work in the industry. As Noah argued: 'We're not trying to outlaw the girls. We realise they're vulnerable, we realise that they need to work. You know, and the far right's going, "We need to abolish all of this altogether". Well no, there needs to be a place for them to be'. On the other hand, residents wanted to live in a peaceful environment. For example, Noah also explained, '[my daughter] gets up at 2 o'clock in the morning in tears because they're yelling at each other. She's got an exam tomorrow'. This resident also described problems with litter, explaining, 'I've grabbed needles out of my hedge on a couple of occasions, and we've got small kids' and he was also concerned about the possibility of children being exposed to sexual activities: '[my son] knows things that he should never know as a 6-year old boy' (Noah). The noise and litter issues were thus relatively easy for this resident to articulate without engaging in any overtly moral discourse. It was a little more difficult to engage in a discussion of the tension of being supportive of sex worker rights, but not in a suburban area, without engaging in a moral discourse.

The home is often referred to colloquially as a haven – a 'safe place' which allows you to 'flourish ... both physically and emotionally – to come home to' (Aha! Parenting, nd). But territoriality extends beyond the walls of the house and some community members, especially those living in solely residential areas, felt threatened by what was happening in the streets and described retreating within the walls of their houses to avoid interacting with street-based sex workers. Some thought that they had lost control of *their* streets and would not leave the house at night: for example, Noah stated 'the main thing is this time of night none of the residents will come out and wander around because it's not *their* street anymore'; and Emma claimed that 'as soon as it hits dark, I won't go to the dairy [store], yeah. Even if I really need something, I still won't. If there's a lot of people out there, I won't'. While some of the residents had experienced verbal altercations with sex workers, none had been physically accosted, but as Goffman (1990) suggests, when they were confronted with the tainted or 'spoilt other', they felt threatened and wanted to distance themselves from them. In trying to separate themselves from the 'spoilt other' they attempted to create boundaries 'beyond which lie those who do not belong' (Sibley, 1995, p 49). The tangible and real boundary for those living in Manchester North was Bealey Avenue. For others, there was an imagined boundary which distinguished them from 'a different part of town' (Ava) or 'more central to town' (Liam).

Imagined boundaries were also drawn between living space and working space. Holloway and Hubbard (2001, p 38) have argued that 'the relationship between people and place varies according to people's understandings of what happens in the place, how it has been designed, what its boundaries are and so on'. Residents, such as Ava, subjectively understood the community to be family- and not work-orientated: 'They're part of the community where they live, but I feel like they don't necessarily live on Manchester Street, so it's hard to associate them with the community when it's their job. Kind of like I go to somewhere else to do my job.' Noah argued that it was not a moral stance – any other form of work, particularly work that created noise, did not blend in with their understandings of what happened in their place: 'It's a commercial activity ... A panel-beater wouldn't be welcome in this community if they worked at night and did what they did. It's not a reflection on the panel-beater.' Some residents saw themselves as the victims of decriminalisation as they felt disenfranchised, no longer having rights to demand that sex workers be removed from working in their neighbourhood. They were concerned that the police and Council did not listen to their complaints. Council members and police were, however, aware that sex workers were legally allowed to be in the areas that they were in, and the Council grappled with understanding how to ensure that all within the community were treated fairly. A Christchurch City Councillor spoke about the 'tightrope' that Council had to walk in making decisions which were fair to all:

> 'You know, we make decisions on behalf of the community. We're all part of the community, and the elected members have been voted in to represent their community and they need to fairly represent everyone. ... And this is a really delicate tightrope that we walk, particularly because it's such a sensitive issue, I think' (Victoria, Councillor).

One of the chief complaints from residents/business owners was that the law has given sex workers rights without any responsibilities and, in doing so, had side-lined their rights. As Sophia stated:

> 'There have been certain rights given now to the industry through legislation, but with those rights comes responsibilities, and it's the same with any other legal activity. You give them the legal right to operate and with that come certain responsibilities. So I think for us it's almost as though they've been given a whole lot of rights, but not necessarily required to be responsible within those rights.' (Sophia, resident)

Public nuisance, offensive to the interests of the community, has frequently been used to justify regulatory action against street-based sex workers in other parts of the world (Campbell, 2015). But such measures serve to drive a wedge between the community and street-based sex workers. You cannot get closer to the 'other' or understand the 'other' without engaging with them (Sibley, 1995). It is widely considered to be more holistic, and more effective to engage with sex workers in a consultative approach to sorting out problems in the community than going down a top-down enforcement route (O'Neill and Pitcher, 2010). Decisions made in a top-down manner most often yield unintended consequences and are rarely effective (Kilvington et al, 2001; Kulick, 2003; Kulick, 2005; Krüsi et al, 2014; Levy and Jakobsson, 2014). In the UK, community engagement has been demonstrated in the managed approach to street-based sex work in Leeds (Brown and Sanders, 2017) as well as in other areas in England

and Scotland (Sanders, 2004; Pitcher et al, 2006; Scoular et al, 2007). It has also been successfully demonstrated in Auckland, as discussed in the previous section.

When an impasse was reached in Christchurch regarding what Council should do about street-based sex work in the residential Manchester North area, regular interagency meetings began between council staff and representatives from NZPC, Youth Cultural Development (who do outreach to young people on the street), the Salvation Army and the Police. The purpose of these meetings was to discuss residents' complaints, as well as other issues affecting street-based sex workers. At this early stage, it was agreed that outreach efforts would be intensified in an attempt both to decrease the numbers of street-based sex workers in Manchester North (there were between 8–14 street-based sex workers reported to be working in this area), and to improve conditions for street-based sex workers generally. The Council then appointed two Councillors to join this interagency group and report back on the viability of a new bylaw clause to regulate the location of street-based sex work away from residential areas.

The interagency group began to expand, with representatives from the Public Health unit in Christchurch, two churches in the area and residents all invited to attend. It was also at this stage that the author joined the group and introduced the findings from this research, as well as findings from research carried out with street-based sex workers in the community in other parts of the world. This helped to inform discussions. NZPC suggested to the group that efforts to remove sex workers from residential areas might be more successful if workers were encouraged to return to Manchester South rather than simply banned from Manchester North. Outreach workers visited the Manchester North area frequently, at different times during the night to urge street-based workers in that area to move to working in Manchester South. They were warned that if they did not do so, it might mean that Council would be forced to regulate street-based sex work and this would impact negatively on all of those working on the street – whether north or south of Bealey Avenue. Residents were provided with the phone number of an outreach worker who lived nearby and were encouraged to phone her at any time of the day or night if they observed any street-based sex worker working in the area. She would immediately drive there to encourage the sex workers to leave. The policewoman on the interagency group also assisted by doing drive-bys and urging any sex workers seen in the area to move across Bealey Avenue. There were positive results, with the numbers of sex workers in this area diminishing significantly and residents feeling less disrupted. Council members on the interagency group were then supportive in recommending that Councillors vote to continue collaborative, non-regulatory approaches, particularly in light of the success that Auckland had when they took a similar approach. For example, one Council representative explained:

> 'There will also be recommendation in there to continue with non-regulatory options, and we're looking to Auckland as a model for that because they have had some success in reducing the issues by taking a partnership approach and working together and with outreach workers, the street-based sex worker community, residents and local businesses, and the police. And that has been working in the sense that they've had a huge reduction in complaints.' (Scarlett, Council representative)

The police advised the Council in September 2017 that they would not enforce any proposed bylaw, citing legal and administrative issues with doing so. This gave the Council further impetus to vote against a bylaw, resolving instead to continue in a collaborative working group approach and encourage street-based sex workers to relocate away from Manchester North, and to monitor and evaluate the actions and outcomes. This has had positive results and, since July 2018, few street-based sex workers have been seen in Manchester North (Law, 2018). On occasions when one does come to work in the area, they are very quickly advised to move. One of the residents in the area has since been cited in a newspaper report as saying that the outreach worker 'was worth her weight in gold' (Law, 2018). The Council also agreed to fund this outreach worker to continue her efforts with street-based sex workers (Law, 2018). Other residents have indicated in interagency meetings and in a wider residents' meeting that they are extremely happy with the current situation. The research presented at the residents' meeting gave the wider community a better understanding of, and empathy for, street-based sex workers. Since then, residents on the interagency group were involved in organising a barbeque for sex workers and the public in Manchester Street to celebrate 'End Violence Against Sex Workers Day' in December 2018, and many community members came out to support this. The interagency group continues to meet regularly to develop strategies to better support street-based sex workers in Christchurch and consider facilities and resources to enhance their safety. Undoubtedly a positive result, this demonstrates that tensions between street-based sex workers and others in the community are far from irreconcilable.

Conclusion

There are two different points regarding street-based sex work in New Zealand's decriminalised environment discussed in this chapter: first, the spaces where street-based sex work is (and is not) acceptable to others in the community; and second, how tensions in these particular spaces have been resolved through community engagement. In summary, it is argued that there is a difference between heterogeneous inner-city and homogenous suburban spaces as to whether or not street-based sex work is accepted and recognised as belonging within a community. The middle-class suburb is constructed as a homogenous, 'pure' space where difference is confrontational. It is hard to get past a discourse of rights when residents argue for their right to a peaceful, family-orientated space, and this conflicts with the rights of street-based workers to work within that space. In such a situation there is little room for recognition and mutual respect. In the homogenous suburban space of Christchurch, it was community engagement and not regulation that was successful in persuading sex workers back into a heterogeneous inner-city environment where they are more readily accepted. In heterogeneous, mixed-use space in Auckland, there was initial discontent among some residential and business community members to having street-based sex workers in the community. This was largely to do with public nuisance related issues, including noise and litter. Community engagement with NZPC and other organisations managed to alleviate many of the issues community members identified and facilitated a greater mutual understanding and respect among all parties. Recognition and respect becomes more possible in heterogeneous, vibrant space, where sex workers are able to become accepted as part of a diverse, inner city area. There are few boundaries to diverse city space – people are able to share space in a more egalitarian way than in bounded homogenous space, the only requirement being that they respect the space, and respect and recognise others in that space as citizens with a right to be there.

Decriminalisation of sex work has seen many positive changes for sex workers in New Zealand (Prostitution Law Review Committee, 2008). Having been recognised as having human rights through the passing of the PRA, police and city councils are required to respect the rights of sex workers. For the councils, this means that they have to be careful when making decisions about bylaws to restrict where sex workers can and cannot work so that they do not contravene the intentions of the PRA. This can cause conflict with community groups who feel that their rights are being sidelined. O'Neill has long argued for participatory methodologies, which includes mediation and community conferencing to inform holistic decision-making in the development of sex work policy:

> Participatory methodologies should include the voices of women, other residents and businesses and respect their expertise/experience (based upon mutual recognition). Such methodologies are also instrumental in helping to create safe spaces for these issues to be raised – and dialogue to take place across the divides between – residents, responsible authorities and sex workers, thus helping to challenge dominant discourses and hopefully feed into public policy at local, regional and national levels. (O'Neill, 2007, p 51).

In contrast to bylaws, community engagement allows the voices of sex worker-led collectives, as well as those of residents/business owners, to be heard, so that solutions which are amenable to everyone can be found. It demonstrates cohesiveness and inclusivity within shared spaces, which everyone benefits from. Community engagement also facilitates a greater understanding of each other. It is through this that supportive relationships are established in the community (Scoular et al, 2007). The residents and business owners who took part in community engagement in both Auckland and Christchurch gained a greater understanding, not only of street-based sex workers, but also of how regulatory approaches could have unintended consequences.

Bannister et al (2006, p 932) have argued that 'through experiencing the "other" we learn of its different values and forms of expression, the uncertain becomes fixed and known and thus less threatening. But more than this, we learn how to interact with otherness to secure a sense of wellbeing as we move through urban space.' Community engagement in New Zealand has proved to be a successful alternative to the use of bylaws when tensions have arisen between street-based sex workers and others in the communities in which they work. It has helped in making the 'other' more familiar. Whether spaces value diversity or family, community engagement has the capacity to bring everyone to a position of respecting otherness.

References

Abel, G. (2014) 'A decade of decriminalization: Sex work "down under" but not underground', *Criminology & Criminal Justice*, 14: 580–92.

Abel, G. (2018) 'Decriminalisation and social justice: A public health perspective on sex work', in S. Fitzgerald & K. McGarry (eds) *Realising Justice for Sex Workers: An agenda for change*, London: Rowman & Littlefield, pp 123–40.

Abel, G., Fitzgerald, L., Healy, C. & Taylor, A. (2010) *Taking the Crime Out of Sex Work: New Zealand sex workers' fight for decriminalisation*, Bristol: Policy Press.

Aha! Parenting (nd) 'Sanctuary: Making your home a haven', AhaParenting. Available at: https://www.ahaparenting.com/parenting-tools/family-life/Sanctuary-haven.

Anon (2017) 'Christchurch residents fed up with sex workers on the street', *The Christchurch Star*. Available at: https://www.nzherald.co.nz/nz/news/article.cfm?c_id=1&objectid=11832954.

Armstrong, L. (2017) 'From law enforcement to protection? Interactions between sex workers and police in a decriminalized street-based sex industry', *British Journal of Criminology*, 57: 570–88.

Bannister, J., Fyfe, N. & Kearns, A. (2006) 'Respectable or respectful? (In) civility and the city', *Urban Studies*, 43: 919–37.

Boreham, J. (2012) 'Street workers headache', *Manukau Courier*. Available at: http://www.stuff.co.nz/auckland/local-news/manukau-courier/6395973/Street-workers-headache.

Brown, K. & Sanders, T. (2017) 'Pragmatic, progressive, problematic: Addressing vulnerability through a local street sex work partnership initiative', *Social Policy and Society*, 16: 429–41.

Bruckert, C. & Hannem, S. (2013) 'Rethinking the prostitution debates: Transcending structural stigma in systemic responses to sex work', *Canadian Journal of Law and Society*, 28: 43–63.

Buckley, T. (2009) 'Locals sweep sex workers off street', *Sunday News*. Available at: http://www.stuff.co.nz/national/2345076/Locals-sweep-sex-workers-off-streets.

Campbell, A. (2015) 'Sex work's governance: Stuff and nuisance', *Feminist Legal Studies*, 23: 27–45.

Chen, X., Orum, A. & Paulsen, K. (2018) *Introduction to Cities: How place and space shape human experience*, Hoboken, NJ: John Wiley & Sons.

Cook, I. & Whowell, M. (2011) 'Visibility and the policing of public space', *Geography Compass*, 5: 610–22.

Cresswell, T. (1996) *In place/Out of place: Geography, ideology, and transgression,* Minneapolis: University of Minnesota Press.

Goffman, E. (1990) *Stigma: Notes on the management of spoiled identity,* London: Penguin Books (original work published in 1963).

Holloway, L. & Hubbard, P. (2001) *People and Place: The extraordinary geographies of everyday life,* Harlow: Pearson Hall.

Hubbard, P. (1998) 'Community action and the displacement of street prostitution: evidence from British cities', *Geoforum,* 29: 269–86.

Hubbard, P. (1999) *Sex and the City: Geographies of prostitution in the urban West,* Aldershot: Ashgate.

Hubbard, P. (2001) 'Sex zones: Intimacy, citizenship and public space', *Sexualities,* 4: 51–71.

Kantola, J. & Squires, J. (2004) 'Discourses surrounding prostitution policies in the UK', *European Journal of Women's Studies,* 11: 77–101.

Kilvington, J., Day, S. & Ward, H. (2001) 'Prostitution policy in Europe: A time of change?', *Feminist Review,* 67: 78–93.

Krüsi, A., Pacey, K., Bird, L., Taylor, C., Chettiar, J., Allan, S., Bennett, D., Montaner, J., Kerr, T. & Shannon, K. (2014) 'Criminalisation of clients: Reproducing vulnerabilities for violence and poor health among street-based sex workers in Canada – a qualitative study', *BMJ Open,* 4.

Kulick, D. (2003) 'Sex in the new Europe: The criminalization of clients and Swedish fear of penetration', *Anthropological Theory,* 3: 199–218.

Kulick, D. (2005) 'Swedish Model', Beijing Plus Ten Meeting. Available at: http://lastradainternational.org/lsidocs/258%20The%20Swedish%20model%20(Beijing%20Plus%20Ten%20meeting).pdf.

Law, T. (2017) 'Pressure builds for Christchurch City Council to ban sex workers from residential areas', *Christchurch Press.* Available at: https://www.stuff.co.nz/the-press/news/91494073/pressure-builds-for-christchurch-city-council-to-ban-sex-workers-from-residential-areas.

Law, T. (2018) 'Prostitutes' Collective gets $40,000 from Christchurch City Council to help sex workers', *Christchurch Press.* Available at: https://www.stuff.co.nz/the-press/news/107029667/prostitutes-collective-gets-40000-from-christchurch-city-council-to-help-sex-workers.

Levy, J. & Jakobsson, P. (2014) 'Sweden's abolitionist discourse and law: Effects on the dynamics of Swedish sex work and on the lives of Sweden's sex workers', *Criminology and Criminal Justice,* 14: 593–607.

Newman, P. (2006) 'Towards a science of community engagement', *The Lancet,* 367: 302.

O'Neill, M. (2007) 'Community safety, rights and recognition: Towards co-ordinated prostitution strategy', *Community Safety Journal*, 6: 45–52.

O'Neill, M. & Campbell, R. (2006) 'Street sex work and local communities: Creating discursive spaces for *genuine* consultation and inclusion', in R. Campbell & M. O'Neill (eds) *Sex Work Now*, Cullompton, Devon: Willan, pp 33–61.

O'Neill, M., Campbell, R., Hubbard, P., Pitcher, J. & Scoular, J. (2008) 'Living with the other: Street sex work, contingent communities and degrees of tolerance', *Crime, Media, Culture*, 4: 73–93.

O'Neill, M. & Pitcher, J. (2010) 'Sex work, communities, and public policy in the UK', in M. Ditmore, A. Levy & A. Williman (eds) *Sex Work Matters: Exploring money, power and intimacy in the sex industry*, London: Zed Books, pp 203–18.

NZPA (2006) 'Manukau council's bill to ban prostitution defeated', *New Zealand Herald*. Available at: https://www.nzherald.co.nz/nz/news/article.cfm?c_id=1&objectid=10405544.

Pitcher, J., Campbell, R., Hubbard, P., O'Neill, M. & Scoular, J. (2006) *Living and Working in Areas of Street Sex Work: From conflict to coexistence*, Bristol: Joseph Rowntree Foundation.

Prostitution Law Review Committee (2008) 'Report of the Prostitution Law Review Committee on the Operation of the Prostitution Reform Act 2003', Wellington: Ministry of Justice.

Robinson, S. (2015) 'Christchurch sex workers: No toilets make us feel like "scum"', *Christchurch Press*. Available at: https://www.stuff.co.nz/the-press/news/67648567/null.

Sanders, T. (2004) 'The risks of street prostitution: Punters, police and protesters', *Urban Studies*, 41: 1703–17.

Sanders, T. & Campbell, R. (2007) 'Designing out vulnerability, building in respect: Violence, safety and sex work policy', *The British Journal of Sociology*, 58: 1–19.

Sanders, T., O'Neill, M. & Pitcher, J. (2018) *Prostitution: Sex work, policy and politics*, London: Sage.

Scoop Media (2015) 'Prostitution by-law bill defeated', Scoop. Available at: http://www.scoop.co.nz/stories/HL1502/S00168/prostitution-by-law-bill-discharged.htm?from-mobile=bottom-link-01.

Scoular, J., Pitcher, J., Campbell, R., Hubbard, P. & O'Neill, M. (2007) 'What's antisocial about sex work? The changing representation of prostitution's incivility', *Community Safety Journal*, 6: 11–17.

Sennett, R. (2003) *Respect: The formation of character in an age of inequality*, London: Penguin Books.

Sibley, D. (1995) *Geographies of Exclusion: Society and difference in the west,* London: Routledge.

Steele, M. (2018) 'City Council turns to residents near sex street for solutions to litter, noise', *Christchurch Press.* Available at: https://www.stuff.co.nz/the-press/news/101114142/city-council-turns-to-residents-near-sex-street-for-solutions-to-litter-noise.

Stringer, E. (1996) *Action Research: A handbook for practitioners,* Thousand Oaks: Sage.

Stringer, E. (2013) *Action Research,* (4th edn) Thousand Oaks: Sage.

Van Doornick, M. & Campbell, R. (2006) '"Zoning" street sex work: the way forward?', in R. Campbell & M. O'Neill (eds) *Sex Work Now,* Devon: Willan Publishing, pp 62–91.

Index

#MeToo 71, 78, 79

A

Abel et al 89, 94, 141
Abel, G. 7, 162
acceptability 158, 159, 160, 161, 163
accessibility 145
Accident Compensation Commission (ACC) 173
Ace Lady Network 69
A'Court, Michèle 61
ActionStation 69
activism *see* sex work activism
advertising 48, 167–9, 172–3
agency workers *see* indoor sex workers
alliances 71
Altink et al 180
Amnesty International 2
anti-trafficking groups 55
anti-trafficking movement 3
Aotearoa (New Zealand) xi, 56n2
Armstrong, L. 96, 101, 104, 107
Arohata Prison 22
Asian women, discrimination against 115–16, 120–1, 129
Auckland case study
 community engagement 205, 206–7, 209
 informal curfew 204–5
 littering 207, 208
 recognition and respect in heterogeneous communities 206–9
 sex workers, education programme 203–4
 vigilantism 203
 working group 204
Auckland City Council 48, 203
 working group 204
Auckland Council 52
Auckland District Court 48
Auckland Women's Centre 69
authenticity 169–70

B

backpackers 119
Bannister et al 217
Barnett, Tim 34
The Bedroom 165
Bernstein, E. 158
Beyer, Georgina 35
Bill of Rights Act (1990) 51
Bindel, Julie 5, 137
Bon Ton 166, 167, 169
bondage and discipline 32
Bones, B. 166, 169
boundaries 210, 211, 212
 living space and working space 212
 sex workers 139–42
Brazilian sex workers 168, 169
brothels 23–4
 certification 48, 50
 high-end 166, 167, 173
 location of 51
 lower-end 166, 173
Bruckert, C. & Hannem, S. 75

C

campaigning 33–5
Campbell, A. 200
Canada 145
carceral feminists 2–3
Carrier-Moisan, M-E. 167, 168, 169
child abuse 72
Children's Poverty Action Group 69
choice 172–3
Christchurch bylaw 52
Christchurch case study 209–16
 boundaries 210, 211, 212
 bylaw proposal 210
 disenfranchisement 212–13
 earthquake 209
 empathy for sex workers 215
 family space 211
 interagency group 214–15
 littering 211

223

living space and working space 212
Manchester North 209, 211, 212, 215
Manchester South 209, 214
moral discourse 211
outreach efforts 214–15
public nuisance 213
pure spaces 211
rights and responsibilities in homogenous communities 210–16
suburbs 210, 211
top-down enforcement 213
Christchurch City Council 52, 210, 213, 214–15
church communities 34
class 21–2
client criminalisation 2–3
clients 31–3, 135–51
  abolitionist feminists 135, 136
  class position 167
  criminalisation of 2–3, 135–6
  men as abusers 135
  research 137–49
    bookings 147, 148
    communication and accessibility under decriminalisation 142–6
    consideration for sex workers 147–8
    ethical considerations 146–9
    findings 139–49
    methods 137–8
    power and control 139
    recognition of sex worker boundaries 139–42
      legal 139
      personal 139, 140
      prosecution 142
    sex workers' safety 145, 146
  under decriminalisation 136–7
  under-researched population 136–7
  violent or abusive behaviour 167
communication, clients 142–6
community engagement 205, 206–7, 209, 215, 217
  in the UK 213–14
community environment 199
community relationships 68
concealing identity 182, 191–3
condoms 27–8, 44, 46, 55, 142
  migrant sex workers 126
consent 142
Contagious Diseases Acts 9, 20
control 139

Convention on the Elimination of All Forms of Discrimination Against Women (CEDAW) 55
  Article 26 (a) 116
  Recommendation 26 116
conventional femininities 171
counter-hegemonic politics 77
Coy, M. & Molisa, P. 137
COYOTE (Call Off Your Old Tired Ethics) 39
creeping neo-abolitionism 3
criminalisation 2–3
  of clients 3
critical discourse analysis 160
Crowe, Bill 23–4
curfews 204–5

D

Dalziel, Lianne 113–14
database of prostitutes 43–4
deadnaming 108n4
decriminalisation
  benefits of 1
  clarity 5
  client conduct 136
  differences from legislation 4–5, 68
  feminist support for 68–9
  impacts of 6–8
  and institutional feminism 64–6
  opponents of 1, 4
  and the police 100–7
  positive outcomes 54–6
  public health 89
  research collaborations 68
  and trafficking 3
  transgender sex workers 100–6
  understanding of 5
  see also New Zealand model; pre-decriminalisation period; Prostitution Reform Act (PRA, 2003); rights of sex workers
Democratic Unionist Party (DUP) 136
Department of Labour 50
deportation 120, 121, 122
discourse representation model 160
discrimination, transgender sex workers 90–1
domestic violence 72
dominant groups 200
dominatrixes 170
The Dominion 43
Donne, T.E. 18

drugs 24
    transgender sex workers 95–6
Dunningham, Justice 54
Dwyer, A. 107

E

economic marginalisation 90
Eldred-Grigg, S. 18, 19
emotional labour 171–2, 179–80, 186, 187
employment discrimination 94–5
enjoyment 169–70, 172, 173
entrapment 27, 143
environmental nuisances 211
escort agencies 95
escort work 26
    risks and hazards 26–7
ethical considerations 146–9
ethnicity 21–2
The Evening Post 43
'everyman' concept 31
extras 24–6

F

Fairclough, N. 160, 163
family space 211
Farley, M. 137
feminism 10
    alliances 71
    fragmentation and dispersal 63–4
    goal 61
    institutional feminism and sex work decriminalisation 64–6
        opponents 66
    issue management 64
    political opportunities 79
    and prostitution 61
    and sex worker activism 61, 61–2
    unique context for 67–9
    support for PRA 34
    waves 62–4, 73
        carceral feminists 66–7
        individualist approach 63
        institutional approach 63
        see also fourth wave feminism
feminist questions 72–4
financial earnings 165–7
fourth wave feminism 10, 62, 68–9, 70, 73, 77
    confronting heteronormative power relations 76
    possibilities for 80

France 136
Funhouse 165, 169–70

G

GAATW (Global Alliance Against Traffic in Women) 116
gender 62
    postcolonial reconstruction of 78
    pre-colonial role 77–8
gender ideology 72
gender wage gap 72
Gill, R. 171
Goffman, Erving 178, 182, 194, 212
Grant, M. 168
grassroots feminism 64, 69
Grey, Sandra 63

H

Habermas, Jürgen 206
Hallgrimsdottir et al 158, 163, 165
Ham, J. & Gerard, A. 162
Hamilton City Council 51
Harassment Act (1997) 54
Harmful Digital Communication Act (2015) 53
Harrington, Carol 67, 68
Hastings District Council 50–1
Hatzenbuehler, M. 194–5
hazards 26–9
Health and Safety in Employment Act (1992) 46
Healy, Dame Catherine 9, 29–30, 142, 194
    consideration by clients 149
    on fight for decriminalisation 49
    garnering support 33
heteronormative femininity 165–6, 171
heteronormativity 65, 75, 76, 80
heterosexuality 76, 77
high-volume brothels 166, 167, 173
HIV/AIDS 29, 30
hoa mahi xi, 78
Hochschild, A. 171–2
HollaBack Wellington 69
Holloway, L. & Hubbard, P. 212
Holmes, Mary 68
home-based sex work 50, 51
home-based workers 48
Homosexual Law Reform Act (1985) 23
Hoskins, Te Kawehau Clea 66, 78
Hubbard et al 102
Hubbard, P. 211

Human Rights Act (1993) 56
Human Rights Commission 53
Human Rights Review Tribunal 53
Hyman, Prue 63

I

Immigration Act (2009) 114
Immigration New Zealand 114, 115
indigenous feminisms 66–7
indoor sex workers 158
    comparison to street-based sex work 161, 163, 172
    making invisible 163
    normalising 163–4
    see also media, study
institutional feminism 64–6
International End Violence against Sex Workers Day
    booklet 53
International Human Rights Watch 2
intersectional radical feminism 62
intersectionalist feminism 69, 73–4

J

john schools 32
Jordan, J. 42, 93, 144
justice 52–4
    sentencing 54

K

Keenan, D. 34–5
Kororareka 19
Krüsi et al 145

L

La Coquille 18
Laban, Dame Luamanuvao Winnie 47
law
    prostitution laws 177
    and stigma 179–80, 180
    see also sex work laws
law enforcement 90
    and stigma 100
    transgender sex workers 91–2, 100–6
legislation 5
legislative change 10–11
Lewis, Lisa 123
LGBT+ people and communities 90, 91
Link, B. & Phelan, J. 178, 195
littering 207, 208, 211
Local Community Boards 52

Local Government Association 50
Lotteries Health 201
lower-volume brothels 166, 173

M

Mac, Juno and Smith, Molly 4–5
MacKenzie, Flora 21, 23
Maher et al 170
mana wāhine Māori (Māori feminist discourses) xi, 64, 66, 67, 77
    definition 66
The Managed Heart (Hochschild) 171
Manchester North 209
Manchester South 209
Manukau City Council 51–2, 52, 203
Māori 41
    feminists/feminism 10, 73, 77–8, 78
    police action against sex workers 42
    representation on NZPC 42
Māori Action Group 30
Māori rangatiratanga (self-determination) 67
Māori tikanga (protocol) 77
Māori whakawahine (transgender women) 42
marketing 165
married men 32
massage parlours 24–6
    duplicity 144
    fears of parlour workers 27
    owners
        exploitation of workers 28
        lists of employees 25, 43
        whims 43
    safety 95
    vulnerability of workers 28, 43
Massage Parlours Act (1978) 24–6
    repeal 50
    Section 18 42–3
McKenzie et al 135–6
McRobbie, A. 171
media
    'acceptable' sex worker 158, 159, 160, 161, 163
    'desirable' kind of sex worker 158
    indoor sex work, representations of 158
    sensationalism and misrepresentation 157
    sex work as a social problem 157, 158
    stigma 158, 163
    study

analysis of texts 161–70
  advertorial frames 167–9
  advertorial nature 172–3
  enjoyment and authenticity 169–70, 172
  financial justifications 165–7
  manufactured identity 168
  normalising identities 162–5
  visibility 161–2
  discourse representation model 160
  indoor sex workers 160–1, 160–70
  methods 159–61
media representations 157
Medical Officers of Health 50
medical profession 34
Migrant Education and Information (MEI) project 42
migrant sex workers 11, 48–9, 55
  communication skills 125
  exclusion from PRA (Section 19) 113–16
  Asian women 115–16, 120–1
  PRA Section 19 study 116–31
    condoms use 126
    denial of human rights 120–1
    deportation
      fear of 120, 121, 122
      notices 121
    exploitation 129
      of non-sex work 118–19
      proposals for reductions in 131
    freely chosen work 118
    methods 116–17
    non-migrant sex workers 123–30
      tensions with migrant sex workers 122–3, 124, 125
    perceptions of 127–30
    stigma 119–20
    temporary/travel visas 118
    threats from non-migrant sex workers 122–3
    unfamiliar with norms and standards 126
    unprotected sex and unwanted sexual activities 122
    working privately 121–2
  trafficking 114–15
  vulnerabilities of 115
    in brothels 115
Ministry for Women 63
Ministry of Business, Innovation and Employment 117, 131
mokopuna xi, 45

Mossman, E. & Mayhew, P. 52
Murphy, Leola 80

N

National Assembly (French) 136
National Council of Women 34
National Council of Women of New Zealand 65
New South Wales 89
New Zealand Federation of Business and Professional Women 34
New Zealand model 4–6
  Prostitution Reform Act (PRA, 2003) 1, 5–6
New Zealand Parliament 56n1
New Zealand Police Association 45
New Zealand Prostitutes' Collective (NZPC) 5, 8, 10, 29–31, 130, 201, 214
  booklet 53
  consultative process with Auckland City Council 203–4
  contracts 40–1
  formation of 30, 39–40
  Māori representation 41
  migrant workers 41–2
  organisational structure 41
  peer-led 41
  resistance to 30
  SIREN 30
  working group 204
New Zealand Reserve Bank 55
Nordic model 2–3, 5, 135
normalising sex work 162–5
Northern Ireland 136

O

O'Neill, M. 217
ONTOP (Ongoing Network Transgender Outreach Group) 30
O'Regan, Katherine 34
Östergren, P. 3–4
outness 182

P

Pākehā xi, 41, 66
  feminism 73, 78
Parliamentary Bills 56n1
pasifika xi, 41, 47
patriarchy, legacy of 179
Pickering, Annah 204, 205

place 200
Plumridge, L. & Abel, G. 95
police
   distrust of 44
   as protectors 52–3
   register of sex workers 43–4
   resistance to reform 91
   sex workers' records, destroying 50
   and transgender sex workers
     disrespect of 103
     harassment of 103
     stereotyping 104
     violence against 103
     workers' distrust of police 102, 104
   see also law enforcement
police entrapment 27
Police Offences Act (1884) 20
politicians 34
politics of solidarity 74
pornography 70–1
poverty 75
power 139
pre-colonial gender roles 77–8
pre-decriminalisation period 9
   campaigning 33–5
   clients 31–3
   early history 18–20
   Māori people 42
   Massage Parlours Act (1978) 24–6
   New Zealand Prostitutes' Collective (NZPC) 29–31
   prior to reform 42–4
   risks and hazards 26–9
   twentieth century developments 20–4
prosecution of clients 142
prostitution
   exploitation of women 66
   home-based 50
   introduction to New Zealand 18–20
     imprisonment, threat of 20
     regulation and control of 19–20
   normalising of 1
   state-sponsored governmentality and surveillance 102
   as a talking crime 169
   twentieth century developments 20–4
     First World War 20–1
     police toleration of 21
     Second World War 21
     threat to family unit 20
   see also sex work; sex workers
Prostitution Law Review Committee (PLRC) 7, 70

Prostitution Reform Act (PRA, 2003) 1, 5–6, 11
   campaigning for 33–5
   harm reduction 65, 70, 73, 75, 76
   implementation 49–52
   justice 52–4
   migrant sex workers 55
   preamble 65
   Section 3 40
   Section 9 55
   Section 11 168
   Section 19 55, 114, 115, 116
     Asian women 115–16, 120–1, 129
     perceptions of 127–30
     racial discrimination 120–1, 128–9
     racialised and gendered 115–16
     see also migrant sex workers
   sex workers' control 139
   stipulations and clauses 34
   success 70
   Supplementary Order Paper 113
Prostitution Reform Bill 40, 64
   Parliamentary process 44–9
     additions 45–6, 47–8
     brothels' certification 48
     condom use 46
     migrant workers 48–9
     oral submissions 45
     Parliamentary election 45–6
     passing of 49
     police search warrants 46
     Second Reading 47
     Select Committee 44–5
     unemployment benefits 46
   rationale for 44
   support for 45
Prostitution Review Committee 52
public health 89
PUMP (Pride and Unity for Male Prostitutes) 30

Q

queer feminism 80

R

racism 22
Radio New Zealand 61, 168
rangatiratanga xi, 67
rap parlours *see* brothels
Rawls, John 206
Raymond, J. 137
recognition 206–9

red-light districts 22–3
Reed, Anna 29
respect 206–9
rights of sex workers 2, 39
ringbolting 22
risks 26–9
Rivers-Moore, M. 166
Roguski, M. 116
   see also migrant sex workers, PRA Section 19 study
Rout, Ettie 20–1

S

Sabsay, L. 102–3
safe sex 27–8, 46, 126
safety 70, 145, 146
   massage parlours 95
Salvation Army 45, 210, 214
Sanders, T. 135, 136, 142, 168, 180
Scarlet Alliance 50, 56n5
Schmidt, Joanna 76
Scoular, J. 164
second wave feminism 63
   indigenous feminisms 66–7
Select Committee 44–5, 51, 52
Sennett, R. 206
sentencing 54
sex industry regulation 6
sex trafficking 74–5, 127–8
sex work
   choice 172, 173
   competition 123
   decriminalisation of 1
   as a form of labour 177–8
   stereotypes about 75
   talking about 181–5
   underground and informal structure 145
sex work activism 61–2
   near-future of 69–77
      shifting feminist questions and tactics 72–4
      next frontiers 74–7
      unique context for 67–9
sex work laws 2
   debates about 2
   tangible impacts on sex workers 3
sex workers 2
   'acceptable' 158, 159, 160, 161, 163
   access to resources and support 101
   allies 2
   arrest and imprisonment 22
   condoms as evidence 27
   class position of clients 167
   communication with clients 142–6
   criminal records 26
   diversity of 10–11
   double lives 178, 179
   exploitative employment conditions 28–9
   fear of discovery 179
   fines 25
   following the gold rushes 19
   good time girls 21
   justice 52–4
   labour rights 43
   and legislation 4
   Māori
      transgender women 42
      violence against 42
   negative stereotypes 159
   as passive victims 177
   perceived as spreading sexual diseases 30
   perceptions of 11–12
   prosecution of clients 46–7
   rights of 2, 39
   safety 145
   STI services 64
   stigma 11, 26, 33, 54, 56, 68
   tensions with migrant sex workers 122–3, 124, 125
   union representation 29
   visibility of 161–2
      strategic invisibility 162
   workplace safety 70
   see also indoor sex workers; street-based sex workers
sexism 22
sexual diseases 30
sexual fantasies 32
sexual health 141
sexual violation 47, 55, 56n3
sexual violence 71, 72
sexually transmitted infections (STIs) 9, 64, 165
ship girls 21–2
Sibley, D. 210, 211
Simpkin, Gay 67
SIREN 30
SlutWalk 69, 71, 78
social discrimination 92
social media 55
social movement feminism 63–4
socially reproductive labour 72–3

soliciting 17, 22, 25, 42–3
  convictions 42
  undercover police officers 42
Soothill, K. & Sanders, T. 140
Souness, Jennifer 169
South Africa 145
South Auckland (Manukau) 203
Speak Up for Women 80n3
state feminism 63, 64, 65, 66
stigma 11, 26, 33, 54, 56, 68, 177–8
  concealing identity 182, 191–3
  and criminalisation 180
  and decriminalisation 194–5
  definition 100, 178
  indicator of 178
  intrigue 187
  and the law 179–80, 180
  and law enforcement 100
  and the media 158
  migrant sex workers 119–20
  negative effects of 100
  openness 182–3
  passing and covering 182
  patriarchy, legacy of 179
  and prostitution laws 177
  research findings
    concealment, pressures of 191–3
    managing reactions from others 185–91
      approval 188
      curiosity 187
      friendships with other sex workers 191
      ostracism 189
      positive and enthusiastic responses 187–8, 190
      shock and surprise 186, 187
    talking about sex work 181–5
  research methods 180–1
  and sex work 178–80
  spoiled identities 178
  transgender sex workers 92, 100, 101, 104, 107
  trust and respect 183, 184
  see also structural stigma
stigma theory 178
Stonewall (1969) 91, 107–8n1
strategic invisibility 162
street-based sex work 42
  characterised as social nuisance 99
  in Manukau 51–2
  public fears 102–3
street-based sex workers 28, 210

community engagement 205, 206–7, 209, 215, 217
  and the community environment 199
  comparison to indoor sex workers 161, 163
  empathy for 215
  police cooperation 53
  research
    Auckland case study 203–9
    recognition and respect in heterogeneous communities 206–9
    Christchurch case study 209–16
    rights and responsibilities in homogenous communities 210–16
    methods 201–2
  rights 199
  and transgender sex workers 92–3
  visibility of 200
structural stigma 75, 194–5
suburbs 210, 211
Sullivan, B. 141
surveillance 103
Swedish model 2–3, 135, 136
  rushed interactions of sex workers 7

T

tactics 72–4
takatāpui xi, 77, 80, 93, 108n2
tamariki xi, 45
tangata whenua xi, 42, 56n2
Te Awekōtuku, Professor Ngahuia 65, 66, 70, 77
Te Ropu Wahine Māori Toko I Te Ora (The Māori Women's Welfare League) xi, 45
Te Tiriti o Waitangi (The Treaty of Waitangi) xi, 10, 67
third wave feminism 63, 73
  indigenous feminisms 66–7
Thursdays in Black 69
tikanga xi, 77, 78
tima tane xi, 21
trafficking 3, 75, 127–8
  migrant sex workers 114–15
  see also sex trafficking
Trafficking in Persons (TiP) Reports 74, 130–1
trans sex workers 10, 23
transgender sex workers 23, 30, 79–80
  absence of research 89–90

decriminalisation, stigma and law enforcement 100–6
 social discrimination and stigma 92
economic marginalisation 90
exclusion and marginalisation 92
experiences of work, discrimination and law enforcement 90–2
law enforcement 91–2
and the police 91
 disrespect of workers 103
 harassment of workers 103
 stereotyping 104
 violence against workers 103
 workers' distrust of 102, 104
and the public space 102–3
qualitative study 93, 106
 abuse from wider public 99
 camaraderie 97–8
 community feeling 98–9
 drugs 95–6
 employment discrimination 94–5
 methods 93–4
 participant experiences 94–9, 100–1, 101–2, 103, 104–5
 violence 96–7
 workplace harassment 99
and street sex work 92–3
women 90–1
The Treaty of Waitangi *see* Te Tiriti o Waitangi (The Treaty of Waitangi)

U

UNAIDS 2
undercover police officers 25, 42
UniQ Victoria 65
United Future 45, 114
United Nations Convention on the Elimination of All Forms of Discrimination Against Women (CEDAW) Committee 55

University of Otago Human Ethics Committee 117, 201
unprotected sex 122, 140–1

V

Vagrancy Act (1824) 20
Van Brunschot et al 158
vice squads 22, 23, 24
Victoria University of Wellington Human Ethics Committee 117, 138, 181
violence 96–7
 see also sexual violence
visibility of sex workers 161–2
 street-based 200

W

Wellington Newspapers Limited 43
whakawahine xi, 42
whanau xi, 98, 108n4
Wilkinson, Maurice 34
Wilton, C. 92
women's organisations 33–4
World Health Organization 2
Worth, H. 93, 98

Y

Yates, Dianne 48
Yingwana et al 3
Young Women's Christian Association (YWCA) 34–5, 65
Youth and Cultural Development 210, 214

Z

zoning 201

www.ingramcontent.com/pod-product-compliance
Lightning Source LLC
Chambersburg PA
CBHW070921030426
42336CB00014BA/2490